RED LEADERS

RED LEADERS

THE OFFICIAL STORY OF
MANCHESTER UNITED'S CAPTAINS

BEN HIBBS and ADAM MARSHALL

SIMON &
SCHUSTER

London · New York · Sydney · Toronto · New Delhi

A CBS COMPANY

First published in Great Britain by Simon & Schuster UK Ltd, 2014
A CBS COMPANY

Copyright © 2014 by Manchester United Football Club Ltd

The right of Ben Hibbs and Adam Marshall to be identified as the author
of this work has been asserted by them in accordance with sections
77 and 78 of the Copyright, Designs and Patents Act, 1988.

1 3 5 7 9 10 8 6 4 2

Simon & Schuster UK Ltd
1st Floor
222 Gray's Inn Road
London WC1X 8HB

www.simonandschuster.co.uk

Simon & Schuster Australia, Sydney
Simon & Schuster India, New Delhi

A CIP catalogue record for this book
is available from the British Library

ISBN: 978-1-47113-992-5

Typeset in the UK by M Rules
Printed and bound by CPI Group (UK) Ltd, Croydon, CR0 4YY

Contents

Prologue
by Bryan Robson

All I ever wanted to do was play football. As a young lad growing up, being a footballer was the only thing I dreamed of doing. But to become Manchester United captain is an honour very few players have the privilege of experiencing in their careers and so I relished the role, never took my responsibilities lightly and always hoped my passion and commitment showed in my performances for the club.

I'm a believer that it takes a certain kind of character to be captain of any club, but especially so at United. I must admit, I'd always been a bit of a loudmouth on the football pitch. In my school teams, where I was captain through all the various year groups, I was often in trouble with referees because I would argue against every decision. Even as a kid, I'd be telling players off, organising and ordering people about.

With the captaincy, though, you come to realise through experience that it's not just about shouting and bawling at people, because sometimes that has a negative impact. Some players can take it the wrong way and it has the opposite effect to what you want: they're demotivated or, as I found in a few cases, they spend their time having a go back at you instead of putting that energy into their performance. So I learned to encourage at the right time, and tell people off at the right time; you've got to get that balance right, because ultimately it's important how people react to you. Saying that, I always found that when it came to shouting at everybody, it came very naturally to me!

Not every captain is built that way, but it takes a rare type of player and personality to lead simply by example. Of course, your actions on the pitch set the tone as much as anything you say, but if you're a manager and you select a captain who isn't particularly vocal then it's a big decision and you have probably very carefully assessed the balance of the rest of the players in the squad. For me, having that voice on the pitch is a vital part of any team. As a captain, you're organising on the field, you're encouraging players and you're giving people both barrels when it's needed. You've got to be able to see the bigger picture of what's going on in a game and get your message across to get your team through the match and ultimately to win.

Playing at Manchester United carries great responsibility, and it comes with a level of expectation that is unlike what you might experience at many other clubs. I found that out coming to Old Trafford from West Brom for a big fee in 1981. There was a lot of expectation on me to deliver. But you have to rise to the challenge of playing for United. Some players embrace it and rise to the occasion, while for others it can be much more difficult.

Being captain is yet another level of responsibility still. I know of managers in football who have gone to players and offered them the armband only to be told that they wouldn't feel comfortable with it and would much sooner just concentrate on their game. I can understand that. Captaincy doesn't suit everybody. I was honoured to take on the role at Old Trafford, I relished it and all the responsibility that came with it, and so to remain as the longest-serving captain at a club like Manchester United, with so many great players and great people to have worn the armband, is a privilege and something I remain immensely proud of to this day.

Introduction

Football supporters all around the world will gladly state with intense pride and great ardour that their team is special, unique and undeniably superior to any other. Yet for anyone caught by the bug, there is something inimitably distinctive about Manchester United. As Tony Wilson, music and culture icon of the city and an ardent Red, once put it: 'This is Manchester. We do things differently here.'

You get a sense of it in the gleaming reflection of silverware in Old Trafford's trophy room, in the echo of the stadium's former heroes and the presence of its current idols. It is there in the tragedy as well as the triumphs of the club's past and in the philosophy of attacking football engineered by Sir Matt Busby, cultivated by Sir Alex Ferguson and fiercely guarded by the club's legions of fans, whose swaggering northern self-assurance extends to the far reaches of the planet.

There is something in the scale and scope of United that takes good players and makes them great, great players and even transforms them into the greatest. But talent alone gets you only so far; character, courage, confidence and more besides are all required to thrive on this stage. Those essential attributes endure in the memory of George Best taking the ball on bobbly pitches against defenders with a licence to kick, in *Le Roi* Eric Cantona's enigmatic magnetism, Cristiano

Ronaldo's stick-it-to-'em shunning of the haters to blossom into a World Player of the Year, or the loyalty and longevity of Sir Bobby Charlton and Ryan Giggs.

For every lionised legend, however, there are others who simply cannot rise to the occasion and are overawed, sometimes defeated, by it. Players in the past – and no doubt more will follow in future – have arrived with talent and willing, yet unwittingly succumbed to the sheer magnitude of the club, the pressure to perform with poise and panache and the expectation to win. All of that is bundled into the non-negotiable bargain of becoming a United player. You thrive or you wilt.

So it stands to reason that to pull on not just the shirt but the captain's armband takes a special kind of player at a very special football club. The honour has been bestowed upon comparatively few men among United's 850-plus players who have run out for the Reds in competitive action, and those who have claimed the title for any extended period of time are scarcer still in the annals of Reds history.

Just ten players have commanded the captaincy for five seasons or more, nine of whom appear prominently in this book: Charlie Roberts, Frank Barson, Johnny Carey, Noel Cantwell, Bobby Charlton, Martin Buchan, Bryan Robson, Roy Keane and Gary Neville. Harry Stafford, leader of Newton Heath in the late 19th century and the very first captain under the club's new guise as Manchester United in 1902, is the other. But Roberts, United's first title-winning captain, represents an appropriate place to start in greater detail the story of the men who, by and large, have led the club to its great glories.

They are joined in this collection by Roger Byrne – a captain of meritorious distinction who would have led United well beyond the five-year mark into the 1960s, and to goodness knows what further triumphs with the Busby Babes, were it not for the devastating

Munich air disaster. Also included are Steve Bruce, Nemanja Vidic and Cantona – an exceptional case after just a year in the role – and, of course, the latest man to take his seat among exalted company at the captains' table: Wayne Rooney. It is an elite group, all boasting different tales to be told, different backgrounds and personalities, but all united by a common theme of leadership.

Compiling a truly definitive list of United skippers is no easy task. Where to start? The club museum records show the first captain to be the elusively named E. Thomas in the 1882-83 campaign – four years after Newton Heath L&YR Football Club was formed, four seasons before the team played its first recognised competitive fixture in the FA Cup, and a full decade prior to joining the Football League. There are no known records of his first name, a common problem in the sepia-tinted early days of the club's embryonic stages, where some details are simply lost to the ages.

Prior to the end of the Second World War, few players other than Stafford, Roberts and Barson had captained United with any great claim to permanence. In fact, the captaincy frequently changed between the two world wars. Sometimes it was a decision made on the day or in the lead-up to a match. The management, or the committee as they were called, would select a team two or three days in advance, usually on a Thursday for a Saturday game, and in the minutes to those club meetings, individual player names would often have an alternative next to it in case of injury or unavailability.

The fact is that from 1912-13, Roberts's final season at the club, to 1945-46, when Carey took on the captaincy, United clocked up at least 20 skippers in a period encompassing 22 unsettled seasons, a deeply unstable period in the club's history in which United experienced managerial changes, faced relegation and promotion six times, very nearly dropped into English football's third tier for the first time ever and almost went out of business, never once winning a trophy.

Even lifting trophies creates an issue of definition when it comes to captains. Denis Law skippered United on the pitch for a sizeable chunk of the mid-1960s, even though Cantwell was the official club captain. Law, who was designated team leader, would in all probability have lifted the European Cup at Wembley in 1968 had a knee injury not prevented him from playing against Benfica. Instead the honour, fittingly, was Charlton's. That image is a deeply poignant moment etched into the club's history, and although it wouldn't have changed the symbolism of the achievement ten years after Munich, Law might have led the team up the Wembley steps instead.

Similarly, Peter Schmeichel raised the Champions League trophy in 1999 – almost lifting Sir Alex off his feet on the Nou Camp podium – while a suited and booted Keane endured suspension for the final. In fact, each of United's three major European triumphs have been won with vice-captains or stand-in skippers lifting the trophy; Rio Ferdinand and Ryan Giggs climbed the steps to jointly claim the prize at a rain-soaked Luzhniki Stadium in Moscow in 2008, with Neville sidelined through injury.

So, for historians and completists alike, there is plenty to debate in assembling a roll-call of United captains. 'You get into uncertain territory and it can be a nightmare to produce anything truly comprehensive,' admits Mark Wylie, the Manchester United Museum curator. 'We've seen examples of it in the last few seasons with Vidic, where Patrice Evra often stood in and quite regularly wore the armband. Then, of course, you have that period where you were wondering who was going to be captain after Roy Keane. Ruud van Nistelrooy had the armband around October to November in 2005, when Keane was out injured and, of course, then when he left the club. Eventually it went to Neville.

'In the 1960s, Law was team captain whenever he was fit, but Cantwell retained his status as club captain. Cantwell was a prominent figure in the Players' Union and was also the man of the

Reserves who was helping to give them a bit of steel at the back and use his experience to show others how to do it. It was felt at the time that he could be the one who was going to take over from Busby eventually. Then he decided he was leaving to take up a managerial role at Coventry – his first game was against us ironically enough. But when Law was fit, he was captain.'

So, while there is a laudable supporting cast of highly reputable leaders, the focus here is on official club captains. The role and its status have certainly metamorphosed in the last century, not just at United but for clubs and national teams around the world. Being captain has perhaps never before been treated with the acclaim and attention that it receives today in the public eye. The position, at least on the pitch, has essentially remained the same – to lead and inspire – but the context around it has altered. Where now it might be to front up to press and public, even in the immediate post-Second World War era captains often acted as an intermediary of a different kind; they were a conduit between the players, generally working-class men, and the manager or even the board of directors, mostly well-off business owners.

'In those very early days there was a big difference between club directors and the players,' adds Wylie. 'There was quite a class distinction. The players might have come from some of the poorer suburbs of Manchester or working-class areas from towns and cities elsewhere in Britain. You needed somebody who could bridge that gap. Carey was widely regarded as very good at being the in-between man. He was Busby's man too, although some of the players at that time believed Allenby Chilton was the real leader in the dressing room. Chilton was hard as nails, a big tall centre-half that you wouldn't want to run into on a bad day. Johnny Morris claimed Chilton was the true captain. But then Morris left under a cloud as he didn't get on with Busby.'

The relationship with the manager, naturally, is an important one. The captain is very often the boss's eyes, ears and voice on the pitch. Different managers covet different attributes in their leaders on the field, and changing managers can often result in instability in leadership on the field too. 'That's another big factor with the captaincy,' says Wylie. 'If the manager changes that often means the captain changes, too. When you have a stable manager you have a stable captain.

'Ernest Mangnall had Roberts. Busby for a long period had Carey, then there was a bit of an issue when it went to Stan Pearson and Chilton. Then Chilton asked to be taken out of the side due to tiredness, because he had played in the region of two hundred consecutive games, and Roger Byrne took the captaincy in his place. Byrne would have remained as captain for the rest of his career but for Munich. After that, there was another period where it was unsettled when you had Maurice Setters and then Cantwell. All the time, the manager is seeking consistency and the qualities that set the tone for his style of management.'

Sir Alex's 26-and-a-half-year reign also featured a well-defined run of captains: Robson, Bruce, Cantona, Keane, Neville and Vidic. Cantona stands out in that feted group, and not only as a one-season wonder when he led his young side to Premier League triumph in 1996-97, before retiring from the game. The Frenchman, on the surface of it, also bucked a trend of what Sir Alex generally sought in his captains: essentially a reflection of his granite-tough leadership. Cantona was considered a flamboyant genius by many, and that virtuoso brilliance inspired the young players around him, but he could never have done it without a fearless, ferocious drive to be a winner. Still, that brand of leadership is rare.

Sir Alex would speak vividly of his more traditional leaders on the field. 'Bryan Robson is a miracle of commitment, a human marvel who pushed himself beyond every imaginable limit on the field,' he once commented. While in 2010, referring to the changing nature of footballers' personalities, he said: 'Some players cry now in the dressing room; Bryan Robson never used to cry.'

In 2001, with Keane perhaps at the height of his powers as a leader in the field of battle, Sir Alex extolled his skipper's virtues: 'If I was putting Roy out there to represent Manchester United on a one-against-one basis, we'd win the Derby, the Boat Race and anything else. It's an incredible thing he's got.' Indeed, reiterating the point about his captains mirroring his beliefs, he commented: 'When I look at Roy I often see myself. He cares, he's a born winner.' No matter how that alliance ended, it cannot detract from how devastatingly successful it was when everything was rosy.

In the modern era, with the proliferation of social media and the instant, vocal reaction of fans and an ever-increasing need for the media to feed the demand to consume football, the role of captain has become a subject of obsessive matter. It is a symbol of status and the storyline of choosing a captain plays to an ever-increasing interest in the fortunes and misfortunes of individuals. Sometimes forgotten amid the sensationalism is the fact that the role is still a practical and purposeful position.

'The role seems to have grown and grown in status in the last twenty years,' says Wylie. 'But the captain of a football club needs to have the respect of the players, the respect of the manager and the respect of the fans and behave accordingly. You're required to be professional, give as good as you get on the field, be good with the media and have the respect of everyone at the club: on the pitch, off it, and in the stands. That, for me, is your perfect captain.'

What makes a great United captain? Passion is a good first port of call. Intelligence on the field is key, too; carrying out the manager's instructions and his vision of how the team should play is essential to the smooth running of the team. That invariably comes with experience, another attribute favoured in captains. Stature within the squad and respect of the other players, consistency and reliability are all a must. Character and courage carry weight, particularly in the moments when things are not going well and others look to their captain: think of Keane against Juventus in 1999, when United seemed to be on the verge of losing in the Champions League semi-final.

Talismanic performances on the pitch are just one part of it. Inspiration manifests itself in myriad ways: the indubitable seniority of Carey or Byrne, grabbing a game by the scruff of the neck like Robson or Keane, the bloody and bruised body-on-the-line leadership of Bruce and Vidic, or United's philosophy visible for all to see as with Charlton and Neville.

Sometimes it is obvious who the team's natural leader is, but at other times there are a handful of suitable candidates. The reasons behind such an appointment require consideration, which is why United's current manager Louis van Gaal refused to make any rash decisions in handing out the armband when he first arrived at the club. He wanted a player and a person he could place his complete faith in. 'Choosing the captain is about characteristics,' he has said previously. 'I choose the captain, not the players, I give them more responsibility so I have to admire him for his personality and his identity. My captains are very professional, very ambitious and also have an honest personality.'

At United, it was one of the first questions people wanted to ask: who would succeed Vidic in the role? 'All the players are possible candidates,' he explained early on in the job. 'I have to get to know them, so I will use four, five or six weeks. Or it could be two months. For me, the captain's role is very important. Therefore, I need time. Sometimes I haven't had the time – then I have to make quick decisions. But quick decisions are not always good. I'll use my time for it. I think a captain is very important.'

In the end, it took the Dutchman almost exactly a month before he came to his decision: 'Wayne has shown a great attitude towards everything he does. I have been very impressed by his professionalism and his attitude to training and to my philosophy. He is a great inspiration to the younger members of the team and I believe he will put his heart and soul into his captaincy role.'

So the torch has been passed on to Rooney and the facts would suggest that he boasts the stature and statistics required to make a success of it: after ten years at the club he is among United's top 20 all-time appearance-makers, having long since joined the 400 club, and he is third in United's list of leading scorers, fast closing in on second-placed Law and the leader Charlton. Even so, the captaincy is another step still and a task that will challenge him to the fullest. He insists he is ready for it, and relishes it, fully aware that he is following in the footsteps of some giants of Manchester United's history.

Chapter 1

The Ghost in Boots

'I don't think any other pre-Second World War captain
had as much influence on the field as Charlie Roberts.'
Mark Wylie, Manchester United Museum curator

Standing at almost 6ft tall, the powerful Charlie Roberts was a striking presence on the football field. Rock-solid defensively and a roaming, dynamic athlete bursting with creative energy going forward, he was arguably the finest half-back of his generation and proved to be a fundamental figure in Manchester United's first great team as he led the club to two league titles, in 1908 and 1911, and a maiden FA Cup triumph in 1909.

Not only was Roberts an imperious leader on the pitch, a pioneering skipper with the vision and authority to dictate games and alter tactics during matches, he also inspired men off the field and played a prominent role in forming the Players' Union. He was opinionated and forthright and, if something needed to be said, he wasn't afraid to air his views or stubbornly stand his ground. He was constantly willing to make sacrifices based on fiercely guarded principles – doing so was occasionally to his detriment but always, he would adamantly maintain, for the benefit of football and his fellow players.

Sometimes that approach came at a cost and his several run-ins with the Football Association appears to have hindered his international career, as he won just three England caps, despite his obvious talents and leadership qualities patently being worthy of many more. Bizarrely, the authorities once admonished him for his preference for wearing short shorts. He wasn't the only footballer going against the ample-fitting style of the times, but English football's conservative rule-makers insisted 'knickers', as they were called, must cover the knee. Sartorial boldness wasn't the only indication that Roberts's mind was his own, nor would it be his only dispute with the FA.

Born in Rise Carr, north of Darlington, on 6 April 1883, Roberts went on to play for Bishop Auckland as a teenager before signing for Grimsby Town at the tender age of 20. His ascent through football's ranks was rapid and he quickly attracted attention from the game's bigger clubs. Just a year later, United beat a host of clubs to his signature by paying a fee of £400. It was a huge sum at the time for a largely inexperienced player, but United and manager Ernest Mangnall were flush with cash and the club was purchasing potential, lots of it.

The *Sheffield Evening Telegraph* said of the deal: 'Everyone realised it would not be long before he was transferred, and at a big figure, for Grimsby were not slow to get rid of their best men if they knew there was a good fat cheque at the end of the negotiations.' Regardless of the financial outlay, United had purchased a rangy, dominant central half-back boasting speed, stamina, defensive nous and excellent distribution. His noticeably pallid complexion earned him the nickname 'ghost in boots'.

Roberts arrived in Manchester in April 1904 and made his debut in a 2-0 win over Burton United at Bank Street, Clayton, in front of a crowd of 8,000 fans. However, a 0-0 draw with Bolton Wanderers two days later finally put paid to United's last hopes of bringing to an end a decade of Division Two football for the club, and even a thumping 5-2 win over Leicester City on the season's final day was too little, too late as Arsenal secured second place behind champions Preston North End.

Roberts would not take the captaincy full time until the 1905-06 campaign, but he was the natural successor to long-serving full-back Harry Stafford, who had brought his Reds playing career to a close a year before Roberts's arrival. Stafford, too, had been influential on and off the field, although arguably his greatest contribution was in his tireless work to alter the destiny of a faltering club's perilous course toward extinction, setting it instead on a more prosperous path to world renown.

Newton Heath LY&R Football Club had been spiralling toward financial oblivion at the turn of the 20th century. At a packed and boisterous meeting at the New Islington Public Hall in Ancoats on 24 April 1902, that was about to change. It was stated that Stafford and four others were willing to offer £1,000 to buy the club. The *Manchester Courier and Lancashire General Advertiser* reported that the rescue party had 'no desire to make anything out of the club. They had come forward in a sportsmanlike manner, and having been told that Newton Heath as a club was practically defunct, they wanted to give it a new lease of life.'

Those words were met with raucous applause from attending supporters. John Henry Davies, a wealthy local brewery owner, would stump up the money to take over the club. At that same momentous meeting, the majority voted in favour of changing the club's name to Manchester United. Davies would become club president and a key influence in an impending spell of success.

But Stafford's role as a beacon in this troubled era is intriguing and, in an age of limited lasting records, it is difficult to distinguish the facts from the fanciful. What is clear is that Stafford was not only captain of the team but champion of the club's future prosperity. How he came to befriend Davies, United's soon-to-be financial saviour, has attracted all manner of tall tales. One story goes that the accountant of Davies's brewery was an avid Heathens follower who got to know Stafford by regularly attending matches. While rushing to the club's Bank Street ground in Clayton, the accountant was knocked from his bike by his boss, Mr Davies, who was returning from lunch. Asked where he was headed in such a hurry, the accountant confessed his love of his football team. Davies was intrigued, met Stafford and an interest in investing was forged.

However, another yarn has passed into legend. Stafford had been diligently seeking public funding to save the club and had helped set up a fundraising bazaar at St James Hall on Oxford Street in Manchester. By his side at the four-day event was Major, his pet St Bernard dog, who had a collection tin around his neck. On the last day, Major went missing and ended up in a nearby pub and was taken in by the manager of the establishment, part of Davies's company. Keen to locate the pet's owner so he could purchase the dog for his daughter, who immediately took a liking to Major, Davies tracked down Stafford and promptly agreed a sale. More importantly, perhaps, they became acquaintances and Davies began to sympathise with the Heathens' plight, eventually invested in the club in 1902 and built the foundations for modern-day Manchester United. All because of a dog, or so the story goes.

Having saved the club from bankruptcy, Davies began to invest heavily in player recruitment. Although, as United, the club did much better in 1902-03, they fell short of promotion, so Davies brought in Mangnall from Burnley as secretary-manager. Initially, the new man's focus was on strengthening the backbone of the team, with Roberts a vital part of that strategy, before he moved to bring in a number of other key players such as wingers George Wall and Billy Meredith and forward Sandy Turnbull. All of these recruits were a result of United's new-found financial power in the early 1900s. However, in March 1903, Stafford made the last of his 200 club appearances. Five years later, in August 1908, his services were recognised when, along with players and club officials, he was awarded a medal to celebrate United's league championship win that year.

Roberts was captain of that side but the fact that, by the time he took the captaincy, United were striving not to survive but to thrive was in no small part due to Stafford's unstinting hard work. Roberts would go on to play a central part in United's first championship-winning team, but first the team had to get out of football's second tier. It took two full seasons after Roberts joined to achieve promotion, finishing second behind Bristol City in 1905-06, with the club skipper playing in all but four league games during the campaign.

He had become a formidable force and United's elevation to Division One was certainly timely, because top-flight clubs such as Aston Villa and Newcastle eagerly sought his signature, recognising the attributes United valued so highly. Roberts, according to Mark Wylie, curator at the Manchester United Museum, was a shrewd skipper and an intelligent footballer, ahead of his time. 'He was noted as somebody who was influential on the field,' says Wylie. 'He altered tactics in games and had the authority to change the way United played. He would tell team-mates where they should be and what they should be doing. I don't think any other pre-Second World War captain had as much influence on the field as Charlie Roberts.'

In the truest United traditions, the club's first league title, just two seasons after being promoted to Division One, was claimed with a swagger and an attacking brand of football that proved the envy of the whole country. Turnbull hit 25 goals in 1907-08, while prolific winger Wall scored 19, and the game's first superstar, Meredith, bagged ten more. But for all United's attacking prowess, the half-back line of Dick Duckworth, Roberts and Alex Bell provided the solid foundations on which everything else was built. The team stormed to the title, nine points ahead of second-placed Villa and with a goal difference of 33 – almost double that of the next-best total from the Midlands club.

United were not resting on their laurels and the following season came sprinting out of the traps and went seven matches unbeaten at the start of 1908-09. But while Roberts and his team had been able to clinch the title even while losing nine games the previous season, 16 defeats during a dismal defence of the crown proved far too costly as United finished way down in 13th place. Roberts missed six of those losses through injury, due in part to his powerful approach to the game. In a 2-2 draw with Nottingham Forest in October 1908, the *Nottingham Post* reported that Roberts 'so severely injured his shoulder in a charge with Marrison that he tore a muscle and is unlikely to take his place for a month'.

A key difference in those two contrasting league campaigns was that famed and formidable half-back line – or lack of it. In 1908-09, Duckworth, Roberts and Bell lined up together just 13 times in the league. The previous season, they played double that number of games as an almost impassable collective, and Roberts was central to it all. Half-backs were positioned slightly ahead of full-backs in a role more commonly aligned to defensive midfield duties today, and United's famous triumvirate were the best in the business, with Roberts marauding everywhere to impose his influence on matches.

While they may have missed many league games, the trio featured in all of the team's six FA Cup ties that season and so it was no surprise United clinched a first Cup triumph that year. Having beaten Brighton, Everton, Blackburn, Burnley and Newcastle en route to the final (Newcastle, Everton and Blackburn would all finish in the top four in the league, so it was a very challenging run), Turnbull's solitary goal was enough to beat Bristol City in front of 71,401 supporters at Crystal Palace to claim the trophy.

Before the final, Colin Veitch of the *Courier* had backed United to win and said of Duckworth, Roberts and Bell: 'By many competent judges they are reckoned the finest trio of halves possessed by any club in the kingdom.' Of the central pillar, Veitch added: 'Roberts, as captain of the team, is the "man of the moment" in Manchester. On the field he is effective both in meeting the attacks of the opposition and in feeding his own forwards. He is top-sawyer in his position, and he used head and feet with equal facility. Of good height and length of limb, he is splendidly endowed from a physical standpoint.'

The league title may be viewed today as the principal prize among domestic honours, but in the early origins of the English game the FA Cup was seen as the absolute pinnacle, the era's Champions League. With 400 clubs entering the knockout competition and a conservatively estimated 1.6 million supporters attending games that season, the final was seen as the highlight of the football calendar.

United beat old Division Two foes Bristol City on 24 April, but didn't return to Manchester until three days later on a Tuesday afternoon for what was a remarkable homecoming. Police struggled to contain excitable crowds at the Central Station when the train carrying United's victorious players and 'the pot' pulled up to the platform. As Mangnall emerged carrying the trophy, the crowd cheered and a band played 'See The Conquering Hero Comes'. Some players were carried shoulder-high to horse-drawn carriages awaiting them outside. Huge numbers of fans were packed outside the station, as Roberts sat proudly at the front of his carriage holding the trophy. The procession then wound its way through a reported 20,000 people outside Manchester's Town Hall, all straining to see the cup decorated in red and white ribbons.

The players and officials were given a Civic Reception, welcomed into the Town Hall by the Lord Mayor. The parade then edged along John Dalton Street, Deansgate, Market Street and eventually on to

Bank Street. All the while fans lined the streets dressed in club colours. Once the players reached their destination it was no time for relaxation. United arrived at the ground just in time to get changed and play the last home league match of the season, against Arsenal. The official attendance that day was 10,000, but newspaper reports suggest there were as many as double that outside the ground alone and they cheered as Roberts and his triumphant team-mates entered the stadium, which had been decked out with flowers. The arrival of the FA Cup in the directors' box elicited more huge cheers from the crowd. Perhaps unsurprisingly, however, all that pomp was hardly ideal preparation for a match as United lost 4-1.

That didn't stop supporters once more lining the streets as the players made their way to the Midland Hotel for a celebratory supper. It was eleven o'clock by the time Roberts and his team-mates sat down to eat, after which United's president, Mr Davies, said: 'The club has achieved the highest honour in the football world,' even if he did add that it was 'not a very handsome trophy'. Roberts later clarified there had been no disrespect in those remarks, but admitted fans would express disappointment at its 'tin pot' appearance when he displayed it in a local shop he owned.

The 1909-10 season brought yet more drama and Roberts, unsurprisingly, was right in the thick of it. In truth, trouble had been brewing between the FA and the recently formed Players' Union, who wanted greater freedom in the transfer market for its members and a scrapping of the £4-a-week salary cap. The situation came to a head when, with United's stubborn band of brothers refusing to budge, it looked like the start to the new season might be postponed, with United's fixture against Bradford in serious danger of being called off.

An emergency meeting was held on 28 August in Manchester, just four days before the season was due to kick off. The previous day in Birmingham all the league clubs expressed loyalty to the FA. They had been told that any remaining members of the Union should be suspended without pay. But United's players resolutely remained unwilling to back down, although they expressed no grievance with the club despite the invidious position such a decision placed them in. The *Observer* newspaper reported the following day: 'The proceedings, which had been most harmonious, then terminated after lasting about two hours. After this decision the Manchester United secretary wired to the Bradford City Club postponing the match arranged for next Wednesday. Roberts, the United captain, said the players were determined to suffer any hardship rather than give way.'

The Reds skipper told the *Daily Mail*: 'The decision of the League clubs to support the Football Association will not alter the determination of the United players to remain loyal to the Union. There would be no going back, whatever happened.'

He also felt the Union had the co-operation of Newcastle, Middlesbrough, Sunderland, Everton, Liverpool and Chelsea among others. It was even posited that he would take the matter to court, while apparently if six clubs could form a breakaway from the FA, a syndicate was willing to pay £10,000 to run them. An invitation had already been made to take a team to South Africa with a percentage of gate money on offer. Matches were also supposedly lined up in England, with players compensated for lost wages.

A photograph from the time shows smirking exiles including Meredith, Wall, Duckworth, Turnbull and goalkeeper Harry Moger among others in a team line-up that features Roberts, designated captain, in front of a chalkboard with their team name: The Outcasts FC.

Roberts felt players' rights were worth fighting for. Four pounds a week was not an inconsiderable sum in those days, but the players felt it did not reflect the interest and wealth in a sport that continued to rapidly grow in popularity. Their second gripe was with the 'retain and transfer' system, which placed all the power with the clubs, who could hold a player's registration and restrict him from joining another team even after his annual contract had expired. If the club decided not to sell, that was that.

Players' dissenting voices had grown in volume since late 1907, when the Association of Football Players' and Trainers' Union, most commonly referred to as the Players' Union, was formed in Manchester. Roberts and his team-mate, Meredith, who had been involved in the Union's predecessor, the defunct AFU, were among the founding members. When the Union, which boasted 1,300 members, made clear its objectives to oppose the salary cap and transfer system, the FA withdrew recognition of the organisation and ordered Football League clubs to suspend players who pledged allegiance to it.

This was of course a very different time, when the relationship between employer and employee was changing. The labour movement and trades unions were both beginning to grow in importance, as they demanded a greater share of the rewards for the country's growing prosperity. As a consequence, employers became wary of being seen to concede to these demands, for fear that they would lose control. The power was still very much in the hands of the owners, but now they realised there was a new challenge to their authority and there was increasing industrial unrest.

Faced with these threats, many players backed down, but Roberts stubbornly refused to set aside the principles he believed in. However, the threat of suspension and pressure from clubs drove many players into submission and membership numbers fell dramatically. This was of course an era when there was no fall-back position for a player, so if their wages were stopped they would have no income. If a player had a family to support, then he would soon be struggling to put food on the table or to pay the rent. It looked as though their plight was doomed, but the tables turned before the start of the season and the impasse was broken when the FA offered the compromise of allowing bonus payments to players to supplement the maximum wage.

Disaster for the league averted, United's players were joined by their Manchester City counterparts on a warm late summer's day as they drove to the ground in a charabanc decorated with club colours and placards that read, 'Success to the Players Union'. The *Manchester Courier* reported: 'The players were cheered all the way to Clayton, and the reception Roberts and his men got when they appeared on the field of play clearly demonstrated in which direction the sympathy of the spectators lies. The cheering lasted for several minutes.' The vocal backing from 12,000 fans helped United to a 1-0 win via Wall's second-half strike against Bradford.

It was claimed that bad blood remained when, in October 1909, United's request to give Roberts the gate receipts from a match against Newcastle as his benefit – essentially a reward for long serv-ice – was apparently refused by the FA. Yet, by summer 1910, all was seemingly well. Writing in Glasgow's *Evening Telegraph and Post*, Roberts extolled the therapeutic benefits of fishing on trawler boats during his summer months, and insisted: 'There are a lot of silly rumours going about just now concerning trouble said to be brew-ing anew between players and the FA. It's simply ridiculous. Trouble, in my opinion, is a thing of the past. We have had enough of that to last us forever. The Players' Union and the governing bodies are now for the good of the game. Ever since a truce was called there has not been a hitch, and only recently the Players' Union was complimented by the powers that be on the manner they have conducted their affairs during the past season. Long may this feeling obtain.'

Contented, Roberts looked ahead to what would be a much more successful campaign than the 1909-10 season, in which United fin-ished fifth in the league, although in itself that was an improvement on the previous year's 13th position. As 1910-11 beckoned, United also had a new mascot to prompt a change of fortunes. Previously the club had used a goat – some reports suggested its name was Billy, but Roberts amusingly referred to 'our poor friend "Union"'. Sadly, the goat died and Roberts said in a newspaper column: 'I had it preserved and it now occupies a prominent place among my football relics.'

The new mascot was a greyhound donated to the club and the skipper declared: 'Manchester United, with the aid of their new mascot, I trust, are in for a long run of successes, and are now once and for all above suspicion in the eyes of the powers that have pestered them so long.' Perhaps more obviously effective was the signing of powerful goalscorer Enoch 'Knocker' West, who would find the net 20 times in his first season, 19 of them in the league. 'I was very pleased to see we secured the services of Knocker West,' Roberts said. 'I have a great opinion of this young fellow, who, on his day, wants some stopping, as I have known to my cost more than once.'

Having also moved to a new stadium, Old Trafford, in February earlier that year, United required suitable success befitting a ground with a capacity that peaked at 65,101 for a 2-1 second round FA Cup tie triumph over Aston Villa a year after its opening. The Villans, however, would very persistently seek revenge in the title race. The Reds began the season with seven wins from eight games and moved into first place in October before dominating top spot for much of the campaign.

By April, Villa still clung tightly to United's coat-tails and when United visited Villa Park in the Reds' penultimate game of the season, the hosts won 4-2, putting them in the driving seat. Villa had two games remaining and one hand on the league trophy. But a draw at Blackburn and defeat on the final day against Liverpool handed United the opportunity to take a second title in four seasons. Roberts missed the final three games of the season through injury, but United made sure of league success at home to Sunderland with a thumping 5-1 win.

As great an achievement as it was, in many ways it was the beginning of the end for this great United team. A second Charity Shield was won in August 1911, but it would be the Reds' last piece of silverware for an astonishing 37 years. Mangnall left the manager's post at the end of the 1911-12 campaign and joined Manchester City, while the team followed up the championship success with 13th and fourth-place finishes in the two subsequent seasons.

The huge cost of paying for and running the new stadium meant there were no funds to keep strengthening the squad. The lack of success on the pitch resulted in the breaking up of United's first great side. There was a need to cash in on the club's playing assets and so in the summer of 1913, when a record offer of £1,500 was made by Oldham Athletic for Roberts, who had just turned 30, United accepted. It brought to an end a seminal chapter right at the start of the Manchester United story.

The great difficulty in replacing a captain of Roberts's calibre was painfully evident as several hapless attempts proved indicative of United's progression on a downward trajectory into something of a wilderness during the inter-war years. Veteran full-back George Stacey took over in 1913-14 for a season before George Hunter, a skilful half-back signed from Chelsea, became skipper. His reign was disastrous. The team ended the campaign in 18th position, narrowly avoiding relegation but, by then, Hunter had been suspended by the club and never played for United again, with just 23 appearances to his name. Hunter had several run-ins with United's directors, attempting to refuse train tickets to travel to an away game and was considered to have set a poor example to his team-mates. Hunter's replacement, Irishman Pat O'Connell, took the honour for the remainder of the season, but with the Great War taking hold and the football calendar due to be wound up, United were drawn into a match-fixing scandal.

During the game in question, a 2-0 win over Liverpool on 2 April

1915, O'Connell had missed a penalty. But that had happened before the betting syndicate's desired scoreline, so there was no evidence to suggest O'Connell was complicit. However, in December 1915 the Football Association handed life bans to Liverpool's Jackie Sheldon and United players West – the only one on the field at the time – Turnbull, Arthur Whalley and Laurence Cook. The latter three had their suspensions rescinded after the war due to service for their country, but, sadly, Turnbull lost his life in the conflict.

For Roberts, he would spend an unhappy spell as Oldham manager when the Football League resumed in peacetime, but he left to pursue his tobacco business, selling a popular brand of cigarettes in Manchester named 'Ducrobel', after the famed partnership of Duckworth, Roberts and Bell. His lasting legacy at United didn't disappear in a puff of smoke, however. Roberts made 302 United appearances, scored 23 goals, won two league titles, an FA Cup and two Charity Shields, and rightfully stands among the pantheon of great United captains.

Chapter 2

The Old Soldier

'Give Frank a rough and a tumble and he'll be delighted for the simple reason that a trial of strength is, to him, a breath of ozone.'

An Outside Right, 'The Whirligig of Football'
newspaper column

As Manchester United struggled to replace Charlie Roberts, the club was in dire need of a new hero. It would take almost a decade for a character of equal billing to assume the captaincy, and Frank Barson's reputation has reached near-comic proportions.

A blacksmith by trade, the fearsome-looking centre-half courted publicity and controversy in equal measure. Many column inches were devoted to a footballer with a strong personality to accompany his obvious talent. Whether some of the stories that have persisted into the modern era are merely apocryphal is surely open to debate, as a selection may only serve to add to the myth of the toughest player in the land.

What is true is that when Barson spoke to the press, the barrel-chested Yorkshireman appeared no headstrong aggressor in print. He argued his case and made his points in measured fashion rather than revelling in any hard-man image. It supports the view that he was an inspirational individual and, above all, a leader of men despite being comparatively mild mannered away from the muck and bullets out on the pitch.

Seven players had taken on the captaincy since the popular Roberts departed and none had truly convinced. In the post-war era, Jack Mew was a goalkeeper prone to flashes of temper and was ultimately replaced between the sticks by Alf Steward. Clarence Hilditch had a longer stint as skipper and would become player-manager in 1926, but was a pleasant chap who did not have the force of personality required as the team struggled.

The First World War caused huge disruption and United suffered the ignominy of relegation in the third season after football restarted, when they finished bottom of the table. Hence, come the summer of 1922 and with the club desperate to clamber straight out of the Second Division, United made a statement of intent in the transfer market by signing Barson. The fee, a record for a defender at £5,000, was settled after weeks of haggling for somebody who had been agitating for a move from Aston Villa for some time.

An FA Cup winner two years earlier with the Midlanders, following another record switch from Barnsley, Barson was irked by being forced to relocate to Birmingham from his Sheffield base and even went on strike to voice his displeasure. A number of clubs coveted the defender, despite a shocking disciplinary record, but United chairman John Henry Davies was determined to land his man and the offer of ownership of a pub if he helped the team gain promotion within three seasons was agreed as an enticing bonus.

It took a matter of days for Barson to be awarded the captaincy, emphasising the importance of his signing for the club. The 31-year-old had a threatening visage, having broken his nose four times, and was 6ft tall and broad shouldered. He looked the part in United's white shirt with a red 'V' and was a welcome addition to the side, with supporters enthusiastic about his arrival.

'A player like Barson is not loved by any but members of his own crowd,' wrote *The Times* during his days as a Villan and a villain. 'But ruthlessly and fearlessly, he manages to break up attack after attack.'

The United team was to be built around the big-money signing but, by all accounts, he took time to settle after being short of fitness when sealing his move. His acquisition meant that Neil McBain, whom United had signed from Ayr United for £4,600 the previous November, had to be moved across to left-half and by January 1923 he decided to move on to Everton. Barson missed the opening four games of the season before belatedly making his debut in a victory at Molineux, the first of two 1-0 wins against Wolves within the space of a week. Some observers reckoned the fault for any failure to gel lay with his team-mates, but he cemented a place in the side when fit, missing only the last two games of 1922 and five of the last six fixtures before returning for the season finale at Oakwell, his old stomping ground.

Barson wrote a newspaper column around that time applauding attempts to reform the appeals procedure for players sent off from the field of play. Perhaps fearing he was a marked man, his logic did not appear to be in keeping with the image that would endure. Arguing 'trying players by correspondence' wasted too much time – 'the system is old fashioned and out of date' – he articulated his support for a committee to review such cases. 'While I agree that there has been a better class of player attracted to football as a profession since the rate of wages increased,' he said in the *Derby Evening Telegraph*, 'there are still very many players who could do themselves and their case far greater justice were they able to give evidence by word of mouth. Many players can speak well and clearly but many of them are not nearly so happy when it comes to putting their case in writing.

'How different it would be were the whole evidence in each case to be taken to a commission. The whole of the facts could be laid bare in one day and soon after the alleged offence. Direct evidence, by word of mouth from the parties directly concerned, could be taken and accuser and accused would have the opportunity of cross-examining the witnesses just as in a court of law. What better example could there be than English Court of Justice procedure which is said, and rightly so, to be the fairest and best in the world.'

While accepting the expense of such a format could provide a barrier to change, he rallied: 'I still hold that a player who is punished should be given the fairest possible trial. The punishment means a great deal to a player – loss of wages, loss of character and loss of reputation. Are all these things to be taken away from a player just to save the expense of giving him a trial which is fair and just? No really sporting player and sporting club wishes to defend the unsportsmanlike player, the man who habitually stops the other fellow by unfair tactics, but all wish to see fair play given to every man. True justice is never a hardship.'

His role as a spokesman for his colleagues began to complement his imposing on-field persona and the side finished fourth in 1922-23, but the following season was a disappointing one as a mid-table position of 14th generated concern about the suitability of the team for gaining promotion. Meanwhile, McBain's excellent form for Everton prompted some criticism, as injury led to Barson being absent for long periods. 'McBain is certainly better than Barson today for the simple reason Barson is hors de combat,' wrote one report.

A serious knee injury at Derby County in mid-February ruled Barson out for the campaign and he was to have ongoing battles for fitness. A crippling back problem caused him to be bed-ridden and would understandably lead to issues for the remainder of his career. However, he remained crucial to United's hopes.

After losing his appeal over receipt of a benefit payment from

Villa, the incentive of the pub from the board would have been an added bonus in its third and final year, but his performances had already illustrated a desire to succeed in Manchester. There was far more to his game than sheer brute force, even if his bone-jarring barges were dubbed 'Barson bruisers'. 'I'd been brought up to play hard and saw nothing wrong with an honest-to-goodness shoulder charge,' he was later quoted as saying.

Exceptional in the air, he could head the ball further than some of his contemporaries could kick it. Legend has it he scored one of the longest-distance headers ever seen in a game against Sheffield United for Villa with some estimating the ball travelled 30 yards. And there was invention in his play, making clever use of throw-ins to exert pressure on opposing defences, and with reference made to his intelligent passing with the outside of his boot.

Understandably, opponents would deliberately attempt to rile Barson and ignite his famed short fuse. 'Since I went to United, I've received plenty of hard knocks but never so many as this season,' he said around Christmas time in 1924. 'My shins are a mass of bruises at the moment.'

A bizarre story emerged soon afterwards, with the Chelsea camp alleged to be the source of a threat to Barson after the Londoners lost 1-0 at Old Trafford on New Year's Day. 'A certain footballer has for long been under almost constant suspicion,' read an unsigned statement to the press. 'There cannot remain any doubt that he should be. Opponents who have played against him have tired of his never-ceasing wrongdoing that there is a movement afoot to send a petition to the authorities in order to prevent the player from crocking others.'

In the event, Barson was injured for another spell, which coincided with ground being lost in the promotion race to Leicester City and Derby County. 'If any further proof of Barson's genius as a pivot were required,' wrote the press, 'it is found here.' The player himself remained confident his team would gain promotion, accurately predicting in February that Leicester would be the other side elevated into the top flight, and stressed he would be ready for the run-in as he was reinstated in the defence in April.

Chelsea's underhand efforts to provoke the United skipper floundered, as the match report for the game at Stamford Bridge in April insisted: 'Barson was a good boy, even though he had to put up with an awful lot.' In the very next match, Bradford City would again test his resolve. 'He got in the wars rather badly,' commented one local reporter. 'But there was no effort to retaliate. "Play the ball," he counselled his players. He is just as astute a general as he is a player.'

Any concerted attempts to expose an obvious flaw in Barson's make-up were proving insufficient to halt the club's march towards promotion. United virtually assured themselves of a return to Division One with a 4-0 thumping of Port Vale at Old Trafford in the penultimate fixture. The players showed their appreciation to their on-field leader at the final whistle by surrounding him and congratulating him for his efforts. It was a mark of great respect and the clearest indication of the esteem in which he was held at the club. A goalless draw at his former club Barnsley ensured second place was mathematically certain and United were back where they belonged.

The story goes that, on receiving the pub in Ardwick Green, Barson was overwhelmed by punters keen to offer their congratulations and thanks, so he handed the keys over to the head barman, vowing never to return. As somebody notoriously reluctant to welcome compliments, it was maybe an illustration that he was not as money motivated as others sometimes sought to portray him.

The redoubtable defender also had a secret command to his pals to urge them on for a final assault on the opposing goal in the closing stages, something the club would become renowned for under Sir Alex Ferguson in later years. Legend has it he would say: 'Now then, let's have a Barnsley rally,' which was effective, if not always pretty, and incorporated 'lusty kicking and hard running, worrying the other side' according to contemporary reports.

The following year saw the club adapt seamlessly to life back in the top flight, but the campaign will be best remembered for a tempestuous FA Cup semi-final with neighbours Manchester City. Even the build-up garnered plenty of attention in the press, with City setting up camp in Buxton in Derbyshire, much to the disapproval of Barson, who accompanied his colleagues to the Ardwick Empire instead to see a show. 'We are not having brine baths or golfing in our training,' he sneered. 'We are keeping to the old-fashioned methods.'

The fact the derby tie was played at Bramall Lane should have meant some local sympathy for the Grimesthorpe native, even if he had been roundly 'hissed' at another Yorkshire venue, Elland Road, before the game had even started, as Leeds United won 2-0 back in October. Again, he would be jeered following an altercation with City's Sam Cowan that left his opponent unconscious, with many later accounts claiming a punch was thrown.

City won 3-0 despite their lowly league position (they would be relegated at the end of the season) and Barson was at fault for one of Tommy Browell's goals. However, his most notable contribution would have greater repercussions as he ended up with a two-month ban, reckoned to be the first-ever case of a player being retrospectively charged with misconduct, after an investigation into the incident with Cowan.

Athletic News offered this view on the challenge: 'Cowan was knocked flat down and out! A merciless crash it was and altogether too vigorous. Cowan lay flat; Barson crouched on his knees and the crowd, suspecting the "old soldier", roared more.' The *Sunday Post* commented: 'Barson was United's outstanding man. In fact, he was the only man on his side to show his real form. The United captain, however, came in for much barracking which, in a sense, was ironical seeing that he was playing before thousands of his fellow townsmen.

'He committed an indiscretion and it was a very severe one. Just after half time, when the City were leading by one goal, the centre-half barged into Cowan, the opposing centre-half. There was no necessity for this clash. Cowan fell like a log and Barson was slightly injured. The crowd set up a derisive howl and referee Barrell cautioned Barson, after which the United captain returned to his previous game, which was scientific, clever and effective. But the crowd barracked him intermittently and he got a lively reception when he came off the field.'

Others insisted Barson performed uncharacteristically badly after the Cowan clash, perhaps more as a result of sustaining a knock rather than any suffocating sense of remorse, and the defence crumbled around him. Another match report from Bramall Lane relayed the opinion: 'It was not a savoury incident but there were others far worse.'

Nonetheless, the FA members in the stands felt the incident warranted further punishment and another suspension was imposed on Barson, even if it amounted only to a loss of earnings in the close season as he would be back by August. However, if he was playing the part of pantomime villain, his post-match chat to journalists did not suggest he was still seething. After clinching promotion, he had declared: 'I have never served a club that could take defeat with a smile as do the directors of Manchester United. It is something which the players do appreciate.' Similarly, the painful 3-0 reverse to City did not bring anger or recrimination, with Barson instead offering no excuses for the performance and allegedly 'laughing at the sorry figure United had cut'. He appeared no sore loser.

Was it simply a case that Barson's reputation preceded him? James Holland of the *Manchester Guardian* argued: 'His vigorous play so incensed the crowds that the moment he stepped on the pitch, he was greeted with cries of "dirty Barson". Yet it might have been a case of giving a dog a bad name. Apart from the strength of play, he had few equals in the matter of heading the ball. To see Barson stand in the centre of the field and direct a full-blooded clearance with his head to either wing was a sight indeed.'

After finishing ninth, the best standing since the war, the club was rocked in October 1926 by manager John Chapman's suspension from all involvement with football due to alleged improper conduct. The Scot, who brought Barson to Manchester, protested his innocence and the vague reasoning behind the punishment was never made public. Although trusty right-back Hilditch became player-manager, Barson was able to exert growing influence on the team, and rumours were rife he even began selecting the XI himself. Fearing Joe Spence was wasted as an outside-right, apparently he took the decision to revert him to centre-forward and it led to five goals in three games for 'Mister Soccer' towards the end of 1926-27. United went unbeaten for the final eight games to arrest a slide that was starting to increase relegation concerns.

Things were even more perilous in the following campaign, and Barson's lengthy absence sparked speculation he was not injured but had fallen out with the club. He was quick to refute this, saying, 'I would give everything to don the jersey again,' as he confessed to feeling much pain following the spinal injury that would require more specialist consultation and treatment.

The battle wounds and scars were taking their toll. He would be 37 by the time the season was out and had been slowing down for several years. He pulled on the shirt only 11 times in 1927-28 and, although offering advice and support to younger colleagues, was no longer the feared warrior of old. His United career ended, perhaps fittingly, when he sustained a broken nose against Portsmouth as even he was unable to play on in the second half with his facial features rearranged once again.

A move to Watford was followed by another suspension for six months, but the punishment seemed incredibly harsh for a tangle with Fulham outside-right Jimmy Temple. 'I asked to be given a hearing but this was refused,' complained Barson. 'The most I had ever dreamed of was a month's suspension and the FA's decision is a terrible blow.'

Once again, it seems as though his reputation counted against him. Writing an opinion column headed 'The Whirligig of Football', a player using the pseudonym 'An Outside Right' informed his readers: 'He would never deliberately crock a player. Give Frank a rough and a tumble and he'll be delighted for the simple reason that a trial of strength is, to him, a breath of ozone. It is a tonic, just as a fight is to an Irishman or an argument to a Scot. The trouble comes when other players go too far with Barson or when other players won't take hard, fair knocks. Then Barson goes too far himself. He is cruelly misjudged in many cases, though no one denies he has transgressed in the past. Barson is the sort of man who never forgets but he can forgive. Mark those words also.'

It is likely he would have earned more than a solitary England cap, awarded against Wales in 1920 when United star Billy Meredith was on the opposing side, had he not garnered such a reputation with the authorities. Yet nothing should detract from his contribution to the United cause and the impact his huge personality had on attracting publicity for the club, albeit unwelcome at times.

'The thing that impressed me was the fact that the United had a real leader,' a Southampton director is quoted as saying in the thoroughly researched *Back from the Brink* by Justin Blundell. 'It was obvious the team would do anything he wanted and it was equally obvious that he was a great positional player. His head was always in the way and he found time to instruct his men. I have not seen captaincy like it in years.'

The club's noted 'chief fixer' Louis Rocca, offered this assessment: 'As a captain, I never knew one who could get more out of his team.' Although also praising an ability to encourage the younger players,

Rocca did add, 'He was a gentleman of firm-set opinion,' according to Jim White's *Manchester United Biography*, alluding to tension between the pair.

As the 1930s approached, the long-serving Jack Silcock took over from Charlie Spencer and had two spells in charge of the team. Left-back Silcock, who had been a miner, signed for United as a teenager in 1916 and went on to make 449 appearances for the club. Capped three times by England, he was another prone to crossing the line when it came to tackling.

'There is only one thing against Silcock,' wrote one newspaper. 'His methods are not always above question.' Another agreed: 'At his best, he can be very stylish and safe, for he tackles with grand intelligence and can kick cleanly under any condition. Is given to losing his temper at times, however, and is rather too robust.'

James Brown (1935-36 and 1936-37) and George Roughton (1937-38 and 1938-39) had a couple of seasons apiece as United skipper, and William McKay held the responsibility in 1934-35 and again in 1939-40 as a world war loomed once more. During this period, the club was promoted twice and relegated once as the weight of debts from building Old Trafford continued to impact on the club.

Things were about to get worse before they got any better, however, as Old Trafford was bombed during the war. The end to hostilities in 1945, and the appointment of Matt Busby as manager, would soon lead to the anointing of another of Manchester United's greatest captains, a player who had already begun to make his mark in the 1930s.

Chapter 3

The Last of the Corinthians

'He was, in every sense, Matt Busby's representative on the pitch.'

Jack Crompton, former Manchester United goalkeeper

'Gentleman' Johnny Carey was Matt Busby's trusted lieutenant on the field, a distinguished character who shared the same values and ethos of his manager and was a man of real integrity. Possessing an immaculate and mature aura that demanded respect, the pipe-smoking elder statesman, who always appeared old before his time due to his balding pate, was the ideal captain to marshal the post-war United side and implement his manager's plans out on the pitch.

A £250 signing from St James's Gate, a team owned by the Guinness firm in his native Ireland, the teenager helped the Reds regain a place in Division One in his first season at the club in 1937-38, as a yo-yo spell of relegation and promotion put the fans through the mill in the 1930s. After serving in the Second World War with the Queen's Royal Hussars, even though active service was not compulsory due to his nationality, Carey returned to Manchester and found the new manager was somebody whose path he had already crossed, having been marked by Busby during a friendly between Eire and the British Army.

'His every action suggested that he was a thinker,' recalled Busby of that encounter on the pitch. 'A student of the game prepared to go to any lengths to achieve his goal – soccer perfection. He was at Old Trafford when I arrived and I quickly made him captain. That was how much I thought of his wisdom and ability and, as a player, he was an artist.'

Carey was deployed at centre-forward in that wartime match and had been an inside-left in the promotion-winning campaign. He would ultimately play in ten different positions for United, even donning the goalkeeping gloves against Sunderland at Roker Park for a 2-2 draw in 1953 when Ray Wood and Jack Crompton were unavailable. Towards the end of the 1949-50 season, a start in attack against Arsenal marked his fifth different role over the course of the last seven matches. Versatility was definitely another of his chief attributes.

Newly installed boss Busby had a clear philosophy and a vision. Only 36 and still fit when he took up the reins in the autumn of 1945, he was able to transmit his ideas to the players on the training ground and the skipper emerged as a key conduit for this information. 'When I joined United before the war, Scott Duncan wearing a business suit was typical of a soccer manager,' said the Irishman. 'But here was our new boss playing with his team-mates and demonstrating what he wanted and how to achieve it. It was unheard of in those days.' Carey was instructed to utilise the long ball to good effect and initiate attacks. 'We now tried to create the game from the back,' said the newly converted defender.

Busby had earmarked Carey as somebody capable of reverting to full-back, where he could provide calm assurance and exert influence from the defence. Such a switch, of course, also freed space for another of the excellent attackers at the manager's disposal, as United emerged from the conflict with its strongest group of players since before the previous war, among them Charlie Mitten, Johnny Morris, Stan Pearson and Jack Rowley, all of whom had been on the club's books prior to the war, plus Jimmy Delaney, a rare signing. Due to the mutual respect between the pair, the positional move was accepted and, in time, he would become one of the leading players in his position.

United missed out on the Division One title by a point to Busby's former club Liverpool in the first season after the Second World War. There was the consolation of a huge personal honour for Carey when he was chosen to captain the Rest of the World against Great Britain in front of 136,000 fans at Hampden Park that May. It provided another platform for his inspirational and organisational qualities and his display attracted acclaim from fellow players and press alike. 'Although unable to hold much conversation with his team-mates, he led them with wonderful skill, setting a superb example,' commented opponent Ronnie Burgess. One reporter, writing under the name Kay Jay in the *Evening Express,* also noted his ability to overcome the language barrier, claiming he 'sent a message through an invisible interpreter and his team responded.'

The following year, the runners-up spot was secured again, this time behind Arsenal, but a fine FA Cup run boosted hopes of winning a first piece of silverware at Manchester United for 37 years. The Cup campaign started on 10 January 1948 in front of 58,683 fans at Aston Villa and it is a match that has been well documented, with United winning 6-4 amid a flurry of goals. When trailing to a shock opener inside ten seconds, eye-witnesses reckon Carey simply put his hand on his hips and smiled as the ball nestled in the net. Exuding belief in the superiority of his colleagues, despite the setback immediately from the kick-off, the captain's confidence proved well placed as his team stormed back to lead 5-1 by half time. Villa rallied to ensure a classic, but the first hurdle was successfully negotiated en route to Wembley.

Liverpool, Charlton Athletic and Preston North End were also overcome to set up a 13 March encounter with Derby County at Hillsborough in the semi-final. Busby's entertainers excelled in a 3-1 triumph, with Pearson scoring all three goals. Local reporter Frank Nicklin was certainly impressed, writing: 'Manchester United [are] the nearest approach to football perfection I have seen since the war. Good luck to them. Their 3-1 shattering of Derby's Wembley dreams was a grand performance by a great team. Every man was an essential part of the machine and there was not one weakness. Carey played superbly, so completely did he overshadow [powerful Scottish outside-left Angus] Morrison, I was rather surprised the Rams persisted in directing most of their attacks down the left flank.'

Allenby Chilton, who was at fault for Derby's goal, was identified as a potential weakness by certain sections of the press, despite performing heroically. Hence, special mention should be made of the respected defender from the North-East, as he would later take over the captaincy. Having made his debut the day before war broke out in 1939, he had kept himself fit by boxing at cruiserweight when stationed in Ireland and was described as 'immense' by Busby.

Goalkeeper Crompton in his autobiography opined that Chilton was 'no shrinking violet' and acknowledged how grateful he was for the protection offered by his burly colleague. Certainly, Chilton played in more matches than Carey in both of the seasons after football resumed and was a pillar of an exciting side, complementing the thrilling attacking guile of the forward line. Some of his peers felt he deservedly succeeded Carey as skipper in 1953 because it was overdue recognition for this service.

The victory over Derby set up a final date with Stanley Matthews' Blackpool, but also sparked a thorny debate over bonuses that would prove difficult to resolve. The Rams had been promised cash incentives to lift the trophy at Wembley and were a wealthy club, causing the United players to feel aggrieved they would not be remunerated for their efforts. Carey was pressurised into meeting with Busby to discuss the matter and was left in an invidious position as he tried to bridge the two camps and reach some form of compromise.

The manager steadfastly refused the request and, although he and his captain tried to redress the balance in other areas – for instance, requesting payment from newspapers for a pre-final photoshoot (an idea that was rebuffed by the press) – it was left to Carey to maintain morale in the dressing room. Thankfully, the defender shared his manager's convictions in elevating football above mere financial reward and, when mischievous reports emerged on the morning of the showpiece game, claiming the boss had described his players as 'swell-headed', Carey apparently approached the Scot at breakfast to tell him not to concern himself because the players did not believe the articles accurately portrayed the manager's feelings.

'The United captaincy was important to Busby,' explained Eamonn Dunphy in *A Strange Kind of Glory*, providing an insider's view as a former apprentice at the club. 'Carey provided the leadership which was symbolic of the ethos Busby had sought to inculcate into his football club from the beginning. Carey was loyal and decent, his behaviour always impeccable. He played the game graciously. Carey was neither militant nor one of the lads. But that was not what was required of him. Like Busby, he came to stand for something by which Manchester United wished to be known: something that was noble rather than feckless; dignified rather than coarse.'

The big day out at Wembley proved to be a memorable success and an exhibition of attacking football. United won one of the finest FA Cup finals 4-2 despite falling behind to a 12th-minute Eddie Shimwell penalty. Chilton conceded the spot-kick for a foul on Stan Mortensen, which appeared to be outside of the area, and even sheepishly asked for a transfer soon after the game as he felt a change in environment might be needed to enhance his work. Busby, illustrating his faith in the defender, refused the request.

Rowley levelled but England international Mortensen sent the Tangerines into the break with a 2-1 advantage. It took a simple but influential team-talk by the Irishman in the dressing room to inspire his troops. 'Don't panic,' he assured his colleagues. 'Keep playing football.' Rowley netted again with 20 minutes left and set up a rousing finale, as goals by Pearson and John Anderson allowed Carey to proudly lift the trophy aloft – the first United skipper since Charlie Roberts to get his hands on the iconic piece of silverware.

A tour of Carey's native Ireland followed in the summer and his popularity back home was glaringly obvious. In fact, the genial skipper was rightly being revered throughout the game, going on to win the Footballer of the Year award in the following year. 'He was seen to embody the values – on and off the field – of Busby himself,' added Dunphy. 'Elan in battle, dignified, modest acknowledgement of the acclaim which greeted victory. Carey was the sportswriters' choice and the people's.'

The club's first major honour since the title triumph in 1911 led to focus switching to the elusive league championship, but the Reds finished runners-up, once again, in 1948-49 as Portsmouth topped the table by five points. At least in 1949, Carey captained Eire to a 2-0 victory at Goodison Park to inflict England's first defeat on home soil to a foreign side and earned himself another place in the record books.

Returning to domestic matters with United, Carey and the rest of his side were finally able to play at Old Trafford after the repairs to the wartime damage were finally completed ahead of the 1949-50 season. The team fell short of their primary ambition as fourth spot was attained in 1950, amid a backdrop of some footballers growing increasingly mutinous over their perceived poor pay. United remained a big draw and looked to exploit the popularity gained from the FA Cup victory, and the team's entertaining style, by embarking on an exotic trip while the stars' salaries remained relatively low.

Unfortunately, things came to a head during the tour of the United States and Canada when Carey agreed to write a diary for the *Manchester Chronicle* and revealed interest in the United stars from South American clubs, specifically Independiente Santa Fe. '£3,500 a year does not tempt us,' he insisted. 'The Millionairos club of Colombia are looking for players to go there. You can take it from me that none of the United players would consider such a proposition because it would mean "finis" as regards our future in Britain.' Yet the comparative riches on offer did ultimately prove too good to resist, and Mitten left for Bogotá after four years in the first team and 61 goals. Stoke City pair Neil Franklin and George Mountford also ended up at the Colombian club.

As other United players were reportedly close to making the same decision to leave, there was a need to unify the squad and for Busby to assert his control over the players, which was not always easy to do with war veterans. The manager would soon embark on a strategy of introducing his fabled Babes into the fold. By acquiring burgeoning talent from further afield within England, he would replace the increasingly agitated senior professionals with youngsters blessed with ability, loyalty to him and United and, in some respects, innocence. Carey would remain an important ally in mentoring this next wave of starry-eyed footballers in his final months at the club, but the draft of rookies would not leave their indelible imprint on footballing history, tragically off the field as well as on it, until after his exit.

Mark Jones, who initially broke into the team as a 17-year-old in October 1950, was an early tyro to benefit from his captain's wisdom and experience. 'Johnny Carey always had time to do his own work and yet look after me as well if I got into trouble,' admitted the Yorkshireman, who was also indebted to Chilton for guidance later in his career. A key role of the skipper was to ensure a smooth transition for any new faces and this was a task handled with relish by 'Gentleman John'.

Bill Foulkes was another young player who came through the ranks at this time, and he told the story of his debut against Liverpool in 1952 in his autobiography: 'He [Carey] may have looked like an old guy, prematurely balding, a bit stooped and with his shorts too long,' said the defender. 'But I left the pitch thanking my lucky stars to have played alongside such a master. Afterwards, he came up to me and asked me my age. I told him I was 20; he looked me in the eye and declared in that soft Irish brogue of his: "I think you'll do well." That's all it was. Nothing to turn a young fellow's head but it made me feel eight-feet tall.'

Another player who looked up to the skipper was Jackie Blanchflower. 'There I was, a sixteen-year-old lost Irish boy standing at the station in Manchester when Jackie Carey himself came to meet me,' he said. 'We were taken under the wing of the more experienced men.'

As with all good stories, there was the perfect ending in many respects when Carey skippered the side to the holy grail of the title in 1952. The previous campaign had ended with a fourth second-placed finish under Busby, and increased fears the Reds would be forever the bridesmaids and never the bride. Mercifully, United saw off the challenge of North London rivals Tottenham and Arsenal to lift the coveted trophy.

The key win against Chelsea was the crowning glory for United, and their captain in particular. It was rather poetic that he should score in the 3-0 triumph at Old Trafford. 'With all the near misses, I remember thinking it's about time that I got myself a champions' medal,' he recalled. 'Against Chelsea, something happened that will never leave my memory. I got the ball near goal and, with all the Chelsea players moving out towards our forwards, leaving me just outside their penalty area and inviting a shot. The ball bounced just right for my left foot which sent the ball high into the goal. At that moment, the league championship was ours and the crowd were all on their feet cheering us for so long that, as Chelsea kicked off again, everyone was still celebrating.'

The unassuming, modest hero was the toast of the red half of Manchester, but legend has it he walked back home to Chorlton after the game and even volunteered to do the washing up rather than join in any of the joyous partying that may have been taking place elsewhere. There must have simply been a sense of overwhelming satisfaction that he had succeeded in leading the team to a first title since 1911.

Much is made of the Irish brogue and dignified manner of such a consummate professional. The Dubliner's gentle demeanour only added to the aura surrounding his personality. This was something he would always possess, with even a player of Johnny Giles's stature admitting he felt in constant awe of his fellow countryman and many of his colleagues felt the same.

Such charisma and standing among fellow football men was not lost on the giants of the game. 'He was a tall, quietly spoken yet loquacious Irishman of commanding presence,' explained Busby. 'A prince among contemporary footballers. People who know me will vouch for the fact that I never indulge in idle adulation, but a certain Johnny Carey was one of the truly great players of all times.'

It is possible to wonder whether Carey never truly understood the respect he engendered in Busby during their time together at Old Trafford. He was so utterly determined to follow the manager's lead that he felt a sense of duty to perform with distinction in every single game and might have been consumed by this professionalism. 'He never used a superlative about something that didn't deserve it,' he said of his boss. 'Very occasionally, after a match, aside, he would come and say: "Well done, skipper," which meant more than a thousand pounds. You had to win his heart. I don't suppose he said it more than four or five times in seven years. I always tried to play in such a way to make him say it.'

In his final season as a player, Carey was sometimes left out of the team, missing ten of the team's 42 Division One fixtures, unlike ever-present Chilton. A new role was offered to ensure he would still feel he was a key figure. Tommy Taylor, a promising striker who had broken into Barnsley's first team, was attracting admiring glances from Busby and his assistant Jimmy Murphy. The boss sought another opinion on the Tykes' target man and requested his senior star should produce a first-hand scouting report on behalf of United.

A positive reference was supplied and the centre-forward joined the Reds soon afterwards for a fee of £29,999 – Busby did not want him to be bracketed as a £30,000 signing – with other clubs left disappointed by the decisive raid on Oakwell. Still an influence as his on-field powers waned, it became clear Carey's role was beginning to change and he knew he could put his experience to good benefit as a manager. Having already coached Ireland at the 1948 Olympics and managed the first XI at his son's school, it was a natural career path to follow and one he had undoubtedly envisaged for some time.

As he was held in such enormous esteem, there was a need to transmit the right signals to the youngsters taking over the mantle and he had clear views on the subject. Writing in an official Football Association bulletin, he explained his ethos to those attempting to make their way into the game. 'Go to meet the ball,' was one instruction. 'Do simple things quickly. There are bitter disappointments, hours of practice and many sacrifices to be made before you can start to climb the precipitous ladder to stardom.' Other prerequisites were to focus on punctuality, conversation, training and taking orders. Sound advice for the budding Busby Babes.

'Johnny was ever so polite and kind,' recollected Dennis Viollet ahead of his debut, a 2-1 win at Newcastle United in April 1953. 'He shook me by the hand and wished me well.' At that point, at 34, he clearly resembled a veteran approaching the end of his career. 'From the moment he led out his side, you got the impression that he was bringing out a pack of schoolboys who were put through their paces under his supervision,' suggested Geoffrey Green in *The Times*.

The end came in May when he felt he was no longer able to hold his own in the team. 'I don't feel capable of playing the brand of soccer for another season,' he conceded and made the decision to hang up his boots. The retirement, inevitably, produced a flood of tributes in recognition of his wonderful contribution to the game.

The esteemed journalist David Meek perhaps put it best in his book *Heroes of the Busby Era* when describing Carey as 'arguably the last of the great Corinthians in professional soccer'. Former team-mate and goalkeeper Crompton was in no doubt about his influence, but may have challenged this perception, hinting his pal also had a mean streak if required.

'He would be one of the first names on my teamsheet,' Crompton wrote in his autobiography when selecting his favourite XI. 'He was an excellent player and a great skipper. He was Gentleman John if the winger wasn't causing any problems! If the opposing forward was a bit of a handful, then he knew just how to deal with them. Otherwise, Carey would be there to do what was necessary to keep his team in check. He was, in every sense, Matt Busby's representative on the pitch.'

The *Manchester Guardian* offered the following assessment: 'The captain has been a model footballer – technically efficient thanks to hard work and a fighter to the last, without ever forgetting that he is a sportsman. A steadier of the younger and inexperienced. An inspirer of the older and tiring and, at all times, the most modest of men, though he has won every football honour open to him.' Other newspapers similarly lauded his achievements, with the *Sunderland Echo* stating: 'His artistic ability on the field and quiet dignity and charm off it combine to make him not only a great footballer but one of the game's gentlemen. His cool, unflustered play and powers as a captain have steadied United on more than one occasion.'

A further measure of the lofty position he held within the club was provided when, for the first time, he was invited to the board-room after retiring. It was a symbolic gesture, one that bridged the gap between the playing staff and the board, and was genuinely appreciated by the United hero. 'No player had ever been respected as him,' insisted Dunphy.

After declining a coaching role at Old Trafford, he accepted the manager's position at Blackburn Rovers instead and then moved on to Everton. Many football fans were outraged by the manner of the Toffees' sacking of the respected figure in 1961. Director John Moores told the boss of the decision to oust him as the pair travelled by taxi to a Football Association meeting in London. Nonetheless, successful stints at Leyton Orient and Nottingham Forest followed and he also managed the Republic of Ireland.

The position as United captain would initially be handed to Pearson, but the inside-forward would soon join nearby Bury. Chilton finally had his chance to lead the side and provided the kind of tutorship to the younger charges that would have been asked of Carey had he accepted the offer to remain on the staff.

'We owed a lot to Chilton, who was then the most experienced player in the side,' revealed Viollet in the much-read *Charles Buchan's Football Monthly*. 'Allenby had to work tremendously hard at centre-half with so many immature players around him. But he was a constant inspiration and held the team together until we found our feet. He dominated the defence, covered up our mistakes and found time to encourage each player. Allenby never minced words. He told us on the field exactly what to do!' This blunt but effective leadership helped the team to finish fourth in Division One, as the Reds remained one of the top sides in the country.

Yet the sands of time were against Chilton, too. In February 1955, he requested a break from first-team duty after an exhausting run of matches – he had set a club record of 166 consecutive league appearances – but never regained his place from the promising Jones. A player-manager's role at Grimsby Town beckoned, but the next incumbent of the captain's role, a man who would be renowned as the leader of the Busby Babes, was ready to step into the spotlight.

Chapter 4

Leader of the Busby Babes

'You looked around [the team] and saw one strength
piled upon another. On top of all this was the
extraordinary leadership of Roger Byrne.'

Sir Bobby Charlton

The pantheon of great Manchester United captains has many distinguished and deserved members, but no such collection of legendary leaders is complete without Roger Byrne. One of the finest defenders to grace Old Trafford, Byrne was a fatherly figure to the pre-eminent Busby Babes and his tragic demise among some of Manchester and British football's most celebrated sons in Munich in 1958 cloaks his unquestionable talent and triumphs in tragedy.

The Gorton-born defender was tough and determined, quiet and sometimes considered aloof by opponents and team-mates alike, but he was a man of staunch principle, exacting standards of professionalism, as well as being a lean and lively presence in defence and attack. He would stand up to anyone, even Matt Busby, who made him his captain right at the formative stage of the emergence into the first team of the feted 'Babes', as they took their positive steps on the road to national and international renown.

Byrne joined United as an amateur in 1948, signing professional forms the following year. Although he would eventually settle in his favoured role at left-back, he initially found opportunities as an outside-left and, in his first season in the side, the title-winning 1951-52 campaign, he scored seven goals in the last six games to help the Reds clinch a first league crown since 1911.

His debut had come in a 0-0 draw with Liverpool in November 1951, at left-back, and he held that position for a further four months before Busby switched him to outside-left away at Burnley on Good Friday, where he found the net in a 1-1 draw to begin an impressive run of scoring form that would account for more than a third of his overall total of 20 career goals for United.

Busby was praised as the 'Master Switcher' in the press for his tactical shift, but the positional to-ing and fro-ing would become a source of contention between manager and player. Byrne was perhaps never considered a technically outstanding footballer, but Busby clearly saw qualities of higher importance in this local lad – he just had to find the best way to utilise them.

Byrne picked up his second trophy with United in September 1952 as the Reds defeated FA Cup winners Newcastle 4-2 in the Charity Shield. However, a 1-0 home loss to their North-East neighbours Sunderland in the following game and Byrne's omission from the team in the match after that against Wolverhampton Wanderers, brought matters to a head. He had flitted between left-back and left-wing that season and his form had subsequently suffered. Now he wanted to a permanent place in the team. The challenge to Busby's authority resulted in a stand-off, and Byrne was placed on the transfer list, but it was perhaps one of the first instances where the great man realised that here was a character who thought for himself, knew what he wanted and was principled, with a clear vision of where his strengths were best suited. The story would pass into legend among the young players emerging at the club who were in awe of both men.

Sir Bobby Charlton relayed the story in his autobiography, *My Manchester United Years*, saying: 'Roger had the feeling that he had been made a scapegoat for a bad defeat and his frustration welled up during a training session when Busby shouted an instruction. Byrne's response was dismissive and his language was quite rough, and the manager retired to his office with something of a dilemma. Could he accept this challenge to his authority – or did he have to impose some discipline? His decision, before it was quickly revoked, was sensational. He put Roger on the transfer list. But not for long, when he pondered how much the team would miss his style and leadership.' Busby had a saying he was fond of using when a player's conduct fell below the high standards he was adamant should always be set: 'That's not United.' But Charlton adds: 'For Byrne, a compromise could be made. Busby knew he had a rare leader.'

The champions finished eighth in the league in 1952-53 as Johnny Carey announced his retirement. He had been a huge influence on Byrne's burgeoning talent and professionalism, but he had also helped develop his emerging credentials as a leader of the exciting crop of youngsters who were beginning to force their way into the Old Trafford reckoning.

The season marked a dramatic change at the club. While the title-winning team 12 months previously had largely been the culmination of Busby's post-war efforts to make United successful, particularly in the league after several near misses, his evolution of the line-up and the realisation of his vision to bring through talented youngsters was finally coming to fruition. From the team that triumphed 6-1 over Arsenal to confirm the title in April 1952, only three players (John Aston, Byrne and Allenby Chilton) survived to start against Portsmouth in the final home game two years later.

By the end of that 1953-54 campaign, Byrne had racked up more than 100 United appearances and earned his first England cap in a 4-2 win over Scotland at Hampden Park. He had caught the eye on his debut, despite being considered partly to blame for one of Scotland's goals and, after impressing in two further friendlies, he was included in the World Cup squad for the 1954 tournament in Switzerland. England made it to the quarter-finals, where the reigning world champions Uruguay defeated them. Nevertheless, it was a huge learning experience for Byrne, whose stature in the game was rapidly on the rise. He would not miss an England game for the rest of his life, playing in 33 consecutive matches.

Change was still afoot at Old Trafford in 1954-55. Despite a promising start to the season, as the Reds topped the table for spells during September and October – before falling and rising to third throughout November, December and January – a poor February (which included a jarring 5-0 league loss to Manchester City, a 2-0 FA Cup fourth-round exit to the same opponents and a 4-2 defeat to Wolves) meant Busby sought further transformations.

Allenby Chilton, who took over as captain from Carey, was about to bring an abrupt halt to an incredible run of 176 consecutive appearances and asked to be rested. The United stalwart, well aware of the impending changing of the guard at the club, was never to play for the first team again, as Mark Jones quickly established himself in the role. That opened the door for Byrne.

With Chilton moving on and 34-year-old Jack Rowley in the last of his 18-year association with United as a player, Busby knew he had the right man to take the captaincy in Byrne. Other than Johnny Berry, he was the most senior figure having just turned 26, and he was surrounded by younger men – Bill Foulkes and Tommy Taylor (both 23), Dennis Viollet and Jackie Blanchflower (both 21), Duncan Edwards (18) and others besides – so his standing in the squad was one of great respect.

Byrne was unflinching as he took on the responsibility. 'Following in the footsteps of Johnny Carey, Stan Pearson and Allenby Chilton was an honour,' he said, and he also admitted to having studiously watched those players to pick up on their behaviour and actions as he felt one day the role as leader would naturally fall to him.

United ended the season by beating Chelsea 2-1 at Old Trafford, but it wasn't enough to prevent the Londoners winning the league as the Reds finished fifth. Hopes were high that the soon-to-be-dubbed 'Busby Babes' would deliver on a second title of the decade. However, the 1955-56 campaign started with less than convincing form in the first eight games, which included three defeats and two draws, but Busby kept faith with the team he was so sure Byrne would lead to glory. His instincts were proved right as results picked up and the Reds claimed top spot in the league with a 1-0 win over Cardiff City on 29 October.

After another early FA Cup exit, this time at the hands of Bristol Rovers – United went out in the third round on three occasions in five seasons – the charge to title glory was relentless. United were undefeated in 14 matches from 22 January onwards, and the team's final haul of 60 points had not been bettered in ten post-war campaigns. Second-placed Blackpool were way back on 49 points, although that sizeable distance had been settled when the two teams met at Old Trafford on 7 April in what was effectively a title-decider.

Blackpool led inside two minutes and United had to endure an hour of applying persistent pressure before the breakthrough came from the spot. Byrne had been a regular penalty-taker for the team, but perhaps recent misses from 12 yards were playing on his mind as he opted not to take the kick. However, the decision could have owed more to a superstitious streak he was not prone to disclosing to teammates or even close members of his family.

His United room-mate John Doherty reported that Byrne

frequently woke in the night having suffered nightmares. The story goes that before the Blackpool match, Byrne dreamed of missing a penalty and, in a cold sweat, swore that rather than put fate to the test, he would not take a penalty were United awarded one. Whether another sign of his superstitions or not, Byrne also insisted on sticking with his trusty and comfortable, but rather worn, football boots. Their condition got so bad that he asked his wife Joy to take them to the cobblers because he was too embarrassed to go himself.

Regardless, Berry stepped up and converted his kick to make it 1-1 and it set up a grandstand finish. Tommy Taylor had suffered an injury earlier in the game and was a peripheral figure until ten minutes from time when the most prolific scorer in United's history popped up with the crucial goal to clinch the win, and the title.

Byrne was absolutely delighted: 'To say I am a proud captain is to put it mildly. I can hardly realise the championship trophy is really ours and the months of tension since we took the lead last December are over.' The United skipper collected the trophy after a routine 1-0 win over Portsmouth at Old Trafford in the campaign's final game and led the triumphant players onto the field to soak up the applause of 38,417 fans. It was a surprisingly low attendance given the, admittedly more crucial, Blackpool game attracted 62,277 supporters. Still, Byrne had missed just three games all season as he presided over an unbeaten home record, boasting 18 wins, 51 goals scored and a miserly 20 conceded at Old Trafford.

United's triumphant players were afforded a civic reception at Manchester's Town Hall, where Byrne paraded the trophy and addressed the thousands of supporters who had lined the streets, acknowledging their patience and support throughout the season. 'During my brief stay at Old Trafford, never has this club been more united,' he was reported to have said.

Important though it was to dominate domestically, United, and Busby in particular, had more far-reaching ambitions. So when the club was invited into the draw for the European Cup – the powers that be in the game, the Football Association and the Football League, could not agree on giving it their approval, with the League concerned it would distract United from their own competition – Busby was insistent United should innovate and be the first English team to make an assault on European success. Six weeks after United lifted the First Division title, Real Madrid won the inaugural European Champion Clubs' Cup after beating French side Stade de Reims 4-3 at Parc des Princes in Paris. With club chairman Harold Hardman persuaded that European football would bring increased profits, the Football League's objections were overcome with the help of the FA.

United and Busby's appetite for adventure was anything but sated by domestic success. The Reds were paired with Anderlecht in the preliminary round and Byrne became the first United captain to lead the team into European competition, and the occasion – a proud one for skipper and club – brought a 2-0 first-leg win. That was one of nine victories in the first ten games in 1956-57, culminating in a 2-0 win over Manchester City. The next match, in late September, saw Anderlecht visit Manchester – all but one of United's home European games was played at Maine Road that season, incidentally, as Old Trafford was yet to install floodlights. The Belgians left Moss Side with their tails between their legs after being hit for ten goals without reply – still a club record today. Dennis Viollet scored four, Taylor notched a hat-trick, Liam Whelan hit two and Berry got the other.

In an example of a captain's pressure to perform with impeccable consistency, Byrne's displays often came under scrutiny. Former goalkeeper turned local reporter Frank Swift, who tragically would be one of the 23 to lose their lives in Munich, commented after a 4-1 league win over Sheffield Wednesday that month: 'If I must single out anyone, then I name Roger Byrne as Man of the Match. Roger has his critics, but this was a streamlined display out of the top drawer.

[Last month] He had Tom Finney, who can be one of the most dangerous wingers in the game, a prisoner on the touchline. Byrne not only kept the Wednesday match-winner out, but also zoomed into attack to start the moves which led to the first three goals. There was England class written all over his display.'

Just a month later, the same commentator berated Byrne for an error in the slender 3-2 first-round first-leg lead garnered against Borussia Dortmund. 'I blame Byrne for the slip which started the avalanche of attacks,' he wrote. 'In the 70th minute, instead of kicking the ball away, Byrne breasted it nonchalantly down for Ray Wood. Alas, Kapitulski was there first and Byrne held his head in disgust as the ball rocketed into the net.'

Byrne again came in for criticism following a 5-2 defeat against Everton but, four days later, he was lifting his second trophy as captain as the Reds defeated City 1-0 in the Charity Shield back at Maine Road. The team's exceptional start might have hit a few bumps along the way, but the saying 'form is temporary, class is permanent' applied and United were soon chasing an unprecedented Treble.

The Reds' skipper dealt with the expectation that came his way, often shielding the younger members of the squad from it, all without showing any cracks in his personality or professionalism. Yet that still didn't bring down his defences in front of his team-mates.

Byrne had been a grammar school boy and continued in part-time education in adulthood, taking a physiotherapy course at Salford Royal Hospital. He was a family man, married, owned a car – one of the first players at United to do so, much to the envy of his peers – and his interests away from football and his general demeanour put what was possibly a healthy distance between himself and the younger members of the team.

'I was never close to our captain, not as I was with almost every other member of the team, but he always had my immense respect,' wrote Sir Bobby Charlton in *My Manchester United Years.* 'I saw him as an aloof master in all that he did. I didn't have the nerve to speak to him freely because he seemed to be operating on another level of life to the rest of us. He seemed so well educated, so cosmopolitan in my eyes, and I marvelled at the fact that he spent most of his free time away from the club working in a hospital.

'He didn't hang around with the lads because he had his own life in Manchester, and was married and not in need of boyish company. On the field, Roger would shout his instructions firmly enough, let you know who was in charge of affairs, but generally he was quiet off the field. He had the aura of a true captain. If you did well, scored a goal, say, you would not expect more than a cursory pat on the back, yet from him it was a gesture you would prize very highly indeed.'

Wilf McGuinness, another young United hopeful at the time, whose career would sadly be ended through injury, described Byrne as a 'loner' and a 'stern disciplinarian' in his book *Manchester United Man and Babe*, but the description isn't a criticism. He added: '[That was] exactly what some of us needed, as we could be a bit daft and boisterous at times. Certainly he seemed quite fearsome to me as a young Reserve. Roger was older than everybody except Johnny Berry. He had a more mature perspective on life than most of us. You could have a joke with Roger but knew you couldn't overstep the mark and Matt Busby must have seen him as an ideal captain. He had authority.'

Of little doubt, it seemed, as United pressed on with the championship charge in the spring of 1957, was that Byrne would get his hands on the league trophy once again. He did so as the Reds racked up a post-war record 64 points, eight more than runners-up Tottenham Hotspur. But it was United's forays into Europe that really caused a stir and created excitement among fans and media alike. With progress being made in the domestic and continental cups, the Treble became a very real possibility.

In the European Cup, having secured a 0-0 away draw to beat Dortmund on aggregate in the first round in November, United overturned January's 5-3 away defeat at Athletic Club – played amid wet and wintry conditions in Bilbao that Byrne described as the worst he had ever seen – as the Reds won 3-0 at home the following month to tee up April's semi-final ties with the pre-eminent reigning champions, Real. Another first-leg defeat, this time by three goals to one at the mighty Bernabeu in front of a colossal 135,000 fans, left United if not a mountain to climb then at least a steep gradient to ascend to make the final.

Byrne had stood toe-to-toe with Real captain Francisco Gento; two great captains of two great clubs. Despite conceding three goals, United were considered to have defended well against the might of the men from Madrid, especially as the Reds left complaining of the opposition's physical tactics. The *Manchester Guardian* protested that Taylor was 'kicked, pummelled, elbowed, shoved, held by the shirt and generally man-handled in a way completely foreign to the English notion'. Don Davies's report continued: 'If this sort of stuff is repeated at Old Trafford – and the referee described this as a "friendly game" remember – then the spectators may prepare themselves for something novel in the way of friendly football. But they'll see some superb stuff as well and if United's five defending heroes play as they played today then as trainer [Tom] Curry said at the close of the match they'll "deserve gold medals as big as frying pans".'

In Manchester, the visitors were keen to press on with their claims to European domination and carved a 2-0 half-time lead at Old Trafford – now it really was a mountain to climb, of Everest proportions. But Byrne and United simply would not give up. David Pegg's cross from the left was met by Taylor and, as the ball hit a post and bobbled along the goalline, Whelan made sure by slamming it into the back of the net. Charlton equalised to make it 2-2 but despite all the toiling it wasn't enough. United were out.

There would be further knockout heartache as Busby's charges lost the FA Cup final 2-1 to Aston Villa. United beat Hartlepool, Wrexham, Everton, Bournemouth and Birmingham City to reach the final, and in the 2-0 semi-final victory against the latter at Hillsborough, Davies heaped praise on Byrne's United, who ruthlessly nullified the contest inside 14 minutes. He wrote: 'At that point, if this had been a boxing match, [the] referee would have advanced to Byrne and raised his arm as the winner, knowing, as we ourselves did, that for all practical purposes the show was over. But custom decrees that the clients shall have their money's worth in time if not in trepidation, and thus at least they were privileged to see five Manchester United defenders tackling and positioning at their very best. To Byrne, as captain, for his inspiring example, his cool directives, his flawless anticipation, and his creative clearances, must go first praise.'

Between the emotionally draining European semi-final with Real on 25 April and the Cup final on 4 May, United also had two games to tie up loose ends in the league, meaning four games in ten days. If tired legs and minds needed to be jolted into action, that was the case in the crudest fashion after just six minutes. Aston Villa forward Peter McParland clattered into Wood and left the United goalkeeper unconscious on the floor with a broken cheekbone. Jackie Blanchflower was handed the keeper's jersey by Byrne and, with no substitutes in those days, United were left to contest the match with ten men.

Wood, miraculously and bravely, returned to the field as an outfield player but as he was suffering from concussion and his injuries, he was a mere passenger, although he did return to goal for the final seven minutes of the game. Interestingly enough, it was seen as Byrne's decision as skipper to bring Wood back to his natural position and give United the extra man in attack. However, by that time, McParland had rubbed salt in the wounds he inflicted by scoring two goals to give Villa a commanding lead. Taylor pulled one back in the

83rd minute and that's when Wood returned between the sticks as United threw everything at Villa, but as with Europe it wasn't to be.

United's FA Cup drama might have been considered a disaster for some clubs, but Byrne and his boys were just getting started. Some players were still a few years from reaching physical and professional maturity, and already the Busby Babes were the envy of England and even of Europe. Byrne acknowledged that Real were the best side United had ever faced in any competition. It was a gracious concession but it wasn't an acceptance of defeat, it was a challenge to himself and the rest of the team that next time United would be victorious.

As with all great captains, the biggest challenges bring out the best in their character. Byrne may only have been of slight build, but that season he stood a little taller. In February's 4-2 Manchester derby win, Byrne was booed throughout, but his performance showed that the precociousness of United's fledgling talents was being coaxed along brilliantly by their leader on the field. The *Daily Mirror*'s match report of that game stated that Byrne 'bullied his men out of a second-half slumber', before adding: 'Here was the captain courageous – a strong man who listened to the crowd's boos and heard a call to action. Here was a captain courageous who listened to two stern lectures from the referee and charged back into the game as if they had been pep talks.'

Byrne was not in the sport to be popular, he was in it to do his job well and to be successful, and he set both heart and mind to the task in a way in which others would gladly give everything to follow. So, any disappointment shelved, United started 1957-58 in imperious fashion with six straight wins and 22 goals. In fact the season, on paper at least, looks strikingly familiar to the previous campaign, as United would again reach the semi-finals of the European Cup and the final of the FA Cup, but the circumstances, the details, and the devastation were utterly different from the previous term's sense of promise and potential.

Despite the bright start, United's league form dipped, with four defeats in the next seven outings, but in October's Charity Shield at Old Trafford – against Aston Villa – there was an opportunity to exact some revenge for the previous spring's frustrations. To say there wasn't any lingering ill-feeling for the challenge on Wood at Wembley would be misleading. In the event, there simply was no contest and the best reprisal possibly was a resounding 4-0 triumph as Taylor bagged a hat-trick and Berry scored the other.

However, Wood soon lost his place as United's leaky defence, which had contributed to the team's shaky league form, needed shoring up and Busby paid Doncaster Rovers £25,000 for the services of Northern Irish goalkeeper Harry Gregg. Remarkably, given the events about to unfold, the new man between the sticks would miss just two games for the remainder of the season and his arrival immediately met with an upturn in results. Gregg's debut in a 4-0 win over Leicester City on 21 December began an unbeaten run that would stretch to 15 matches and well into March.

Gregg briefly stayed at Byrne's family home while he settled into life in Manchester and realised that his perception of a player he had faced at international level with Northern Ireland and, on the surface of it, found somewhat aloof and distant, was nothing like the man.

The turn of the year, as always, brought with it the focus of the cup competitions and Red Star Belgrade travelled to Manchester in January. Charlton and Eddie 'Snakehips' Colman gave United a 2-1 lead in the tie – hardly a commanding advantage ahead of a difficult second leg in Yugoslavia three weeks later, but a lead nonetheless. United followed that victory with a 7-2 league win over Bolton (Charlton scoring three, Viollet two, and both Edwards and Albert Scanlon one apiece), and then beat Ipswich Town 2-0 in the FA Cup before playing out one of the most entertaining matches in the club's history against Arsenal at Highbury.

The Reds led 3-0 at half time and were even applauded off the field by the home fans, but Arsenal hit back to level matters after the break. An injury to Byrne put even more pressure on Busby's men, as the skipper completed the match with minimal input, but the visitors scored twice more before Arsenal pulled another back, completing a 5-4 win for the Reds – that team's last game on English soil.

Byrne was subsequently a doubt for the trip to Belgrade for the second leg of United's European Cup quarter-final, but he received intensive treatment before the squad departed and, indeed, once they arrived at the team hotel. Nevertheless, he would line up with the rest of the team at the open-air Stadion JNA in Belgrade in front of a 55,000-strong crowd.

United started brilliantly, as Viollet scored after 90 seconds before Charlton added two in two minutes to make it 5-1 on aggregate at the break. The Reds, playing in a white change strip, looked to be cruising, but Red Star hit back to make it 3-3. It was a nervous wait for the final whistle and Byrne wasn't shy in revealing his relief when it finally sounded and United's path to the semi-finals in successive seasons was confirmed.

Celebrations that night, however, would be tragically tempered by the following day's horrific events as the plane carrying United's squad, club staff and journalists failed in its third attempt at take-off on the icy slush of Munich-Riem Airport. The air crash sent the city and the football world into deep shock and mourning.

John Arlott, a sports journalist for the *Manchester Guardian*, had initially been drafted in to replace the unavailable regular Don Davies, whose beautifully descriptive musings were signed off 'Old International'. At the last minute, Davies decided to travel, sealing his sad fate. As No.2 on the Manchester beat, Arlott had the tearful task of piecing together events for the newspaper. His story read: 'Yesterday on Munich airfield, Association Football shrank to a small matter. Twenty-four hours before, Manchester United had drawn with Red Star Belgrade to pass into the semi-final of the European Cup on aggregate. It was yet another triumph for the finest club team ever produced in Britain. For the moment that victory seems slight, at best, a memorial to young athletes now dead.'

The loss placed a deep void at the heart of the club, which simply could not be filled. Of the 23 people who lost their lives, the team that Busby had built led by Roger Byrne and including Geoff Bent, Eddie Colman, Duncan Edwards, Mark Jones, David Pegg, Tommy Taylor and Liam Whelan, had been cruelly snatched away. Busby would later remark with a voice cracked with emotion: 'You could say that the first few years affect you more – or you are more aware of it – but time doesn't heal these things; it doesn't for me anyway.'

Just 13 days after Munich, with Duncan Edwards about to lose his brave battle with the injuries he suffered, and Busby still in hospital, United had to play an FA Cup fifth-round tie against Sheffield Wednesday at Old Trafford and Bill Foulkes, a survivor of the crash, led the team out. United won 3-0 in a sombrely emotionally game and somehow, after going on to beat West Brom and Fulham, a broken team made it to Wembley for the final, where Bolton ran out 2-0 winners.

The much-changed United side's European campaign had to continue too, although the semi-final with AC Milan, held in May after the league and cup games had finished, ended in a 5-2 aggregate defeat. Foulkes would retain the captaincy the following season, before it passed to Viollet and then Maurice Setters before a new era would be ushered in.

Life, somewhat brutally, carries on in even the most devastating circumstances. But Byrne and the Babes will never be forgotten and, in fact, the daring of youth, the brilliance of that team, shine as a beacon of the club's past and of its unique identity – a point to which Byrne evocatively subscribed – of doing it the United way.

Chapter 5

The Thinker

'He was always a leader. He always had that way about him and he had an air of authority that made him a natural captain.'

Johnny Giles, former Manchester United midfielder

Noel Cantwell arrived at Old Trafford with a reputation as a deep thinker on the game and, potentially, a top-class coach of the future. Later in his Reds career, when he often found himself out of the side, he went on to become United's first-ever club captain, holding on to the position even though someone else would be the match-day leader. The shrewd signing from West Ham United had led the Hammers to promotion in 1958, but lost his place at Upton Park to John Lyall and, after asking for a move, cost the Reds £29,500 when he signed for them in November 1960 – a record fee for a full-back. He would soon be asked to maintain harmony in a dressing room containing big personalities and even bigger talents.

After less than two-and-a-half years at the club, he replaced Maurice Setters as skipper in March 1963, ensuring he would be the man who lifted the FA Cup at the end of that memorable season.

However, the deposed captain was also part of the successful XI at Wembley on 25 May and continued to live up to a hard-man image and play an important role.

Setters' method of captaincy was to be vocal and belligerent, barking out orders to his colleagues and sometimes embracing confrontation. When a suspension was imposed for arguing with the referee, it opened the door for a change. Matt Busby still had his ideals and handed the responsibility to a calmer figure in Cantwell – the Irishman was also tough and resilient but more controlled. Setters won the battle to regain his place in the team, but it was felt he might operate more effectively without the added responsibility of the captaincy.

Within a couple of months, Cantwell was leading the side out at Wembley against Leicester City. It was the perfect way to compensate for a league programme that had been so poor that a talented side, featuring Bobby Charlton, Johnny Giles, David Herd and Denis Law among others, flirted dangerously with relegation. United finished only three points above the drop zone as neighbours Manchester City were demoted to Division Two with Leyton Orient.

'I had only taken over the captaincy earlier in that season,' Cantwell later said in an interview with broadcasters RTE. 'The turmoil at the club was reflected in how many times the captain changed. But it was a very special day at Wembley.' Leicester were favourites to lift the cup after a fourth-placed spot in the top flight, but United could at least play with freedom after the relief of avoiding the drop.

Cantwell clearly relished the task in hand and set the tone for the team ahead of the showpiece event. 'Even I, as manager, had to admire the common-sense way he conducted his conference with the lads on the eve of the 1963 final,' admitted Busby. Leading by example, he conducted TV interviews in a relaxed mood and exuded confidence.

Yet the nerves were still fluttering among the players as 100,000 fans packed inside the national stadium. Setters popped out for a pint of beer at a nearby pub and new signing Paddy Crerand wandered outside in his jockstrap to listen to traditional hymn 'Abide with Me' in order to compose himself. 'If I had known that a drink of beer would have done the trick for Maurice, then I would have ordered him to take that stroll and have it on me,' Cantwell insisted.

The match itself went very much to plan, Law scoring as usual and Herd netting twice in a 3-1 win against a fancied Foxes side, as United earned a first major honour since the Munich tragedy. 'As the proud skipper of a proud team, I had to give fewer instructions than I sometimes have had to do in the first thirty minutes of many ordinary league games,' stated Cantwell.

'We set our stall out to keep possession as much as possible from the start. Even if the chances did not come. Leicester, accordingly, had to do a lot of chasing – something to avoid at Wembley – and, once we began to use the ball well, our confidence returned.' On an individual basis, *The Times*'s match report described him as a 'captain of influence and presence.' Giles said of his fellow countryman: 'He was always a leader. He always had that way about him and he had an air of authority that made him a natural captain.'

The defender initially forgot to collect his medal from the Queen and an FA official instructed the joyous skipper to relent from hurling the trophy around as the celebrations reflected the excitement over the accomplishment. 'I've played cricket for Ireland so I'm pretty sure I'll catch it,' was his measured response (he had won five caps in the sport for his country between 1956 and 1959). The players celebrated by drinking milk and, more appropriately, Moët in the changing room as they reflected on a landmark victory for the club – one that signalled the start of a new era after the dark days of tragedy five years earlier.

The following season saw United finish as runners-up behind Liverpool in the table, even if there was some incredible inconsistency in terms of results. Ipswich Town were hammered 7-2 at Portman Road, but Everton and Aston Villa thumped the Reds 4-0. A 6-1 loss to Burnley at Turf Moor on Boxing Day was avenged, just two days later, by a 5-1 victory in the corresponding fixture. Naturally, some thrilling displays of attacking football attracted many admirers and second spot was, of course, a vast improvement on finishing positions of 15th and 19th in the previous two years. United were back among the domestic elite and deservedly so.

Cantwell's personal campaign was marred by an incident in a pulsating European Cup-Winners' Cup tie against Tottenham at Old Trafford. While United successfully overturned the two-goal deficit from the first leg, the game will also be remembered for Dave Mackay breaking his leg during a bone-jarring collision with the United skipper. Some of those present claim the awful crack echoed around the stadium.

The granite-tough Mackay refused to forgive his opponent for what he deemed to be a reckless challenge and, for somebody who was never recognised as a dirty player, it was an unfortunate affair for Cantwell to become embroiled in. 'Dave was understandably bitter about that,' said Spurs striker Jimmy Greaves. 'They made up after they both retired but, for the rest of his playing career, he was planning a revenge hit.'

Law, who was watching from the stands, saw things differently despite his allegiance to Scotland colleague and pal Mackay. He came down to console his stricken friend but attached no blame to his team captain. 'I don't think Dave should have gone for it,' he stated. 'I'm not saying it was his fault though and it certainly wasn't Noel's either. It was just one of those freak accidents that can happen in sport.'

It can only be speculated as to whether the matter did have any psychological effect on Cantwell. Certainly, he struggled to maintain his place thereafter, as Busby moved Tony Dunne, who could operate on either flank, across to left-back, while right-back Shay Brennan was also in the mix, as the manager sought the perfect blend of the talents at his disposal.

Law took over leadership of the team when Cantwell was absent, famously locking horns with opposite number Charlie Hurley as Sunderland were overcome in a classic FA Cup encounter that is still talked about today on Wearside. After entertaining 3-3 and 2-2 draws, the Scotland striker hit a hat-trick in a 5-1 second-replay romp at Huddersfield Town's Leeds Road to knock the Roker Park outfit out and once again showcase his class.

As the cup run illustrated, the Reds guaranteed entertainment but much has been said about alleged friction between Cantwell and Busby over the team's tactical approach. Busby famously had simple directions for his side, urging his men to play football and pass to a red shirt. The club captain had developed a passion for the theoretical side of the game at West Ham and was good friends with Malcolm Allison and John Bond. The so-called 'footballing academy' founded in East London had spent many an hour discussing formations and modern coaching techniques, and Cantwell believed the team needed to adapt accordingly.

Indeed, Cantwell had been sat with Allison and Hammers legend Bobby Moore, whom he mentored and recommended for elevation into the first team, when he heard the sad news of Duncan Edwards' death in 1958. The three men shed tears as they processed the awful truth that the world had lost potentially the greatest of all the Busby Babes.

Cantwell recalled of Busby: 'I enjoyed Matt's company a lot. My first recollection was after signing from West Ham, when I was in his car, and I asked him: "How do we play?" He was amazed. "I just paid thirty thousand pounds for you. How do we play? We play football." At Matt's United, you blended in. You were a footballer and that was it.'

Yet the Irishman clearly respected a manager who had achieved so much in the game and survived the Munich air disaster, returning to his job after fighting for his life in a German hospital. 'He seems a dour Scot but he's a very kind and tolerant man,' wrote Cantwell in his autobiography. 'He is, without any shadow of a doubt, a father figure to us all at Old Trafford. He likes us to play the game simply but effectively. He is probably the complete soccer-minded man and he is a manager who wants to win all the time.'

Other players offered similar assessments of Busby's team-talks. For instance, Allenby Chilton insisted: 'He never told you how to play. Well, you've got to play your own way.' However, Law did offer an alternative view: 'We worked as diligently as most clubs on set-plays. We were well aware when we conceded a free-kick who should be in the defensive line-up, where we all were in relation to the play and who to pick up when we were not in possession. We all had our jobs to do. Had we not mastered the basics, it would have fallen apart and we would have been chasing our tails. It was often like a game of chess at times.'

Nonetheless, the thought prevailed that Cantwell tried to push his new, more structured, ideas through at Old Trafford and they met with resistance from some of the senior professionals and those on the coaching staff. The arrival of George Best onto the scene during that season – a precociously gifted youngster who could clearly not be harnessed to a rigid tactical system – perhaps only complicated matters further. The winger's individual brilliance could also render others' tactical plans useless, and he benefited from playing with the shackles off. It is worth pointing out that the Northern Irishman had huge respect for Cantwell.

Before too long, the Reds would have three of the biggest stars in the world in Best, Law and Charlton representing United, and so the dressing room needed a firm hand at times. Busby was happy to delegate this responsibility to his captain who would quell any friction between various players, just as he ordered his sparkling talents to perform off the cuff out on the field.

Cantwell clashed with Law during a five-a-side session in training, an occurrence pretty commonplace in the world of football, and insisted they became firmer pals afterwards. 'Naturally, I like to think we are above silly feuds at United,' said the Cork-born defender. 'Certainly, we have our squabbles but they are resolved openly and not allowed to lie festering into something bigger. This reduces dressing-room atmosphere, as it is called in the newspapers, to a minimum.'

A solution to maintaining a harmonious group was surely rather more difficult to find. Others, including keeper Harry Gregg and coach Jack Crompton, told a different story and there was at least one meeting of all the senior professionals in a bid to clear the air when arguments arose over the training methods at The Cliff.

One man who was indebted to Cantwell for his hands-on approach was David Sadler, who had joined from non-league Maidstone United in 1963. 'Some of the bigger stars were a bit daunting, but that certainly wasn't the case with Noel,' he stressed. 'He would go out of his way to put you at ease. He was one of the game's great thinkers and talkers.'

Unfortunately, Cantwell was restricted to only two appearances in the entire 1964-65 campaign, but he still performed his off-field duties as club captain, with Law appointed to carry the fight on the pitch, sometimes taking this instruction too literally. There seemed no problem with the arrangement and it afforded respect to the Irishman, even if he had lost his place. 'Noel was a leader of men,' Law commented many years later. 'You wanted to follow him.'

As for the prolific striker, he was a very different character altogether. 'Some call him a big head,' said Cantwell. 'He isn't. He simply has a slightly cocky confidence in his own ability. He is a great club man. A big practical joker, too. He will always have a lark around in the dressing room or on the practice pitch but, when the game starts, it's all action and no nonsense.'

Law may have been a superstar, and earned a relatively large salary at United, but his demeanour away from the pitch was far removed from some of the classic captains of the past. 'I'm a bit shy when I haven't got my boots laced up,' he conceded, but his cheerful outlook helped lift spirits. There was no timidity on the field as his temper often exploded, when provoked by aggressive opponents, and he had long been a marked man with referees.

Two bruising FA Cup semi-finals with Leeds United may have dashed any hopes of the Double, but the league title was clinched with a run of seven consecutive victories, culminating in a 3-1 triumph against Arsenal. It was a remarkable run-in and Cantwell certainly played his part after coming in from the cold.

On 19 April, a visit to Birmingham City saw the Irishman thrown into the attack, a position he filled more often with his country, in place of the injured Herd. It might have been his first game of the season but he responded well and headed the final goal in a 4-2 victory that condemned the Midlanders to relegation, after two previous seasons where they had finished one place above the drop zone.

Five days later, he reprised the role as makeshift attacker in the tense clash with Liverpool at Old Trafford. Law had six stitches in a knee injury sustained in a clash with Ron Yeats and had to leave the field, but United won 3-0 with 'The King' having scored twice. It may have been tough on Cantwell that he was no longer required for the game that clinched the title as, 48 hours later, Arsenal were beaten 3-1. Not only was Law patched up, but Herd was also fit enough to feature. Law was instructed that he was required to play through the pain barrier by Busby and, following his manager's orders, he netted another brace. 'I thought there was no way I should be playing,' he admitted, 'but what choice did I have?'

A final-day defeat to Aston Villa ensured only goal average sep-
arated the Reds and Leeds United at the summit – due largely to a
superior defensive record, despite the team's considerable attacking
prowess. Rumblings of discontent in the dressing room faded as Law
enjoyed the thrill of parading the championship trophy in front of
the ecstatic fans before the Inter-Cities Fairs Cup tie against
Strasbourg the following month, even if he was still concerned about
his knee injury at the time.

'It was a wonderful set-up at Old Trafford with a fantastic team
spirit and a lot of that was down to Denis,' revealed John Connelly,
the winger having joined United at the start of the season. 'Usually,
he had a big grin on his face and he kept everyone bubbling.' It was
smiles all round and there was still a chance of more glory in Europe
after Strasbourg were dismissed in the quarter-finals, but Ferencvaros
shaded a play-off after the aggregate scores were level at the end of the
second leg. Notably, the Inter-Cities Fairs Cup games were the final
five fixtures of the season, which finished on 16 June – the longest
in the club's history.

Cantwell was back in action more frequently in the following
campaign, but 11 players still made more than his 23 league appearances, 29 in all competitions. Despite worries he was losing a yard of
pace, he provided reliable cover for full-backs Brennan and Dunne,
and also centre-half Bill Foulkes. He certainly made a worthy contribution, even if a fourth-placed finish was a disappointment and
Everton won a tight semi-final at Bolton Wanderers' Burnden Park
in his absence to end the club's FA Cup hopes.

Cantwell admitted such painful defeats in semi-finals only
strengthened Busby's resolve to land more silverware and made him
realise the conviction of the man and, indeed, the club. Meanwhile,
Law's situation was complicated at the end of the season when he
demanded a pay increase and was even placed on the transfer list
by Busby. It was later revealed the ace marksman received his

£10-per-week rise when the dispute was resolved, even though this was a closely guarded secret as the manager did not want to increase any disharmony in his squad.

In 1966-67, as United successfully chased league glory again, Cantwell managed only four outings as he again found himself out of the side. Law led the Reds to another title, clinched in stunning fashion with a 6-1 win at West Ham, with the irrepressible forward bagging another double – the rampant Reds had gone unbeaten in the league after a Boxing Day reverse at Sheffield United.

Cantwell featured in none of those games after the festive period. Three-quarters of his appearances were made in October and the other in November. United won three and drew one of those games, but he could not force himself back into the regular starting line-up. Meanwhile, the last of his 36 international caps came in February 1967, just a few days before his 35th birthday. By now, he was exerting his influence on the Reserves and developing younger players at that level. It was clear he was cutting his teeth for a move into management and was looking to the future. Already the PFA chairman, he was embracing other areas of the game and refused to retreat into his shell when struggling for first-team football. In fact, quite the opposite was true.

There was no disputing the respect in which he was held, and his manager was also keen to praise his ability to deal with established stars and fledgling talents alike. Writing in the foreword to Cantwell's 1965 autobiography, Busby opined: 'Besides being a great and versatile player, and a wonderful marshal of our side, he is also one of the best-informed theorists and thinkers in the game. Noel is a big, strong lad with a big personality, on and off the field – and a heart to match. He is a man who can use the ball intelligently; and a man who can remain cool, calm and unflustered even under pressure. Keeping his defence in line, he is almost like a general on the battlefield.

'His charm and intelligence and loyalty have not only made their impression on me but also on the many big names in my side whom he has skippered. This influence on the players runs right down the line – from the top international down to the lads on the ground staff. Noel takes a tremendous interest in the youngsters, the lads who aspire to get into his top bracket. This probably stems from his innate belief in the coaching and theory side of the game.

'He has what we Scots call a good "head-piece" for the game – a man of character and talent who has been an invaluable help to me in my job as manager. When he says something – in that wonderful soft brogue of his – it means something. And his approach to people, from those youngsters with stardom only in their eyes yet, to the world-class players he knows, is always just right.'

It had been expected that Cantwell might succeed Busby as United manager and it looked a sound bet that he would at least remain on the coaching staff. Even the Scot himself had forwarded this notion to his captain during their lengthy discussions in his office. 'I was thinking that it was time to move on and I remembered Matt telling me that he wanted me to be coach at Manchester United,' said Cantwell. 'I was very, very excited.

'There had been numerous times when I had taken the training when somebody wasn't available, and I'd always had it in my mind that the training could have been better and more entertaining and exciting for the players. But, unfortunately, things never materialised. The reason being, I think that, although Matt appreciated me, and thought I knew something about the game, and could lead men, I don't think that he wanted to upset the balance of the whole club.

'The Jack Cromptons, the Jimmy Murphys and the rest of them. I think he might have thought that, by bringing in this young upstart, it might just upset the rest of them and the balance. He used to have long conversations with me in his office. He would call me in and it would be friendly but secret and we'd talk about the club and the game and it would never go any further. And he did say to me: "Noel, you can stay at Old Trafford." He wanted me there but I was ambitious. I didn't want to play in the Reserves too long.'

After rejecting the assistant manager's post to Tommy Cummings at Aston Villa, he left for recently promoted Coventry City in October 1967, and succeeded *Match of the Day*-bound Jimmy Hill as Sky Blues boss. Busby described the move to the West Midlands as a 'fantastic opportunity' and Cantwell departed Old Trafford with his blessing. 'I did not need much of a push as I had been hoping to become a football manager and this was why I turned down the Villa job,' the 35-year-old stated. 'I did not think it was ideal for me.'

The first assignment for the young coach was a return to Manchester for a game against his former employers and United ran out 4-0 victors. John Aston scored twice, with Best and Charlton also hitting the net, providing a tough baptism in football management for their former colleague, who was also lined up for the Republic of Ireland job.

With Cantwell gone, Law remained skipper, when fit, and this became pertinent as he battled knee trouble owing to a persistent problem that related to a piece of cartilage left over from an operation in his Huddersfield days. He struggled through a European Cup tie against Hibernians of Malta, but it became clear surgery was required and he would face a lengthy spell on the sidelines.

Curiously, the striker is rarely prominently considered when discussing the club's finest leaders, although he will always be foremost in any debates about the Reds' greatest players. Perhaps this is because he did not like to elevate himself above others on the team or maybe it was simply because injury was to rob him of the ultimate triumph in the role. Another factor is his sheer ability overshadowed many other elements – he was, after all, voted European Footballer of the Year back in 1964.

'I was proud to lead out my team, whether at schoolboy, club or international level,' he stressed. 'But I never saw myself as one fellow in charge of the rest. Every good team needs a few captains, motivators who will keep the lads going at all times. We were lucky having the likes of Paddy Crerand and Nobby Stiles, who were shouting directions to the rest of us the whole time.'

Although he led the team out for the 1968 European Cup semifinal against Real Madrid at Old Trafford, admitting it was a real thrill to be shaking hands with the great Francisco Gento in the centre circle beforehand, he would be forced to watch the epic final encounter with Benfica at Wembley from his hospital bed. The skipper on that glorious night would not be Crerand or Stiles but another icon of the club – Bobby Charlton.

Chapter 6

The Symbol of Manchester United

'My own approach was to try to provide leadership on the training field and the pitch by example.'

Sir Bobby Charlton

Like Manchester United, Sir Bobby Charlton's story is indelibly marked by and inextricably linked to the Munich air disaster. It is neither mawkish nor morbid to set his career or life in such context, it is simply that the events of 6 February 1958 defined him, some say changed him, and he carried the burden of the unfulfilled hope for that great team as a torchbearer for everything they, and subsequently Manchester United, stood for. He has performed the task precisely as he played the game – with grace and class, a humble nod to his working-class roots and indubitable dignity, all of which, when placed beside his many successes, nudges his status well beyond that of the captaincy.

In that sense, Charlton is utterly unique in this cast of captains because, while others perhaps defined their respective eras through their leadership on the field, he transcends his own reign as skipper.

He led the side during one of the club's most turbulent periods, and his five years in the position (from 1968 to 1973) struggle to compete with his vast and incredible achievements in the game before and after that spell. Charlton is, in many respects, the symbol of Manchester United: he represents the club's rich history, he has achieved the profession's highest honours, and he is rightly recognised and respected around the world.

A winner of the European Cup, Ballon d'Or and the World Cup – the only Englishman ever to claim all three coveted prizes – Charlton is a rare talent and a gentleman of the sport. His 758 appearances for United was a record that stood for 35 years until the equally exceptional Ryan Giggs surpassed that epic tally, and a haul of 249 goals still shines like a beacon at the top of the scoring charts in late 2014, neither eroded by time nor conquered by a host of challengers to the throne. As with all records, even the loftiest targets, it is likely to fall one day – United's current skipper has it in his sights – but, in lasting so long, it has helped to preserve the magnitude of what Charlton achieved. For a younger generation who have never seen 'Thunderboots' bursting the net with a fearsome shot from distance, or his balance and poise in possession or his fine cross-field passing with either foot, the figures at least give some sense of how special he was.

Those talents were obvious from an early age, although that is not to say young Charlton did not have to work on his skills – tireless hours spent on the training pitch honing his play under the tutelage of men such as Jimmy Murphy would prove vital in his progression, and would highlight his dedication and determination to make the very most of his abilities.

Charlton's United journey began back in 1953, when he signed schoolboy forms at Old Trafford as a 15-year-old. His pedigree was unquestionable; he hailed from football-mad Ashington, a mining village in Northumberland which, through the famous Milburn family, produced a host of league footballers. Jack, George, Jim and Stan Milburn, Bobby's uncles on his mother Cissie's side, were all league players, and her cousin was the legendary Newcastle striker 'Wor Jackie' Milburn. Football was in his blood.

Charlton signed in the summer of 1953 and was part of the precocious junior United sides to win the FA Youth Cup in 1954, 1955 and 1956 – the middle three years in a straight run of triumphs in the tournament's first five seasons. But despite easily being the best footballer in his school, his district and his county, as well as being an England schoolboy international with clubs queuing for his signature before scout Joe Armstrong snapped him up for United, he wasn't considered the best young player at United. Few would dispute that crown had a deservingly lofty perch in Duncan Edwards.

Despite being just a year older than Bobby, Duncan had already made his first-team debut by the time Charlton arrived at Old Trafford and had notched more than 50 appearances when, on 6 October 1956, just five days shy of Bobby's 19th birthday, his younger team-mate's United bow arrived. There was no shame in that, of course, as Edwards was a boy in a man's body. With a more slight and slender frame, Charlton was still considered one of United's brightest young talents, as evidenced on his first outing for Matt Busby's men, against Charlton Athletic neatly enough, as he scored twice in a 4-2 win at Old Trafford.

That contribution was unsurprising in some respects as, back then, young Bobby was a prolific inside-forward and he scored 12 goals in 17 games in his debut campaign. But it wasn't until December 1957 in the following season that Charlton began to command a regular place in the side. Apart from a run of five consecutive matches in late 1956-57, he was embarking on his first sustained spell in the team, and he made a hugely impressive impact. Charlton scored in a 4-0 win over Leicester City on 21 December 1957 and right through to the 3-3 away draw with Red Star

Belgrade on 5 February, which clinched a place in the European Cup semi-finals, he scored 12 goals in 11 games.

At 20 years of age, Charlton wasn't exactly a late bloomer, but he was blossoming in his own time. Against Red Star, in front of 55,000 baying home supporters, Charlton delivered a performance of staggering maturity for someone so young, scoring two crucial goals – he would have bagged a hat-trick had another effort not been disallowed – in what was only his third appearance in European competition, and he rightly drew praise from the press.

Don Davies, 'An Old International', writing in his match report in Belgrade for the *Manchester Guardian*, picks up the story after Dennis Viollet had given United the lead inside 90 seconds: 'Further success for United was impending. Charlton, this time, was the chosen instrument. Dispossessing Kostic about 40 yards from goal, this gifted boy leaned beautifully into his stride, made ground rapidly for about ten yards, and then beat the finest goalkeeper on the continent with a shot of tremendous power and superb placing. There, one thought, surely goes England's [Steve] Bloomer of the future.

'Further evidence of Charlton's claim to that distinction was to emerge two minutes later. A smartly taken free-kick got the Red Star defence into a real tangle. Edwards fastened on the ball and did his best to oblige his colleagues and supporters by bursting it but he muffed his kick and the ball rolled to Charlton, apparently lost in a thicket of Red Star defenders. Stalemate, surely. But not with Charlton about. His quick eye detected the one sure route through the circle of legs; his trusty boot drove the ball unerringly along it: 3-0 on the day; 5-1 on aggregate. Nice going.'

United faced an onslaught as Red Star fought their way back to 3-3, but the Reds held firm to progress. They were, after all, the team that could do anything. The world was seemingly at their feet. Then, disaster. As Sir Bobby movingly describes 'that hellish scene at the airfield' in his autobiography, *My Manchester United Years*, his world as he knew it tilted on its axis amid the snow, slush and horror of the runway at Munich-Riem Airport, as the aircraft carrying United's heroes stopped for refuelling on the homeward journey the following afternoon but failed to find flight at the third attempt.

'With my first glance, I saw that one beloved team-mate was dead after suffering injuries I could never bring myself to describe – and then Matt Busby groaning and holding his chest as he sat in a pool of water,' he recalled. 'I could delve into so much that has been a joy to me before I come to the sight of seven of my team-mates laid out in the snow. That, however, would be an evasion, a cosmetic device to obscure the truth I have lived with since 6 February 1958: that everything I have been able to achieve since that day – including winning the European Cup and the World Cup and being linked with two of the greatest players the world has ever seen, George Best and Denis Law – has been accompanied by a simple question: why me?

'Why was I able to run my hands over my body and find that I was still whole when Roger Byrne, Eddie Colman, Liam 'Billy' Whelan, David Pegg, Tommy Taylor, Mark Jones and Geoff Bent lay dead, and Duncan Edwards, who I loved and admired so intensely, faced an unavailing battle for his life? Why had I been picked out to inherit so much of what they, in the first surge of brilliant youth, had achieved so beautifully? One of the few certainties that replaced my original belief that anything could be achieved in the presence of such great footballers is that I will never stop asking that question – no more than I will be able to shed those feelings of guilt at my own survival which can come to me so suddenly at any moment, night or day.'

That guilt, however misplaced, and pervading sense of loss would never leave him. But his role in honouring his team-mates, friends, or brothers as he described them, had only just begun. Frank Taylor, a sports journalist for the *News Chronicle*, also survived Munich and chronicled the aftermath in his seminal book *The Day A Team Died*.

He wrote: 'Three men, in my opinion, saved Manchester United from oblivion. They are: Jimmy Murphy, the loyal lieutenant of Matt Busby; Bobby Charlton, who was in such a dazed and shocked condition himself immediately after the accident that it seemed he might never play again; and Busby himself.'

Charlton did return to the football field after initially being hospitalised; he played in the 2-2 FA Cup sixth-round draw with West Bromwich Albion on 1 March – less than a month after the accident and barely a week after his good friend, his idol, Duncan, lost his brave fight against the injuries he suffered in the crash.

Busby had asked Murphy to 'keep the flag flying, Jimmy, until I get back', and with the help, in particular, of Harry Gregg and Bill Foulkes, who played in United's next game after Munich against Sheffield Wednesday on 19 February, and Charlton, who joined them two weeks later in the Cup, that is exactly what he did and United eventually reached the FA Cup final against Bolton Wanderers. Just weeks before Munich, Charlton had hit a hat-trick – his second of seven for the Reds – in a 7-2 hammering of Bolton that showcased United's frightening potential, even despite a season that had delivered inconsistent league form from the champions. But Bolton proved too strong in front of 100,000 at Wembley and won 2-0, while in the delayed European Cup semi-finals against AC Milan in May, United triumphed in the first leg 2-1 but lost the return fixture in Italy by four unanswered goals.

The long and winding road to recovery was not going to be an easy journey; in fact, it was in no way a given that Busby would ever place his team back on its previous trajectory to greatness. The 1958-59 season remarkably saw the Reds finish second in the league, but Busby's men trailed champions Wolverhampton Wanderers by 14 points. It was, however, the best of Charlton's 19 seasons in front of goal as he scored 29 in 39 matches.

United's transformation took place gradually, as might be

expected after such devastation. The Reds followed that campaign with consecutive seventh-placed finishes before plummeting to 15th in 1961-62 and 19th in 1962-63. Charlton had won league championship medals in 1956 and 1957 and must have then thought many more medals from England and Europe were inevitable, but his chances of adding to them seemingly grew slimmer by the season.

However, change was around the corner and United's so-called Holy Trinity was about to be formed. In many ways, the divine convergence of Charlton, Denis Law and George Best perfectly described United's approach after Munich. Charlton represented United's link to the past, Best its commitment to the future, and Law, a £110,000 record signing from Torino, the club's willingness to spend big to restore the team to the top of the game. Busby stated that it was signing Law in 1962 that convinced him United were once again on a path to greatness. Best's debut against West Bromwich Albion in September 1963 completed the trio.

Charlton's game was changing too. With Law and David Herd banging in the goals in the mid-sixties, Charlton could drop deeper, adding more creativity in a central role, and this would be the position in which he would become world renowned. His goal contribution would still be healthy, but he would only once break the 20-goal barrier after 1960-61, whereas previously he had done it three times in four full seasons.

The 1963 FA Cup final win over Leicester City was a landmark in United's recovery and reinstatement as a team capable of claiming silverware, and league titles duly followed in 1965 and 1967. But it was in the return to continental competition that United hoped to fully find redemption, first in the European Cup Winners' Cup in 1963-64 (United lost in the quarter-finals to Sporting Lisbon), then the Inter-Cities Fairs Cup in 1964-65 (losing to Ferencvaros in the semis) and finally the European Cup in 1965-66 (defeated in the last four by Partizan Belgrade).

However, having fallen at the crucial latter hurdles on each occasion, doubts crept in. That trip to Belgrade had been a painful retracing of steps, a repeat visit to the city from which United had made a doomed homeward journey. The emotion clearly affected United, as did the strapped knee of Best, who had been hailed 'El Beatle' after his devastating destruction of Benfica in the 5-1 quarter-final second-leg win. The Reds lost 2-0 to Partizan, a result that could not be overturned despite a 1-0 win back at Old Trafford. 'I'm sick at heart,' Busby said, despairing, 'sick at the great chance we have missed.' He would despondently question whether winning the European Cup was now impossible.

Charlton led United's representation, alongside Nobby Stiles and John Connelly, at the 1966 World Cup with England, and Bobby would subsequently be named European Footballer of the Year later that year to accompany global glory. He subsequently finished second in the vote by *France Football* magazine for the famous Ballon d'Or trophy in 1967 and 1968. Still, there was unfinished business with United.

A fourth-placed finish in the league in 1965-66 meant no European football the following year, but United reclaimed the title from Liverpool in 1967 and embarked once again on a continental journey. By the time Hibernians Malta had been dispatched and United prepared to take on Sarajevo, Charlton had turned 30 and as he looked around a dressing room at players of a similar age, there was a feeling that this might be the last chance to achieve glory for this team.

Charlton needn't have worried – United were on the cusp of true greatness and he would play a central role. He hit 20 goals and played in all but one of United's 54 matches that season – missing a 2-0 win over Arsenal at Highbury in February. And while he didn't score in any of the early rounds against Hibernians Malta, Sarejevo, the quarter-final's troublesome Polish opponents Gornik Zabrze, or in the epic semi-final battles with Real Madrid, there was still time to address that particular statistic.

Against Real, those great foes of old, United led 1-0 in the first leg from Best's fine goal, but the Reds were without the injured Law at the Bernabeu and were trailing 3-1 on the night by half time. Had the dream evaporated into harsh reality amid the heat of Madrid? Charlton, captain for the night, cites not his own powers of motivation but the brilliant and typically defiant and pugnacious performance of Nobby Stiles as the jumpstart for the team's belief. Paddy Crerand and Charlton both watched powerful shots fly narrowly wide, but United were in the ascendancy. David Sadler bagged a scrappy effort to level the aggregate scores. Then, to confirm United's passage to the final, Best cut the ball back for the unlikely figure of Foulkes to secure a 3-3 draw and ensure a place in the final.

Charlton collapsed on the pitch, drained and dehydrated due to the oppressive evening heat in the Spanish capital, but with a final waiting at Wembley, even against Benfica and the might of Eusebio, he allowed himself to believe that destiny was finally on United's side. Perhaps in another twist of wicked fate, Law's knee surgery meant Charlton would again take the captaincy and with it the opportunity to finally grasp the trophy United had given so much to attain.

On that balmy night at Wembley on 29 May, United and Charlton could dwell on many motivating factors – Munich being one, of course, to honour those who had died attempting to realise the Reds' dream as pioneers in European football, doing it for 'the Old Man' Busby, to avenge past semi-final defeats against AC Milan, Real Madrid and Partizan Belgrade, and naturally because it was on home soil. That didn't stop Charlton worrying as United completed preparations for the final at Great Fosters, a hotel in serene Surrey countryside. 'As captain, I felt a heavy responsibility,' Charlton later recalled. 'I had to do everything that was expected of me, and I had to make sure the others didn't forget their responsibilities for a second. In the end, all you could guarantee was that you would run, on and off the ball, until you were ready to drop.'

As he had done in Madrid, Charlton was ready to run himself into the ground, almost literally. He had already set out to the press how he thought the team should play and how the big game might pan out against opponents whose style he respected and relished playing against, as opposed to some of the tactics employed by Real Madrid's players, for example. 'You see, with that sort of game they play, that slow, smooth, passing game, they've got to wait for things to happen,' he said. 'If it goes for them – fine, they can be devastating. But if things go wrong, they can't do much about it. With our more physical game, we can force things to happen. If it goes against us we can change it, impose ourselves on it.'

Determined to shape this particular storyline, Charlton glanced home a rare and beautiful headed goal in the 53rd minute to get the scoring started. United were 1-0 up and seemingly en route to victory when Jaime Graca stole in at the far post to equalise with seven minutes remaining, and, with tiredness taking its toll, Eusebio, who had earlier hit the bar, had two late efforts saved by Alex Stepney. The latter left the Portuguese forward applauding in awe.

That late let-off and the full-time whistle offered a much-needed opportunity to regroup before extra time began. 'We were really gone,' recalled Charlton. 'None of us could run. It was a terrible, helpless feeling. My legs were killing me, both of them. It wasn't like ordinary cramp. They just sort of seized up and there wasn't a real stoppage in the last quarter, so that you didn't get a chance to get down and give them a shake to loosen them. It was murder. When they scored, it looked on for them, considering the state we were in, but we held on somehow and when full time came they had lost their advantage. It was starting all over again and we had a breather, a chance to get ourselves going. [But] we were flopped out there, like dead men, but we were ready to go when we had to. Matt said: "Just keep going, you can still beat these." We were more like ourselves again when extra time began.'

Best brilliantly unlocked the Benfica defence within two minutes of the restart, before Brian Kidd added a third and, before the first half of extra time was over, Charlton had delightfully nipped in front of his man at the near post to clip a beautiful finish past Jose Henrique in the Portuguese goal. With the contest practically won, United just had to see out the clock, which was easier said than done in humid conditions after such epic physical and emotional endeavours. Charlton admitted to 'not being able to run to save my life' in those last few moments, and when the final whistle came it was sheer elation and relief.

Otto Gloria, the Benfica manager, magnanimously admitted: 'The title is in very good hands.' Very good hands, indeed, as Bobby shrugged off the exhaustion and dehydration that had drained his body to climb the famous 39 steps and finally take the trophy. The players had wanted Busby to go up to receive the Cup he had strived so hard to win, but he waved them away and reportedly said: 'It's your day. Go on, Bobby, it's your day, son.'

Busby's insatiable hunger had been sated: 'I've chased and chased this European Cup with many disappointments, but here it is at last. I am the proudest man in England tonight. The boys have done us proud. They showed in Madrid that they have the heart to fight back and tonight they showed us the stuff that Manchester United are made of. I am proud of them all.'

Charlton could fully appreciate those sentiments and that he started and completed the scoring was utterly fitting and a sign that, when it was required, he would step forward in the most decisive moments. And while it was disappointing for Law not to be there and to experience the glory as team captain, there was something symbolic about the honour falling to Charlton to hold aloft football's big cup. He would miss the parade into Manchester and on to the

Town Hall, as a reported 250,000 fans lined the city's streets. He had to join up with the England squad beside his good friend Nobby as they prepared for the European Championship in Italy.

Before that, celebrations continued into the small hours that night at the Russell Hotel in London. Charlton was conspicuous by his absence, and journalist Frank Taylor recounted: 'I looked in vain and couldn't see him. Then his wife came through the door. "Where is our Bob?" I asked. For a split second, she looked embarrassed, and then whispered in my ear: "It has all been a bit too much for Bobby. I think you would understand better than most people. He is just too tired physically and emotionally to face up to all this. He couldn't take it, with complete strangers coming up and slapping him on the back and telling him what a wonderful night it is . . . He's remembering the lads who can't be here tonight."'

Charlton later claimed that dehydration – the two beers he downed in the dressing room immediately after the game might not have helped – had caused him to faint three times. Regardless, whether it was emotional or physical exhaustion, or both, nobody would deny Charlton his moment of reflection. He had reached the absolute zenith of his career, but it had come at a price.

Despite everything he had achieved to this point, his journey as captain was only just beginning. The cups and consistency afforded him an irreproachable stature within the game and at the club. It was almost impossible that anyone else could lead the team now. He would be awarded an OBE the following year and his experience would be all the more important, in Busby's eyes, when 'the Old Man' decided at the end of the 1968-69 season that he would move upstairs. Busby had informed Charlton of his intentions as the pair went on a golfing trip to Scotland – an unusual move for manager and captain, even for two men with such shared history, but Charlton was never going to rebuff the wishes of his boss.

As with the departure of Sir Alex Ferguson, the abdication of the

Old Trafford throne by a great figure in the club's history creates an almost impossible act to follow. The pillars of the European Cup-winning team naturally would not stand forever, and the careers of Foulkes, Stiles and Crerand, among others, were winding down, while Law, Best and Charlton all produced flashes of brilliance but perhaps not the same ruthless consistency of old. Still, at the time, Charlton wouldn't let go of the hope that things would turn around as he led the team into a new decade.

The tenure of his good friend Wilf McGuinness was not to fare well for various reasons. Hugely passionate about United and with the gift of the gab, McGuinness knew the club and the culture like few others and had coaching experience with England and United. He led the Reds to two semi-finals in 1969-70 – losing to Manchester City in the League Cup and Leeds in the FA Cup, as well as finishing eighth in the league. The bootroom policy of promoting from within has its merits, but equally its pitfalls, as Wilf explained in his book *Man and Babe*: 'Was it a problem that I'd grown up alongside some of the players who would now be in my charge? I got on well with the players, both personally and professionally. Of course, I had close pals at the club, but although I realised I would have to treat some of them with a bit more detachment than in the past – certainly I could not be seen to have favourites in my new position – I saw the friendly relationships as a positive.'

Nevertheless, he was in a somewhat invidious position when things did not start well in autumn 1969. Wilf had signed for United as a young lad on the same day as Bobby aged 15, and now here he was managing a player who was 14 days his senior and who had made over 500 appearances for the club. It cannot have been an easy transition to manage, despite both men only ever wanting the best for the club they loved. United drew the first game of 1969-70 against Crystal Palace and followed it with consecutive home losses against Everton and Southampton. Something had to change and

Wilf felt his midfield had been overrun against Everton, so he rang the changes for the return fixture at Goodison Park later that month. He informed Charlton and Law that they weren't in the team. Law was injured, but Charlton was left out for tactical reasons. When Wilf broke the news, Bobby accepted the decision without recourse. But a 3-0 defeat attracted huge criticism from press and supporters.

Wilf insisted he wasn't trying to show the senior lads who was boss. 'If I had been seeking to prove a point, a bollocking in front of the other players would have done the trick, but I never felt the need to do that. Nothing could have been farther from my mind.' Nevertheless, captain Charlton was seen as being a vital ally and he remained in the team for the rest of the campaign, missing just one more game that season – and nobody played more than his 57 matches across three competitions.

One oft-cited incident has been overplayed but perhaps best sums up how difficult it was for McGuinness to complete the trans-formation from player to coach to manager. Alex Stepney claimed McGuinness had a rule about players putting their hands in their pockets. It was a matter of professionalism – be prepared to work at training, be serious, committed and ready. The rule was, if you were caught with your hands in your pockets, you did ten press-ups in front of the group. Dressing-room jokers Shay Brennan and Stiles were fond of pointing out offenders and one day, when Charlton had asked to leave training early for a prior engagement, he returned briefly to the training field in a suit to listen to McGuinness's team talk. Out of his training gear, Charlton absent-mindedly placed his hands in his pockets and Brennan and Stiles gleefully pointed it out. McGuinness had no choice but to tell Charlton to face his forfeit, but he insists it was all in good humour, Charlton didn't have an issue with it and rejected any notion that it harmed their lifelong friendship.

McGuinness would later say: 'I'm delighted to report that it never remotely threatened a breakdown of my long-lasting relationship with Bobby. We understood each other far too well for that to have been a possibility. True, there were times towards the end of my managerial stint when he wasn't happy with the way things were going, and he said so, but there wasn't a moment when I felt our friendship had been damaged. When I was in charge there had to be some demarcation line, but before and after that we have been very close.'

Wilf, unlucky with certain results that season and frustrated by a lack of backing in the transfer market in summer 1970, was eventually relieved of his duties in December, with Busby stepping into the breach. Frank O'Farrell would follow him and, although United shot to the top of the table in his first autumn, the Reds were trading off the increasingly unpredictable and wayward genius of Best. O'Farrell's tenure lasted just 81 matches, six fewer than McGuinness.

The case of Best was a difficult one for Charlton, as senior player and captain. He could not condone the absences from training and felt it created divisions within the squad, but equally discipline wasn't in his hands and he could perfectly understand the dilemma that faced all three of Busby's immediate replacements (Tommy Docherty succeeded O'Farrell): the difficulty was that, with United in such evident decline, the team desperately needed Best's talents to lift them out of the mire. Charlton, reflecting on that period in his autobiography, neatly summed up the quandary: 'He was hard to live with, in some professional terms, but could we live without him?'

In contrast, Charlton saw it as his duty to lead by example on the training pitch and in games, maintaining that ever-consummate professionalism for which he was famed, and largely steered clear of any of the internal politics at United that seemed to characterise that period off the field and which was created by the vacuum of power upon Busby's stepping aside – or, more precisely, upstairs.

By the time Docherty entered the fray, Charlton was already asking questions of himself about his future and began addressing the gnawing doubts about whether he had the motivation to carry on, at the age of 35. Charlton's reign as captain had not been one littered with success, that magical night at Wembley aside, of course. Semi-final defeats to AC Milan in the European Cup, Leeds in the FA Cup, Manchester City and Aston Villa in the League Cup, were aligned to league positions of 11th, three eighth-placed finishes and 18th in his final season – hardly fitting for his glorious career. But as has already been stated, it is not his captaincy nor the fortunes of the team during that period that define Charlton – more that everything he achieved simply made him deserving of the title, and more.

After finally informing Docherty of his decision to leave the club, which went unchallenged, the end of his final season in 1972-73 loomed and his last game was played in front of a sell-out crowd at Stamford Bridge against Chelsea on 28 April. At the Russell Hotel, where United always stayed in London and where the players had cel-ebrated in 1968, chairman Louis Edwards wandered the halls muttering, 'Sad, sad, sad.' Docherty had declared: 'I want a good open game and a win for Bobby.' Charlton, himself, was much less fussed about the occasion, adding: 'I only want the whole business to be over. I feel I really said goodbye in Manchester last week. London doesn't mean too much to me.'

Jeremy Bugler wrote in the *Guardian*: 'But Charlton meant something to London. At Stamford Bridge, queues for the Chelsea match began forming at 9.30am and the gates were closed 45 min-utes before the kick-off with many supporters locked outside. Twenty-one players formed a circle in the centre of the pitch. In the middle, Chelsea chairman Brian Mears presented Charlton with an inscribed cigarette box. Charlton is a non-smoker. Well, the thought was there.'

Charlton was widely celebrated for his 758 appearances, 249 goals, his England achievements and countless club trophies, but also for his sportsmanship and the media were keen to press the point home. Bugler added: 'He was booked only once, for delaying a free-kick. Tommy Docherty recalled the incident yesterday and said: "The cheek of it! The referee should have been booked!"' The Chelsea crowd gave Charlton a rousing send-off, a sign of his wide-reaching acclaim in a game he gave everything to serve, and served brilliantly. As Charlton had pointed out, however, he had already said goodbye at his spiritual home, at Old Trafford two weeks previously, in a 2-1 defeat to Sheffield United.

Paul Fitzpatrick, also of the *Guardian,* described Charlton as 'arguably the outstanding footballer of his generation, and certainly the best loved', before adding: 'Having seen Charlton score two goals on his first appearance for United against Charlton Athletic at Old Trafford, it was gratifying to see his last appearance there. He is a different person now, a different footballer, from that highly promising youth who played his first game in 1956. But, in between times, first as an orthodox scoring inside-forward, then as an orthodox outside-left, and latterly as a midfielder, he has enriched the game and the watching of it, with his abundant skills and impeccable sportsmanship.

'At the end, the crowd gathered in a swaying, almost uncontrollable mass in front of the stand. Charlton made a brief appearance and then made an equally brief speech, which was drowned by the chanting of the crowd – and the last surviving member of that great pre-Munich side had gone. It is sad that he will not be seen again at Old Trafford.'

That was true on the pitch, perhaps, but Charlton's virtually life-long association with United was not about to end there, of course. Charlton's final act in a United shirt actually came in an Anglo-Italian Cup match, beating Verona 4-1 on 2 May and, fittingly, he ended his career as he had begun it all those years ago against Charlton, scoring twice. Newcastle would win the tournament by beating Fiorentina in the final, but as United stayed on the shores of Lake

Garda, Charlton took time to reflect on his incredible journey. 'I had scored two goals and played well enough to wonder, if only for a second or two, whether I had made the right decision to retire. It was so hard to think that I would never do this again. The accompanying press were most concerned with the shape of Tommy Docherty's new United, and it was a little strange to read about a future in which I no longer belonged.'

The emotions Charlton felt came bubbling to the surface in a local restaurant after the game when the United squad gave him a standing ovation and presented him with an Italian clock they clubbed together to buy. 'Inevitably, I choked up when I made my speech of thanks and attempted the impossible task of explaining what all the days I had spent wearing the shirt of Manchester United would always mean to me,' he said. The clock, which still resides on his mantelpiece at home, was an appropriate gift because his contribution to Manchester United is not constrained or lessened by the ticking of time – he stepped beyond being a player or captain and into unforgettable legend.

Chapter 7

The Cool Customer

'It was a great honour being Manchester United captain. A captain must lead by example.'

Martin Buchan

'I like to be different,' Martin Buchan once said, and the linguistics-loving, guitar-playing defender, who, in some respects, was the antithesis to the archetypal footballer off the field was, as always, true to his word. An educated, thoughtful Scot hailing from the Granite City of Aberdeen, Buchan was unafraid to speak his mind or go against the grain and was a hugely respected figure in United's squad. He had the character to command, the consistency to back it up and consequently was liked by team-mates and supporters alike. 'The Fonz is cool, but Buchan is cooler,' read a banner created by United fans, highlighting his popularity throughout the troubled 1970s, which offered more lows than highs.

Frank O'Farrell urged the club to stave off interest from Leeds United and Liverpool to capture the £125,000 signing from Aberdeen in March 1972, breaking the club transfer record set previously by Denis Law's £115,000 move from Torino in 1962. It was a record fee for Aberdeen too, and the highest for a player leaving Scotland. Buchan was arguably O'Farrell's finest legacy from an ill-fated reign at Old Trafford as he gifted United one of its most dedicated servants, a player who remains comfortably among the club's top 20 all-time appearance makers.

To complete the deal, O'Farrell travelled north with Sir Matt Busby, club secretary Les Olive and chief scout John Aston Sr. to meet Buchan at a hotel in Bellshill, North Lanarkshire – the town just outside Glasgow where Busby was born. Aberdeen were keen to sell only because a fire had ravaged the main stand at Pittodrie, a blaze in which the Scottish Cup Buchan helped the club win as the country's youngest cup-winning captain had to be rescued by firemen.

O'Farrell knew full well that United's squad needed overhauling if the Reds were to scale anything like the heights Busby had conquered, and Buchan was seen as an essential piece in the jigsaw. O'Farrell proudly described his new addition as 'a skilful, enthusiastic and determined player and one possessed of exceptional talent. He will be a tremendous asset to United.' He wasn't wrong. Buchan said of his move: 'I did not need any second thoughts. I am very pleased indeed to be joining Manchester United where good football is encouraged.'

However, during the negotiations, Buchan did require a nudge in the right direction as he made a brief exit to seek the advice of his former coach and mentor, Eddie Turnbull, who had given him his break at Aberdeen before moving back to his beloved Hibernian. Buchan counted Turnbull as a revolutionary coach way ahead of his time, someone who had fully prepared him for life in England's top flight.

Leeds and Liverpool both had established defensive figures, while United were crying out for reinforcements, which Buchan took to mean chances would be fully forthcoming. Not that he was looking for an easy ride – if anything, it would prove to be the opposite as United were in a sticky period of transition in the post-Busby era. Such situations in football require quality and character, and Buchan was lacking in neither department.

With Turnbull giving his blessing, the cool and classy Scottish Footballer of the Year – won at the age of 22 – moved south of the border to see what the English were made of. A typically forthright Scotsman, Buchan didn't pull any punches when it came to what he witnessed on arrival in Manchester. 'I was amazed to find people in the first team who wouldn't have got a game in Aberdeen's reserves,' he said. 'I couldn't believe that there could be such poor players in a side containing George Best. Worse still, there were those who lacked dedication and pride.'

Strong as those words were, he perhaps had a point. United were nosediving towards relegation in 1972-73, the farewell season for Bobby Charlton and Law, while the increasingly wayward Best approached his last dozen games, and the Reds ended up finishing 18th. O'Farrell had been dismissed in December that season after a 5-0 loss at Crystal Palace and, although new boss Tommy Docherty steered United through choppy waters to safety come spring, he couldn't prevent them hitting the rocks the following season as United tumbled out of the top-flight for the first time in 36 years. Buchan refused to jump ship, saying: 'There was always a feeling that we would stay up, by hook or by crook, but we didn't and it would have been easy to ask for a move. But when relegation happens, you owe both the club and yourself an extra year to put it right.'

Charlton had been captain when Buchan arrived, before the role was passed to a fellow Scot and another new signing in George Graham. The chances of Docherty choosing a countryman of Buchan had increased somewhat as the new boss formed a little Scottish enclave at Old Trafford. Graham's leadership, and his stay at

United for that matter, didn't last very long before wing wizard Willie Morgan took on the role.

But Buchan was the natural candidate; a pillar of consistency he was utterly dependable. He took the captaincy midway through United's dalliance with Division Two football in 1974-75, and continued to be a reliable defensive foundation upon which the Doc's Red Army built the swashbuckling attacking football that would return them to the top league rejuvenated. Buchan heartily disagreed with Lou Macari's claims that the step down was something of a breeze for the team's quality players, as he was fully aware that opponents desperately sought United's scalp. Perhaps it was understandable that captain Buchan and team joker Macari, who both got on despite differing personalities, held a contrasting view on the matter.

Buchan's elevation in status under Docherty was far from guaranteed and the pair experienced something of a rocky relationship at first. Buchan had been unhappy at shifting positions within the side. When he was asked to play at left-back, he made the point that if he had to play full-back at all, then he would be better used on the right, being a right-footer, although he strongly felt he was best in the middle. Docherty didn't take kindly to being challenged and threatened to sell Buchan to QPR – managed by Dave Sexton, the man who would eventually replace Docherty at Old Trafford. Buchan called his bluff and verbally agreed to a move, only never to hear of the matter again. His future remained resolutely Red.

In December 1973, the *Guardian* reported that Buchan had 'expressed his dissatisfaction to Docherty'. The paper added: 'A request to wear the No.6 shirt was refused and Buchan has again been to see the United manager who said: "Buchan will continue to play at right-back for the club." Docherty denied that Buchan will be leaving Old Trafford but it has never been the club's policy to keep an unsettled player. Buchan, to achieve his ambition, might return to Scotland.' And yet, a year later, such transfer tittle-tattle seemed like folly, as the *Observer* said of Docherty: 'There may be anxieties concerning his defence, only because it owes so much in match after match to Buchan's capacity to read and resolve situations almost instantaneously.'

On the pitch Buchan was beginning to exert his authority and character, and he was equally noticeable off it. His education – he passed his entrance exams at Aberdeen University but never took his place because football took priority – his devoted professionalism and his organisational skills set him apart from the standard footballer, and those qualities also made him ideally suited to the captaincy. He was keen to ensure the team bonded so that everyone pulled in the same direction, which was essential considering the squad that had begun the decade quite visibly bore fault lines of disharmony. He wasn't new to the requirements of being a leader; he had captained every team he played and was Aberdeen skipper aged 20, becoming the youngest captain to lift the Scottish Cup at 21.

He was delighted to take on the role, handed to him with very little ceremony by Docherty, when Morgan picked up an injury. Buchan was born for the job, stating: 'It's a great honour. I believe that a captain must lead by example, especially as there is far more that goes on off the field than there used to be. I am not the most experienced player in the United side, by any means, and that is why it is important to take notice of what other players do and say. If play-ers spot weaknesses or faults, then it is their duty to point them out and we can thrash them out together. I felt terrible when we were rel-egated last year, but I think we can get back again. We've learned our lessons.'

While he excelled on the pitch and relished the role behind the scenes, not all the off-field obligations proved appealing. Buchan rarely gave interviews to the press and, even today, seldom succumbs to nostalgic reminiscing with journalists. 'I didn't talk to the press,' he said in Andy Mitten's book on that era, *United! United!* 'I didn't not get on with any of them, but I didn't give my number out like Macari did. It was to my detriment that I didn't. I think I might have got an award if I'd been more pally with some of the press.'

Buchan gave the air of being cerebral in his play and beyond the 90 minutes on a Saturday. He would be considered by some as a bit of a loner, because he would read on the team bus while others played cards. Not only did he read books, he read play brilliantly, too. He had pace as a young defender but could anticipate danger effectively, had excellent positioning and timing in the tackle and possessed a distinct ability to grasp what the team had to do tactically.

There are numerous stories alluding to his individuality, from signing a boot deal with adidas after the rest of the squad had agreed to wear Gola, or on the 1975 pre-season tour, when he refused, unlike his team-mates, to hand in his passport to the club so that nobody lost their identification. Here was a man who would think and act for himself, he didn't need to be mollycoddled. It is intriguing to wonder what he must make of some of the footballers of the current day he comes across in his role working with the Professional Footballers' Association.

Promotion from Division Two was guaranteed at Southampton on 5 April 1975, before Buchan collected the league trophy later that month, showing it off around Old Trafford before fans ran onto the pitch. That entire season has been mythologised, with good reason, by fans who followed the Reds up and down the country but, for the team, it was a mere stepping-stone to what they were confident would be much greater triumphs back at the top of the domestic game. Not satisfied with consolidation, Docherty sought to immediately build upon the momentum United had gathered, and his much-loved brand of free-flowing attacking football was given yet more impetus with the signings of wingers Steve Coppell – whom Buchan had great admiration for – and Gordon Hill a few months apart in 1975.

Coppell's consistency and class and Hill's unpredictable wing-play would be a feature of a more dynamic team, for which Buchan thoroughly enjoyed playing. 'In 1974-75, the Doc cleared out a lot of dead wood and brought in new players,' he said. 'We went straight back up and, for two seasons, the football was wonderful to watch and to be part of. I had my difficult moments with the Doc but, looking back, those first two years back in Division One represent the summit of my career. They were the happiest years of my time in football.'

Now firmly established at the heart of United's defence, Buchan just needed a partner alongside him. On the terraces, fans chanted: 'Six foot two, eyes of blue, Big Jim Holton's after you,' but injury soon halted his short spell in the side and created an opening that was filled by midfielder Brian Greenhoff. The popular Yorkshireman sadly passed away in 2013, which prompted Buchan in his role as a PFA executive to warmly recall the alliance they had struck up. 'Our partnership came into being by sheer chance,' he said. 'It came about when Jim Holton was injured in a freak accident before a pre-season friendly at Old Trafford against Red Star Belgrade in the summer of 1975. Brian, previously a midfield player, was a quick learner and settled in very quickly.'

United boasted the second-best defensive record on home turf in 1975-76, conceding just 13 goals at Old Trafford in the league and losing only once. Yet while home form put the newly promoted Reds right in the frame for a pop at the title at the first time of asking, it may have been a case of too much, too soon. The Reds were in second place in the league following a 3-0 win over Middlesbrough on 27 March, a point behind leaders QPR with a game in hand heading into an FA Cup semi-final clash with Derby County at Hillsborough. Two goals from Hill secured victory in Sheffield, but the looming final would prove distracting, as would the players' pool – the pot of funds shared out between the squad at the end of the season. There were reports that players were demanding fees for interviews in the lead-up to the final. Buchan certainly disapproved of such behaviour.

Regardless of the impact that did or didn't have on United, the fact is that three of the five league games between beating Derby in the Cup semis and facing Division Two side Southampton at Wembley ended in defeat, and resulted in a rapid tailing off of United's title hopes. Needless to say, however, the Reds were still expected to bring home the FA Cup. Despite starting brightly and creating several scoring opportunities, the game seemed destined for extra time when Bobby Stokes struck an 83rd-minute winner to steal an unlikely victory.

Still, thousands upon thousands of fans congregated in Manchester city centre and outside the Town Hall for what was supposed to be United's glorious homecoming. Docherty made a promise to supporters that day that his players would return again next year, this time with the trophy. Buchan had no reason to doubt the size of the club he captained, but this welcome for defeated finalists left a lasting impression on him about the scale of United's support and the passion of the club's fans.

Liverpool clinched the title as United ended a promising campaign empty-handed, but optimism still abounded. The team was legitimately challenging for honours again and the dark days of being plunged into English football's second tier were seemingly very distant. Buchan's role in it all was crucial as a close-knit group emerged and threatened to challenge the might of the Liverpool machine, while his partnership with Greenhoff solidified into the sturdiest of foundations. That was led by Buchan's coolly authoritative demeanour but also his apparent omnipresence – he missed just one league match between August 1972 and May 1976.

By this stage, Buchan's influence on the team had never been stronger and he was more than willing to put team-mates in their place when required. A famous incident occurred between Buchan and Hill in January 1977 during a 2-0 win over Coventry, one that caused a fuss in the press. The skipper felt United's free-spirited winger wasn't paying due care and attention to his defensive duties and gave Hill a whack on the back of the head as he ran past him. Hill hit back and, in the absence of Docherty, who missed the game through illness, nobody was there to quell the argument. Inevitably, the tabloid sports press picked up on it.

Nevertheless, today Hill reflects respectfully when discussing Buchan's leadership style, stating unequivocally: 'Martin was a great captain. Disciplined, demanding, and wanting. Disciplined – you do your job and do it well. Demanding – you better work and he made sure everyone gave their all. Someone like him is an ideal captain. He wouldn't take any rubbish from anybody, but would also let you know if you weren't performing.

'Martin knew his job and did it well. I think he knew the job that everyone else did but didn't appreciate sometimes what they were doing. He was never a person to shy away from letting you know his views, but he was also there to help you if he could. He wasn't one of these captains who shouts all the time but he spoke with a very calm voice, in an authoritative way, to say: "Guys, listen, we've got our work cut out today and if you don't do your job . . ." Well, I won't tell you what he said, because the language we used in the changing room wasn't what you use every day! Let's just say he got his message across!'

United had been expected to kick on in 1976-77 and, while the FA Cup remained an obvious target, the Reds had shown that, late capitulation in the league aside, the Doc's side were not far off challenging for the title. However, when Buchan's almost ever-presence came to an abrupt end as winter 1976 approached, the impact was telling.

The Scot picked up a thigh strain shortly after United had edged to the top of the league on 2 October 1976 following a 3-0 win over Leeds at Elland Road. Buchan steered the Reds through a League Cup third-round replay against Sunderland, but missed the league clash with West Brom, which United lost 4-0. By the time Buchan returned for a 3-1 away defeat at Arsenal in mid-December, Docherty's team had plummeted to 16th in the table, losing four and drawing three of seven matches without their influential skipper, while also bowing out of the UEFA Cup at the hands of Juventus and the League Cup at the expense of Everton.

A ten-game unbeaten run after the turn of the year was impressive, but a 0-0 draw with Liverpool at Old Trafford in February was described by Docherty as 'our worst performance of the season'. The *Guardian*'s match report read: 'United's defence is always likely to creak under pressure and last night it suffered one of its more alarming experiences, frequently being pulled out of position and growing in disarray the longer the game went on. Buchan was the notable exception. If he made an error it was not obvious, but his colleagues fell some way below his impeccable standard. The debt that United owe him is immeasurable.'

League form once again tailed off as United finished sixth, ten points behind champions Liverpool, whose miserly back four ensured the Merseysiders remained undefeated at home to deservedly deliver the title to Anfield. Again, it was the FA Cup in which United excelled, seeing off Walsall, QPR, Southampton, Aston Villa and Leeds to reach the final to face the champions on 21 May, just four days before Bob Paisley's side were due in Rome for the European Cup final against Borussia Monchengladbach. It was the second leg of what would have been an unprecedented Treble, and few expected them to surrender the opportunity to achieve it.

It was set up to be an intriguing final between two teams at very different phases of their development, summed up neatly beforehand by Docherty. 'Liverpool are the best team in England, but we're the best to watch,' he said. Such was the clamour to be among the 100,000 supporters at Wembley on a baking hot afternoon that there were unverified claims of 4,000 forged tickets said to be in circulation on the black market, while one opportunistic scamp in London appeared in court after placing an advert in a national newspaper offering 'Cup final seats' for £15. Applicants were reportedly sent canvas stools purchased from Woolworths for £3 with the words 'Cup Final' crudely scrawled on them.

More seriously, Buchan was a major doubt for the game after injuring his knee against West Ham in the final league match of the season. He had told Docherty to send him back to Manchester in a bout of defeatism but, after leaving it to the last minute, he passed himself fit despite managing only light training in the lead-up to Wembley's showpiece occasion. The opportunity to fulfil the Doc's promise to deliver the Cup was not to be missed. Meanwhile, supporters craved a first major honour since 1968, during which time the team down the East Lancs Road seemed intent on winning anything they could lay their hands on.

Sports journalist David Lacey commented: 'The best news for United was not only that Buchan, who injured a knee at West Ham on Monday, would be fit, but also that he had signed a new three-year contract. The absence of United's captain would have lessened the chances of the game's succeeding as both a spectacle and a contest. Buchan may not be 100 per cent fit and spent yesterday's practice match keeping goal. But the fact that he is able to appear gives United a greater chance of winning than if he had had to drop out as appeared highly likely on Tuesday.'

A crunching 50-50 tackle with Liverpool hard-man Tommy Smith early in the game proved to Buchan that the risk of passing himself fit had paid off, and he excelled in snuffing out Liverpool's attacking threat. In the event, the contest was decided in one hectic spell early in the second half as goals by Jimmy Greenhoff and Stuart

Pearson fell either side of Jimmy Case's effort for Liverpool. Finally, United had delivered a major trophy, while also scuppering Liverpool's Treble hopes.

Buchan and his triumphant team-mates returned to Manchester in suitably high spirits, and if the Reds skipper had driven away from Manchester's Town Hall reception following defeat to Southampton a year earlier marvelling at the dedication and depth of his team's support, the reported 750,000 who lined the city's streets to welcome home the FA Cup winners took his breath away. Indeed, such was the scale of the turnout on crowded streets that 1,000 casualties were treated and local authorities said they would have to consider an alternative to the Town Hall for such parades in future.

Docherty instructed his captain to take care of the trophy and so, that night, Buchan took the famous cup with him to the Wheatsheaf pub in Altrincham. He had no need for the velvet-gloved team of security guards that follow trophies everywhere today, and he returned it unharmed to the club the next day.

Babysitting silverware wasn't the only responsibility that came with the captaincy. Buchan was also in charge of handing out match tickets to the players each week – an onerous task as any skipper will tell you. Players received two season tickets each year, plus two tickets per game if they were in the team. Buchan also kept tabs on players' lounge tickets after matches. It was an important part of the squad camaraderie to be able to have a beer after the game and socialise, but Buchan imposed strict rules on entry when he found that he was struggling to get served because there were no glasses left as the lounge was full with hangers on.

Buchan couldn't complain too much because he was thoroughly enjoying life and the prospects of more trophies. Little did he know that was the end of his trophy-winning days. The self-belief instilled by Docherty and his assistant Tommy Cavanagh, the attacking play and feisty support, home and away, made it a great period that promised plenty. But the roof caved in when Docherty departed under a cloud of controversy to be replaced by Dave Sexton. He arrived with a strong reputation as a quality coach but, perhaps not unexpectedly, United had gone for a polar opposite character. Far more introverted than the Doc, Sexton's reign was another huge step-change, just as the team seemed to be heading places.

United struggled in the league and finished tenth in 1977-78 as Sexton made several alterations to the side, with Gordon McQueen and Joe Jordan his most high-profile recruits. The following season wasn't much better as the Reds finished ninth in the league and Liverpool once again took the title. Not even two rare goals from Buchan that season – half his total tally of four for United – made any impact, although his thunderous long-range effort against Everton in September is still fondly talked about. The saving grace heading into 1979 was an FA Cup run that yielded wins over Chelsea, Fulham, Colchester and Tottenham to tee up a semi-final against the old enemy from Anfield, who were out for revenge.

At Maine Road, after a see-saw battle that ended 2-2 to prompt a replay at Goodison Park, a disappointed Buchan said: 'It was as though we had lost. We'd had the feeling that this was going to be our day. We'd gone behind, drawn level immediately, they'd hit the post with a penalty and then we had gone ahead … it was very disappointing not to win. But now, what is it, an hour after the match? And the spirit is coming back.'

Buchan, now 30, was outstanding in resisting what Sexton described as 'the Liverpool steamroller', a reference to their machine-like manner of winning. The *Observer*'s Ronald Atkin wrote: 'Kenny Dalglish, for me the Player of the Year, will not again find his skills so intelligently stilled in two successive matches as they were by his Scotland colleague, Martin Buchan.' Sexton also enthused: 'Probably of all the centre-backs in the country, if you wanted to find somebody to play against Kenny, you would choose Martin. His strong point is the last third of the field, just like Kenny's, and he is as quick at turning as the bloke he is marking. We were blessed, really, to have him.'

Buchan didn't feel so blessed in the final. He felt sluggish, and wasn't the only one. Arsenal were cruising at 2-0 up heading into the game's dying stages when McQueen hauled United back into life four minutes from time to make it 2-1. Sammy McIlroy's stunning solo effort drew the scores level and extra time beckoned. Then Alan Sunderland's 89th-minute strike put Arsenal back in front and broke United hearts.

Alongside McQueen, Buchan had formed another impressive centre-back partnership and, in 1979-80, they were formidable when flanked on either side by Arthur Albiston and Jimmy Nicholl as United narrowly missed out in the title race with Liverpool, who topped the league by two points. That was Sexton's loftiest finish but, once again, he missed out on a major trophy and that would ulti-mately cost him his job a short while down the line. It would also be the last time Buchan played what could be considered a complete season. Although he went on to make a further 68 appearances in a United shirt across three seasons, as Ron Atkinson took up the reins at the start of 1981-82, Buchan's time was coming to an end. 'Ron was building his new United,' he said. 'He considered me past my sell-by date, though I felt he wrote me off earlier than necessary.'

Buchan still captained the side when he played, but his chances were gradually diminishing and in his last season, in 1982-83, he made just six appearances as United reached the FA Cup final and beat Brighton via a replay. Buchan had played no part in the Cup run and later claimed he discovered the captaincy had been handed to Ray Wilkins when he read it in a newspaper.

Buchan moved to Oldham Athletic on a free transfer that summer and stayed at Boundary Park for two years before trying his hand at management with Burnley. He quit the job after 110 days and blamed the cut-throat nature of the job for his disillusionment – he had to tell a dedicated young player that he wasn't going to make it. 'It hurt me,' he said. 'I wasn't as hard as I'd thought and it made me realise that management wasn't for me.'

It was a brutally honest admission, which took toughness itself, a quality Buchan had shown with astonishing consistency at United. In 12 seasons spanning a colossal 456 appearances, he took in three Wembley finals, an FA Cup triumph and a Division Two title. Silverware was much harder to mine during this fallow period, but as many United fans would recall with a nostalgic glint in their eyes, it was made all the better by the presence and poise of quality performers like Buchan, who led with such distinction.

Chapter 8

Captain Marvel

'Bryan Robson epitomised everything I thought a United player should be. He gave blood, sweat and tears.'

Gary Neville

Bryan Robson set the perfect mould for a captain, the type of all-action hero that gets the blood pumping among team-mates and supporters alike; he was a battling, never-say-die talisman who repeatedly hauled his team out of the mire, sometimes seemingly single-handedly, leading the way to era-defining triumphs. With superhuman efforts like that, it is no wonder Robson acquired the nickname Captain Marvel. At times, through his lionhearted will, stubborn resilience and unquestionable quality, it was as though he was the instrument for an entire club's desire to emerge from two decades of underachievement, to end the long, arduous wait to resume being Britain's premier football power and bring them back among Europe's elite.

It is fitting then that, in his final four seasons, he helped oversee both targets as club skipper when United won the European Cup

Winners' Cup in 1991, ended a 26-year wait to be named league champions in 1993 and, the following season, stepped back into the European Cup, or Champions League as it had recently been rebranded, for the first time since 1969.

By that point, Robson's battle-weary body may have been creaking somewhat due to the ravages of time and a series of wounds inflicted through his uncompromisingly committed style, and he was used sparingly as Steve Bruce took up the reins in his stead. Yet that in itself was a sign of his commitment to the United cause: he gave every last drop of effort to see through the task. It was a towering legacy and set of standards he left behind – continued by another player in a similar vein, Roy Keane – against which all Manchester United central midfielders are now compared.

These impossible giants of the game are not only magnificent players on a technical level – good passers, tacklers, goalscorers too – they are also a touchstone for the teams they lead, the influential tone-setters on the field and off it. Think Manchester United in the 1980s, you think Bryan Robson. The two elements, the great player and the great leader, when aligned are a devastating combination, as Robson would so emphatically prove.

Robson, much like another great export from the North-East football stronghold, Bobby Charlton, seems such a vital part of United history now. His journey to Old Trafford, however, was not as direct as Charlton's. Born in Chester-le-Street, County Durham, Bryan grew up in nearby Witton Gilbert and, like a lot of young lads from the area, was obsessed with the game, first kicking a football aged five. It didn't take long for his natural talent to begin to shine through in his school team and eventually football league clubs from up and down the country started scouting him.

After trials at Burnley, Coventry and the club he supported as a boy, Newcastle, Robbo – a nickname given to him by his father, Brian – decided instead to join West Bromwich Albion, where he felt welcomed, well looked after and, most importantly, well coached. He was taken on as an apprentice, but Don Howe, manager at The Hawthorns at the time, had serious misgivings about young Bryan's size and strength. So, at 15, he was placed on a 'special' diet, which his coaches felt was going to add the necessary height and bulk to make the most of his abilities in a sport more brutally demanding then than it is today. Breakfast subsequently consisted of a bulk-building concoction of a pint of milk, raw eggs, sherry and sugar, while evening meals often amounted to a huge pile of potatoes and meat, washed down with an obligatory bottle of Guinness, which Robson hated. But he went diligently along with it all and his efforts in the gym soon paid off, too.

Bryan grew in stature and signed his first professional contract at The Hawthorns aged 17. Just a year later, when Howe was dismissed as manager towards the end of the 1974-75 season, Reserves coach Brian Whitehouse took temporary charge and, with just a few matches remaining, made sweeping changes to the Baggies' line-up, including giving Robson his debut against York City. Aged just 18, he helped West Brom to their first victory since Christmas, a 3-1 win at Bootham Crescent. He scored on his home debut against Cardiff City and again in a 2-1 defeat to Nottingham Forest on the final day of the season to earn sixth place in Division Two, 16 points behind champions United. It was some start for an inexperienced teenager and a sure sign that here was a plucky young player capable of rising to meet any challenge thrown his way.

West Brom were promoted to the top flight the following season and Robson scored in his first game at Old Trafford, netting in a 2-2 draw in March 1977, which actually marked a sharp decline in form for the Reds and with it went United's title hopes. Bryan also played in the oft-referenced 5-3 Baggies win in Manchester on 30 December 1978. That victory under Ron Atkinson was a sign of how well the Midlanders were progressing, peaking that season with a third-place finish, 14 points ahead of United in ninth. That progress hadn't gone unnoticed and the Reds came calling for Big Ron in 1981 to replace Dave Sexton.

Robbo had, by that point, become a full England international and was talented enough to expect that whichever club he played for would challenge for trophies. West Brom, it seemed, having previously threatened to break into the domestic elite, were now heading in the opposite direction as they sold off a number of their best players, including Laurie Cunningham to Real Madrid. Robson had been given no indication that he would follow his old boss to Manchester.

Atkinson knew that he wanted the midfielder to rejoin him, but when an initial offer of £2 million from United for Robson and team-mate Remi Moses was turned down, it looked like he might not move at all. It threatened to become a drawn-out affair, but with Liverpool also circling, offering £1 million for Robson alone – and given that the young midfielder wasn't against moving to Anfield – things accelerated. Eventually, United's superior offer made up West Brom's mind to sell and Robson went to Old Trafford for a record fee of £1.5 million in October 1981.

The move was somewhat bittersweet for Robson because he was impressed by West Brom's reluctance to sell him despite the enormous fee on offer, yet he was worried by their unwillingness to spend to progress their own status towards the big league; and then there was his own desire to take his club career to the next level. In the end, he said: 'It's a fantastic move for me and a relief. I am sure it will be of benefit to everyone concerned.' Atkinson clearly thought so, as United's ebullient boss beamed: 'It's a hefty price, but one I consider to be realistic. Bryan is the best midfield player in the country. He can serve Manchester United for the next ten years – six of them in midfield and four at the back. I have wanted him since I took over at Old Trafford.'

Robson had played in a variety of positions during his fledgling years at West Brom: full-back, left midfield, central midfield. But, at 24, he had matured into a commanding presence in the centre of the pitch, and that is precisely where a perm-haired Robson signed his contract at Old Trafford before watching United batter Wolverhampton Wanderers 5-0 on 3 October 1981. Sammy McIlroy, a player whose position was apparently now under threat due to Robson's arrival, scored a hat-trick alongside goals from Garry Birtles and Frank Stapleton. He'd been given such a grand entrance, but after that display Robson harboured doubts that he could force his way into the team.

A 1-0 defeat in the League Cup against Tottenham Hotspur wasn't the ideal debut, but solid contributions in a 0-0 draw with Manchester City and a 2-1 win at Anfield against Liverpool in his first five matches certainly wasn't a bad start. He would miss just one match through to the end of the season as United finished a creditable third, albeit nine points behind champions Liverpool and five adrift of runners-up Ipswich Town.

His instant status as a regular in the side was a mere prelude to his rapid rise to become skipper barely a year after arriving in Manchester. The incumbent captain, Martin Buchan, was one of many players who had helped Robson feel instantly at home at Old Trafford, but he was also edging towards the end of his career and, as Robson explained in *Robbo: My Autobiography*, a change was on the cards. Of the Scot, he said: 'He was very much his own man and not everybody's cup of tea. An intelligent, thoughtful guy, he specialised in put-downs. I thought his sarcastic sense of humour could be funny and he was OK with me but not everyone found it so easy to get on with him. Some felt he was too cold and aloof. I think it's fair to say he and Ron were always heading for a clash of personalities.

'Martin took his position as captain really seriously. At the end of a match, he would rush off the pitch, put on his tracksuit and stand at the door of the players' lounge, collecting guest tickets. If any guests turned up without one, he would turn them away. If there was anyone in the lounge he felt shouldn't be there, he would throw them out. When I took over the captaincy, the lads said, "This is a bit different!"'

Buchan remained at the club until summer 1983, but United already had two credible candidates to replace him in the role. Robson was clearly one and had been touted as England's next skipper after an impressive showing at the 1982 World Cup in Spain, where he scored twice against France in the group stage – his first after just 27 seconds to stop the clock on one of the fastest-ever goals in the finals – before the Three Lions bowed out in the second round.

However, Robson's midfield partner for club and country, Ray Wilkins, was chosen as England skipper – with Bryan named vice-captain – and he took the role at Old Trafford too, as Buchan was gradually edged out, playing just six times in his final season. Wilkins had joined the Reds from Chelsea in 1979, and had been their captain before his move north. He had already captained United before taking the armband permanently for his country for the first time against Denmark in September 1982.

Then, just a few weeks later, he suffered a broken cheekbone during a 2-2 League Cup second round, second leg draw at Bournemouth and was ruled out for two months. By the time he returned for a 3-0 league defeat at Coventry on 28 December, Robson had taken over as captain at club and national level, and he wouldn't look back. Buchan later admitted that he felt Atkinson wanted to offer the role to Robson anyway, but couldn't overlook the more senior Wilkins.

Nevertheless, Robson recalls the moment he was made skipper, saying: 'I was sat in the dressing room preparing for kick-off when

Ron walked over and handed me the captain's armband. There was no great fanfare and no press conference or media statements like you might expect today. I just remember feeling proud to be wearing the armband for United.'

Robson continued by saying: 'I'm sure it was disappointing for Ray [to lose the captaincy of England and United] but he dealt with it with a lot of class and dignity, which is nothing less than you would expect of him.

'I'd never been captain at senior level, only with England's youth teams or a couple of times in West Brom's Reserves. At West Brom we had a really experienced captain in John Wile, who played over 600 games for the club and was a real warrior, so he always led the team. But I felt ready to take on the role and being made captain of my club – not just any club, but United – was an incredibly proud moment for me. I was fortunate that I kept the armband with United and England right throughout my career. That's a real honour.'

If a twist of fate handed Robson his chance as skipper, it snatched away his first shot at lifting his maiden trophy within months of taking the armband. The League Cup clash at Bournemouth, in which Wilkins had been injured, was the start of a path to three trips to Wembley that season and, having beaten Bradford, Southampton, Nottingham Forest and Arsenal, the Reds booked the first of those visits to the capital against inevitable league winners Liverpool. But Robson had damaged his ankle ligaments in the 2-1 semi-final, second leg win over Arsenal at Old Trafford, which clinched a 6-3 aggregate victory. He was subsequently ruled out of the League Cup final and Wilkins took the armband, only for United to lose 2-1.

Still, Big Ron's Reds were continuing the club's recent reputation as a cup team and, with Robson back in the side, United once again saw off Arsenal in a semi-final, this time in the FA Cup at Villa Park in April, having already defeated West Ham, Luton Town, Derby County and Everton. Against the Gunners, Tony Woodcock had put his side in front, but Robson came to the rescue and Norman Whiteside added another to seal a final spot against Brighton & Hove Albion.

Back on league duty, four defeats and three draws in the last ten matches once again saw United's title hopes prematurely fade to black, which painfully served to show the ruthless consistency which Liverpool seemed so readily able to apply to see out the championship. Subsequently, and somewhat typically, Atkinson took his players to Majorca for a few days' training and relaxation so as to press the reset button ahead of the impending Wembley final. Robson approved of the move as captain, showing that manager and skipper were very much in tune when it came to the balance between encouraging team spirit while demanding professional match preparation. In the Balearic sunshine, Robson could rightly reflect on an incredible first full season at the club – and as captain – but he wasn't fully satisfied without delivering success, and subsequently he took his season stats to 15 goals in 49 games when he scored twice in the 4-0 final replay win over Brighton, having initially drawn 2-2.

Stuart Jones, writing in *The Times*, noted: 'Wembley's ancient rafters trembled last night as Manchester United, the club with the biggest and most expectant support in the land, won the FA Cup. As Bryan Robson, their captain and scorer of two of their goals, lifted the glittering silverware, the flash of a thousand cameras captured the long-awaited moment and a mighty roar of emotional delight echoed around the packed national stadium.' He added: 'Robson has few rivals as Europe's most complete all-round player.'

The Reds skipper could have bagged a hat-trick to neatly round off the scoring and an impressive first campaign as skipper. United were awarded a penalty just after the hour-mark, with the scoreline seemingly comfortably poised at 3-0. Certainly United's raucous support among the 92,000 who made the journey to London on a Thursday night had only one man in mind. But Robbo thought it prudent to make absolutely certain of victory rather than seek further personal glory – especially after Brighton, sensing certain defeat, had thrown caution to the wind and forced a couple of good saves from Gary Bailey.

Robson stated afterwards: 'When we got the penalty, one or two of the lads shouted for me to take it to give me the chance of completing a hat-trick and I suppose I could have taken it. But, at three-nil, teams can still come back at you. So it had to be Arnold Muhren who took it.' Spot-kick specialist Muhren insisted: 'I didn't really think about letting Bryan take the penalty. We had talked about it before the game and it was my job.'

After successive third-place finishes and a first trophy in six years, United had a sense of purpose (and no shortage of hope) that Atkinson's hefty outlay on players, characterised by the inspired and influential Robson, would bring sustained success back to Old Trafford. That sense of optimism, coupled with the ability and desire of the team's leader to achieve it, was reinforced when Robson struck twice again at Wembley during a 2-0 win over Liverpool in the Charity Shield in August ahead of the new season.

In 1983-84, however, United's domestic cup dominance was conspicuously absent as a fourth-round League Cup tie with Oxford required two replays, before the Us won 2-1 following a pair of 1-1 stalemates. Then Bournemouth dumped the Reds out of the FA Cup in the third round. In the league, United finished six points behind Liverpool, an improvement on the previous season's 12-point chasm, but dropped a place to fourth behind Southampton and Nottingham Forest. Despite topping the table in March, United's inability to see out victories on the road proved costly, with 11 matches drawn away from Old Trafford, eight of which came in the second half of the season. Combined with another poor run late in the campaign – one win in the last eight – this all put a stop to United's title ambitions.

However, that season will most fondly be remembered for United's run to the semi-finals of the European Cup-Winners' Cup, which included epic quarter-final ties with Barcelona and Diego Maradona. In the first leg at the Nou Camp, a Graeme Hogg own goal and Juan Carlos Rojo's brilliant volley in injury time left United staring down the barrel, with a European exit almost a certainty. That prompted the press to speculate further on a rumoured £3 million bid for Robson from Italy, with a host of interested suitors including Sampdoria, Torino, Fiorentina, Inter Milan and Juventus.

The Times's David Millar pontificated: 'If and when the rumoured Italian bid for Robson gains more basic temptation with money on the table, from Internazionale or any other club with a lust of success greater than United's, the decision will depend upon three men: Robson, Atkinson and the chairman, Martin Edwards. For differing reasons, all three of them will, I suspect, decide it makes sense to accept.' Atkinson, Millar proffered, faced a difficult dilemma: 'Frankly, he says, he would not really wish to part with such an outstanding player, who is potentially the difference between an ordinary side and a good one. Yet if the offer is made – approximately doubling Robson's value during a two-year period in which domestic fees have moved sharply downwards – then it would make practical sense "provided the money all goes back into new players".'

Tycoon Robert Maxwell's attempts to buy out Edwards's stake in United had failed but merely heightened talk that, following Atkinson's spending, the club had to deliver league or European silverware to offset the large financial outlay. Robson later admitted to having his head turned by the prospect of moving to Italy, especially given the wages on offer on the Continent. At that moment, though, he had more pressing matters to attend to. He had missed a gilt-edged chance in the second half in Catalonia, which would have cancelled out 19-year-old Hogg's unfortunate faux pas on his European debut. Robbo had missed a one-on-one, so unlike him given that he gave a career-best return of 18 goals that season, and he was determined to make amends.

In a night that shook Old Trafford – from the roar of the crowd and the excitement generated on the pitch – Robson scored in either half to draw the teams level on aggregate. His first was to bundle home a corner, before sliding in bravely to pounce on a rebound from the goalkeeper after the break. Within a minute of his fist-pumping celebrations in front of the Stretford End, Frank Stapleton smashed home a third goal from close range and a baying home crowd turned delirious. Despite Barcelona's inevitable rally, United saw out the win and Robson was carried shoulder-high from the field. Some say it was his finest performance, a brilliant midfield all-rounder at the peak of his powers – and all this against the might and glamour of Maradona's Barcelona.

Robson prefers not to be so self-congratulatory: 'Every man in our team played a heroic part that night, and so did every one of our fans. All night, the atmosphere had been fantastic, the best I ever experienced in my time at Old Trafford. The packed ground was shaking with the noise. The passion of the crowd, the drama and the excitement were unbelievable, and at the end, the explosion of joy just about took the roof off the place. The players hardly had time to congratulate each other before they were mobbed by thousands of fans, spilling on to the pitch. I was lifted off my feet and carried shoulder high. My name was being sung and my back was slapped till it hurt – or at least it would have done if I hadn't been so elated. It was one of those nights you dream about and treasure for the rest of your life.'

Many supporters there that night feel exactly the same way, and

Charlie Roberts was United's first great captain, seen here leading out the team for the 1909 FA Cup final. He was never afraid to take on the football authorities to help his fellow professionals.

Frank Barson was a teak-tough defender in an era when United struggled to make any impact on the field.

Johnny Carey is congratulated by United fans after he had led the team to their first major trophy in 37 years following a thrilling FA Cup final against Blackpool in 1948.

Roger Byrne, skipper of the Busby Babes, was a father figure to his team-mates and a link between them and the manager.

Maurice Setters and Noel Cantwell proudly display the trophy on their return to Manchester after winning the FA Cup by beating Leicester City 3-1 in 1963.

Bobby Charlton shoots for goal against West Ham United. He took over the club captaincy in the aftermath of the European Cup success of 1968, but could not halt United's decline in the 1970s.

Bobby Charlton continued to be the perfect ambassador for the club long after he had hung up his boots. Here he reminisces with Benfica's Eusebio about the 1968 European Cup final.

Despite injury concerns, Martin Buchan did a fine job in organising the team to beat Treble-chasing Liverpool to win the 1977 FA Cup final.

All-action 'Captain Marvel' Bryan Robson clashes with Jimmy Case during the 1983 FA Cup final, watched on by his predecessor as skipper, Ray Wilkins.

Steve Bruce and Robson lift the Premier League trophy on the way to a historic first Double in 1994.

Eric Cantona inspired a new generation of young players, including David Beckham, who emerged in the double Double season of 1995-96. He was captain at Wembley in 1996 and led the side in the following campaign.

Roy Keane's stunning performance against Juventus helped get the Reds to the Champions League final in 1999, but it was Peter Schmeichel who lifted the trophy on that extraordinary night.

Roy Keane and Patrick Vieira shake hands before the start of the 2003-04 Old Trafford clash. The big games always brought out the best in the inspirational Irishman.

Gary Neville celebrates John O'Shea's winning goal at Anfield in March 2007, as United close in on yet another title. Rarely has the club had such a passionate skipper.

Only one winner. Nemanja Vidic rises high above Gareth McAuley of West Brom as the skipper led his side back to the summit of the Premier League in 2012-13.

Vidic and Patrice Evra display the Premier League trophy in front of Old Trafford, after the Reds signed off Sir Alex's career with a 20th league title.

Wayne Rooney, the club's latest official skipper, leads from the front as he scores United's third goal against QPR in September 2014.

it is perhaps the fact Robson so visibly and evocatively shared that vision of United in its defining moments that aligned fans with their hero. Or perhaps, for supporters, it was simply that here in their midst was a world-class player capable of so colourfully writing epic moments into United folklore.

Robson was in the form of his life and on a run of seven goals in ten games between February 1984 and the start of April, having been encouraged to push higher up the pitch behind the two strikers to make the most of his goalscoring potential. His eye-catching performances did little to quell the transfer speculation, although he stated that occasions like the one against Barcelona could only persuade him to stay. However, disaster struck after achieving that scoring run in a 1-0 league win over Birmingham on 7 April, as Robson pulled a hamstring in training before Juventus's visit to Old Trafford in the Cup-Winners' Cup semi-finals.

With Robbo ruled out for a month, it meant he would miss the home and away ties against the Italians. That certainly impacted on the outcome, and although the rejigged Reds, also missing Muhren and Wilkins for the first leg, drew 1-1 in Manchester and were holding Juve by the same scoreline as the second leg veered towards extra time in Turin, Paolo Rossi struck late on to secure victory for the Old Lady.

Having travelled to Italy to watch the game, Robson was cleared by United to meet Juventus to decipher their intentions in the market. Atkinson had told his captain that he wanted him to stay and that he was a central part of his plans to turn United into a European force, but added the caveat that, if a £3 million offer was made, it would have to be accepted. Robson later recalled: 'In the end, all the talking led to nothing. None of the Italian clubs would go to three million pounds, so I stayed at Old Trafford. That certainly wasn't a problem for me. I shared Ron's desire to take United back to the top and was happy at the club. I never asked for a transfer and never instigated the discussions for a move.' United did sell to an Italian club that summer, but it was Wilkins who joined AC Milan for £1.4 million.

It was a loss after his impressive 1983-84 campaign, and Barcelona's World Cup-winning manager, Cesar Luis Menotti, felt Wilkins rather than Robson had turned the tie around earlier that season. The truth is both players had been influential. Now more responsibility was certainly being heaped on the United skipper's shoulders. At 27, he was at peak maturity and, as captain, he was at his most influential, revelling in the responsibility that came with it. 'Some players will tell you that their form suffered after becoming skipper because they found the added responsibility a burden and a distraction from their own game,' he said of the captaincy. 'Others shy away from it because they feel it's simply not for them. But I never found the job a burden or a handicap. In fact, I relished the responsibility and believe I thrived on it.'

The profile of the club means there is additional focus on United at the best of times, and this is even greater when things aren't going to plan. When the scrutiny is at its greatest, that is the surest test of whether a player has the temperament to excel at Old Trafford and can live up to the expectations placed on him. It takes immaculate determination and resolute focus to stare down those moments of uncertainty with unflinching nerves, and Robson proved utterly adept at it. In fact, it wasn't just on the field that Robson excelled as player and leader. Away from the matchday maelstrom, he understood the essential impact he could have as club skipper in managing and influencing the spirit and focus within the squad.

'The role of being captain extends beyond ninety minutes twice a week,' he says. 'I always thought the part you play off the field is just as influential as the one you perform on it as skipper. I learned at a young age at West Brom that the bonding of a team is important.

That is the captain's job and it might have been as simple as saying, "Right, we've not got a midweek game so we're going out for a meal together."

'We used to go to the races, or we would play golf or we went go-karting . . . whatever it was, that type of bonding session helped you find out about your team-mates much better than just going into training through the week. You get into that cycle of training, going home to rest, then you come in and do the same thing the next day and it becomes routine. When you go out as mates and enjoy your-selves, get to know each other, you have a stronger bond and a better trust when it comes to matches. I always thought that was my responsibility as a captain to encourage that atmosphere of trust and a strong bond as a group.'

There was a feeling of collective optimism on the dawn of the 1984-85 season after United signed Gordon Strachan from Aberdeen, Jesper Olsen from Ajax and Alan Brazil from Tottenham Hotspur. Robson had also put the interest from foreign clubs behind him and signed a seven-year deal at Old Trafford, said to be worth in excess of £1 million. He was effectively committing the rest of his career to the club and it firmly cemented his association with United.

That show of loyalty brought with it a reward, as Robson and United would go on to clinch the FA Cup come May 1985, but Manchester's premier club had to emerge from epic battles with Merseyside's dual powers to achieve it. After beating Bournemouth, Coventry, Blackburn and West Ham to reach the semis, Liverpool were waiting at the neutral Goodison Park. United twice took the lead, through Robson then Stapleton, but Ronnie Whelan inside 90 minutes and Paul Walsh in extra time both equalised. In an unforgettable replay at Maine Road four days later, Paul McGrath's unfortunate own goal put Liverpool in front, but Robson grabbed hold of the tie in the second half, bursting forward from midfield and arrowing a 25-yard shot past Bruce Grobbelaar, who got a hand to the ball but was never going to stop it. Mark Hughes wrapped up victory when Strachan brilliantly carved out space to set the United front man through on goal, and he finished with aplomb.

Fans flooded onto the pitch after the final whistle and once again held Robson aloft as he twirled a scarf above his head. 'We're really pleased because Liverpool are the team to beat,' the skipper said magnanimously. 'They've done it for years. They never give you a moment's peace when you're playing against them. So it's a great result. I said recently my shooting hasn't been very good at all, so it was lovely to see that one fly in! Liverpool might still have come back after Hughesy scored because they did it twice before in the last game. Our supporters were great. They turned out in fantastic numbers again and they stick by the team whether we're winning or losing. So they're great fans.'

If defeating Liverpool wasn't tough enough, Everton were next up in the final and, as newly crowned runaway league champions (they'd finished 13 points ahead of Liverpool), they were eyeing a Double. A fairly uneventful final erupted with little more than ten minutes remaining when Kevin Moran became the first player to be sent off in an FA Cup final for a challenge on Peter Reid. That tipped the numerical advantage in Everton's favour, but the perceived injustice was fuel to the fire raging inside Robson and his men. Whiteside had missed a couple of earlier chances to break the deadlock but, in the most difficult of the three big opportunities that came his way, he scored in extra time, steering a beautiful left-footed shot past Everton goalkeeper and Football Writers' Footballer of the Year, Neville Southall.

So Robson held the famous trophy aloft at Wembley for a second time, and while again tailing off in the league, the United squad was buzzing from another epic Cup run. The mood was only tempered on the parade back home in Manchester by fusty FA rules that had denied Moran a winner's medal on the big day, though he would later be granted one after an FA committee relented in the unprecedented scenario of a player being dismissed in a final.

With no European distractions the following season due to English clubs' continental ban after the tragic Heysel disaster, United had to focus solely on domestic matters. Despite losing 2-0 to Everton in the Charity Shield, Atkinson's side made a blistering start in the league, winning the first ten matches and scoring 27 goals in the process, including a 4-0 thumping of Aston Villa on the opening day and a 5-1 demolition of West Bromwich Albion. Everton had broken the monotony of the Liverpool machine grinding out championship wins, but Robson dearly wanted Manchester to end Merseyside's dominance, while the large and looming reality was that United were hurtling towards a third decade without a league triumph.

United extended that promising start to 15 matches unbeaten but, as that run ended in a 1-0 defeat to Sheffield Wednesday in November, the season quickly began to unravel. Robson had missed four games prior to that loss with a hamstring strain and suffered a calf muscle problem after just 14 minutes at Hillsborough. He missed the next 12 matches, including a League Cup exit against Liverpool, but the focus was on the league. The team's leader returned to league duty for a 2-1 defeat at West Ham in February, but United remained near the top of the table. Even a 1-1 draw against Liverpool a week later kept Atkinson's side in second place, equal on points with Everton but behind on goal difference, two points ahead of Liverpool.

United just couldn't find any consistency, and neither could Robson, who played in half of the Reds' remaining fixtures, in which the team slipped to fourth as once again the league campaign fizzled out and Liverpool reclaimed the title from runners-up Everton, while West Ham – United's conquerors in the FA Cup and against whom Robson had dislocated a shoulder – edged comfortably into third spot come May.

Robson's injury issues continued at the World Cup in Mexico when he dislocated his shoulder again, which required surgery and meant he missed the first four games of 1986-87, none of which United won. A 5-1 win on Robson's return to action against Southampton was followed by defeats to Watford, Everton and Chelsea in the league. Just three wins in the first 13 league games left Atkinson's hopes of continuing as manager hanging by a thread and a 4-1 exit against Southampton in the League Cup third round confirmed his departure.

Big Ron was dismissed and in came Alex Ferguson, who had been linked with the United job after his impressive work in Aberdeen's shattering of the Old Firm duopoly north of the border. Ferguson was immediately intent on a culture change at the club that, he hoped, would help rid players of injury problems and bring about a new era of league success that had proved so elusive. He just had to find the right way of pitching it: 'You can't go into a club and tell people their fitness is terrible, they're bevvying, they're playing too much golf and their ground is filthy.' Strachan's reaction to Ferguson's arrival had simply been: 'Och, no!' Things would change, ultimately for the better, but Robson fervently denies a drinking culture existed at the club, simply that Ferguson was more of a disciplinarian than Atkinson and preferred his players not to drink alcohol at all.

Regardless, when Ferguson arrived, one of his biggest battles was getting Robson out on the pitch at all due to injury. Robbo's run of absences had not been solved earlier in the year by a visit to a clinic in Amsterdam for a week's intensive treatment and training, but the injuries also prompted some to suggest – and this was an idea floated by Atkinson – that Robson might drop back into defence, where the lack of strenuous physical output working from box to box would be considerably less demanding on his body. This notion was rebuffed by Robson's international manager and name-sake, Bobby. 'He still has a great future, providing he is clinically fit,' said the England boss. 'But he's best in an area where he can win a match, not save it. I wouldn't consider playing him anywhere else.'

With Robson now 30, almost a year into his new job Ferguson was willing to give it a go to prolong his captain's influence on the team. In a 1-1 draw with Luton in October 1987, the Scot trialled Robson in a deep-lying role and declared: 'The idea was for him to break into the middle of the park and control the tempo for us.' It was an experiment 'with the pitch and the way Luton play in mind [but] we might see it again.' That was the case when United hosted Norwich a couple of weeks later, but a dire team display in the first half forced a rethink and Robson shifted up into midfield, inevitably scoring the winner in a 2-1 triumph.

That Robson's game was changing was beyond doubt, and perfectly natural given his age, but the fact he was England's best performer at the European Championship in West Germany as a midfielder suggested he could still cut it there, and a powerful display in a 3-3 draw with Liverpool at Anfield showed he still influenced games. The idea of him becoming less of a rampaging warrior and more an all-seeing midfield general, though, applied sound logic.

The 1987-88 and 1988-89 campaigns saw Robson largely avoiding injuries in two heavily contrasting seasons. While in 1988 Robson reflected on 11 goals in 43 appearances in all competitions and a runners-up finish behind Liverpool, the following year his eight goals from the same number of appearances helped United only to 11th in the league, 25 points behind winners Arsenal. The promise shown in challenging for the title with Robson leading the way a few years earlier was slipping away, and while Merseyside's grip on the title had slipped, it was not because of United's doing. Ferguson's rebuilding of the team and the club was in desperate need of reaching fruition.

The turning point would come in 1990. How influential Mark Robins' goal against Nottingham Forest in the FA Cup third round actually was has been met with claim and counter-claim from the main protagonists. What is not in doubt is that United won the FA Cup later that season, with Robson lifting the trophy for a third time, notably battling past Oldham Athletic in a semi-final replay and then again in a second match in the final to see off Crystal Palace.

The times were changing. Liverpool won the league that year and United had reached a nadir by finishing 13th, but it would be the end of the Anfield club's domestic dominance. The European ban on English clubs had also been lifted and Old Trafford hosted continental football once more, while Ferguson's side were steadily climbing the league ladder. This new journey began with an unfortunately familiar scenario as Robson missed a huge chunk of the start to the 1990-91 season after suffering a bad Achilles tendon injury on duty with England at the World Cup.

Only once more would Robson play more than 30 games in a season for United, but he was a relatively regular presence in the side in the second half of the season. Robson and United had to overcome the disappointment of losing the League Cup final 1-0 to Sheffield Wednesday – it was an unlucky competition for him having missed the 1983 final, losing in 1991's showpiece and missing the 1992 triumph over Nottingham Forest. That said, the defeat to Ron Atkinson's Owls side was the only final or semi-final Robson ever lost in United colours. By then, Robson had hit form and bagged a first goal of the season against Derby five days before the trip to Wembley. United were willing to show faith in their skipper by offering an extension to his contract to the summer of 1993.

The final defeat to Division Two Wednesday irked Ferguson, who said of his team before taking on Barcelona in the European Cup-Winners' Cup final: 'We are capable of beating the best and losing to the worst.' In Rotterdam, there was another shot at glory and a chance to win a European trophy for the first time in 23 years. United had beaten Pecsi Munkas, Wrexham, Montpellier and Legia Warsaw to reach the final, but Barcelona were a different proposition altogether. Although the dramatic 2-1 triumph conjures images of Mark Hughes wheeling away in celebration, it was one of Robson's finest performances in a United shirt.

David Lacey, writing in the *Guardian*, praised the Reds skipper for a disciplined display: 'Bryan Robson was an inspiration as United refused to allow Barcelona to lull the game into a tempo which would have better suited their purposes. Practically all the drama was compressed into the last 20 minutes, but equally important for United was the way Robson and Paul Ince, locking horns with Eusebio and Bakero, preserved a parity in midfield which often isolated Laudrup and Salinas in the Barcelona attack.' To cap an impressive display, Robson's angled pass set Hughes racing free to round the keeper and score his second of the night.

On a wave of optimism created by that victory, Ferguson's team was finally slotting into place and United mounted a serious challenge for the title in 1991-92, only to surrender the crown to Leeds with a poor run at the end of the season which garnered just two wins in the last eight games. That included the League Cup final loss against Forest and consecutive league defeats to the Midlanders, West Ham and Liverpool, gifting the title to United's cross-Pennine rivals. Robson had played in 38 games that season, and while he would go on to notch just 17 appearances in all competitions the following year and make just ten league starts in his final campaign, there was no doubting that the United skipper still commanded the respect of his peers and had played an integral role in leading the Reds' resurgence under Ferguson.

As captain, Robson saw it as his duty to protect his team-mates out on the pitch, particularly the younger members of the squad that started to come through during the 1990s. 'Trust is a key factor as captain,' he says. 'I read a story from Ryan Giggs about a situation in a game against Sheffield United – I think it was in 1992 when Ryan had just broken into the first team. He was having a tough time against their right-back who was trying to intimidate him, to get inside his head by making threatening remarks, which happens in football. So I said to Ryan, "I'm going out to play on the left wing for a while, you stay in here in my position." I was experienced and could look after myself and put a few tackles in where some people maybe couldn't. Ryan could tackle but we weren't to know that when he was just a young lad. So I went over and tackled the guy and just said: "There's going to be more of that if you kick the kid again." That's football, particularly at that time. The game has changed a wee bit these days but it comes back to that bond again, looking after your team-mates and all players, but especially so as captain. You have to have it in you.'

Having a keen awareness of the various characters in the squad, and of each player's temperament, was also a key facet of Robson's leadership style. 'As a captain, it's very similar to being a manager,' he explains. 'You've got to work out what makes the people around you tick. You have to gauge their personality and respond to it accordingly. You've got to know who you're going to get a response from if you have a bit of a go at them, and who might go into their shell rather than rise to the challenge if you give them a telling off. Some players need encouragement rather than a rollicking. So it's important you work that out so you can be as effective as possible with the things you say, whether it's out on the pitch or in the dressing room.'

Sir Alex set out the parameters he believes set his greatest captains apart in his autobiography, saying: 'In all my time, the strong personalities have helped shape the team's actions. Bryan Robson, Steve Bruce, Eric Cantona: those players have enforced the will of the manager and the club.' That relationship with the manager had proved key, and while Robson wasn't afraid to stand up to his boss, being aligned with his principles and philosophy was essential. 'The coach sets everything out,' he said. 'What you try to do as a captain is make sure the players on the pitch are doing what the coach has asked you to do. It is about being disciplined and motivating yourself to keep the shape and follow the instructions of the manager.'

Robson's part in the United story was coming to an end, although his presence remained an integral part of the squad's identity. As such, despite just 14 league appearances (five as a starter, nine as substitute) in 1992-93 in the first year of the Premier League, it was fitting that, when United lifted the trophy after beating Blackburn Rovers 3-1 at Old Trafford in May, Bruce, who captained the side in Robson's absence, called on the club skipper to hold the trophy aloft alongside him. The pair repeated the scene a year later, when Robson made 27 appearances as United clinched the Double in 1993-94.

In the final months of that season it became clear that Robson was moving into a different phase of his career. He had already played a part in United's Reserves, stirring the pot of rich talent bubbling under the surface at Old Trafford. In February 1994, at 37, he was called into the England coaching set-up to assist Terry Venables. It was a move fully countenanced by Ferguson, who said: 'We would help Bryan to meet the commitments involved, if that is what Terry wants. Bryan is perfectly capable of organising his life to include some international duties. He wants to complete at least this season with us and with luck we will have a lot of games, so he is sure to play a part.'

By March, Robson was attracting interest as a manager not as a player, as Wolves sought a replacement for Graham Turner. He insisted he wanted to see out his contract at United until the end of the season, adding that he didn't want to regret missing out on something special at Old Trafford, but he said: 'If Wolves approach me, I'll take the matter from there. That's all I can say at the moment.' The job in the end went to Graham Taylor.

Robson's departure as a player was confirmed before United faced Coventry in the final game of the league season on 8 May. He said: 'I'm leaving but I'm not sure what I'm going to do. I have offers as a player and manager, but I don't want to decide for a week or two.' That just left the FA Cup final against Chelsea to contend with to complete United's Double and to bring the curtain down on an incredible 13-year career with the Reds. But there was no guarantee that the club skipper would play.

In the 4-1 semi-final replay win over Oldham, Robson had been tactically deployed, playing in a three-man midfield. Ferguson said after the win, in which Robson scored United's third goal: 'Semi-finals are meat and drink to him. He has scored in every semi-final he has played in . . . at least, that's what he says! At thirty-seven he never showed any sign of being second to any ball. It typified the old Robson.'

However, picking a team for the final was a different matter. Ferguson had a well-established and formidable XI: Schmeichel, Parker, Bruce, Pallister, Irwin, Kanchelskis, Ince, Keane, Giggs, Cantona, Hughes. It was difficult to see him breaking up that canonised collection, but even for a place on the three-man bench competition was fierce. Before the final, Ferguson's stomach churned over making a choice of two from Robson, Brian McClair and Lee Sharpe. 'I face a decision I wish I didn't have to make,' he said. 'It's horrendous.'

In the end, the substitute places went to goalkeeper Gary Walsh, plus Sharpe and McClair. Ferguson confessed to 'agonising for hours' about leaving Robson out. 'It was a tragedy he wasn't on the bench,' he said. 'But I needed McClair's flexibility because I couldn't be sure if Cantona would be able to complete a whole game. Robson has been a fantastic player for us and I hated leaving him out, but he's going to be a manager soon. I asked him what he'd do in a similar situation. He said he'd still pick himself!'

United beat Chelsea 4-0 at Wembley with two penalties from Eric Cantona and a goal apiece from Hughes and McClair, while Robson watched in his club suit in the stands. The club offered to have a medal made for him, but it was politely and proudly declined. Robson recalled: 'Despite my disappointment over the final, I could look back on a fantastic career with United. I had three winners' medals in the FA Cup, two in the championship, and one in the European Cup-Winners' Cup. I played my part in taking United back to the top of the English game.'

Nobody could argue with that, but just as importantly, he left an indelible mark on the club through his indomitable character, the way he played the game and in setting phenomenal standards of quality and commitment to the United cause. That legacy would stretch out for years – and still echoes prominently at Old Trafford today.

Gary Neville made his debut in the UEFA Cup in 1992, but his second match for the Reds was in the European Cup against Galatasaray and he played alongside a player he had always idolised. 'Bryan had a huge bearing on how I turned out as a player,' he said. 'I remember being there at Old Trafford the day he signed, when United played Wolves, so for him to then praise me when I was in the youth team was unbelievable. I remember it like it was yesterday. He said about me: "I'll be amazed if he doesn't become a top player." At the time I was only eighteen and I thought, "Really?", and I never looked back from there.

'To me, Robson epitomised everything I thought a United player should be. He flogged himself to the end of every game and gave blood, sweat and tears. He was a leader and the spirit on the pitch in what was a pretty disappointing period for the club. When he used to burst into the box, it was like everything mattered. You could see it in his face and his running style, everything was a fight and a battle and that shaped how I wanted to play the game myself. You go to the last minute, give your all, give your maximum.' Those standards still abound today.

Chapter 9

The Media Man

'You cannot train a captain. The man either has leadership qualities or he has not.'

Steve Bruce

Being passed the Manchester United armband by the iconic figure of Bryan Robson, the ultimate 'Captain Marvel', should have been enough to fill any man with dread. However, with Robson still on the playing staff and operating as club captain, genial Geordie Steve Bruce became an instant success in an increasingly demanding role.

Not only was he an ever-present in the epochal 1992-93 season, but that campaign marked the end of a torturous 26-year wait for the league title. More glory was to follow when he made history a year later by lifting both the championship and FA Cup as the Reds did the Double for the first time, and he was still a major contributor when the remarkable feat was repeated in 1996.

'If you were to create the perfect club captain, who wasn't Bryan Robson, it would be Brucey,' commented Roy Keane. 'In my early days at United, he'd gone out of his way to help me feel I belonged. Strictly speaking, that wasn't his job but he made it his business.'

A self-effacing character who embraced the position with a sense of dedicated duty, he acted as though every aspect of the job was a privilege and one to be savoured. Fearless in dealing with intimidating centre-forwards – he admitted losing count of the number of times his nose was broken – he remained dignified and approachable away from the physical confrontations on the field when facing the media's microphones and journalists' notepads.

Maybe Bruce's stewardship marked a real change in the responsibilities that came with the captaincy. Yes, Robson wrote a regular column in *Shoot* magazine and was comfortable when facing the TV cameras, but the launch of the Premier League brought with it much greater razzmatazz and fanfare to support an ever-increasing amount of attention given to the sport. There was a new hunger to consume football and the stories behind it that had never before been seen. Not only were the matches themselves regularly screened live, but players were handed greater media commitments – not least the skipper – and those duties became an essential and largely unavoidable task. 'Steve is always talking on the pitch as well as being good with the media,' suggested Robson when backing the appointment. 'It all adds up to being a good captain.'

If anything, perhaps he was too accommodating with the press and the demands from wider areas of the media. Certainly, he would always front up after any defeats, often shielding his team-mates from any criticism, and would foster relationships with trustworthy members of the press. Performing the duty with a smile, he did once concede: 'We've all got to do our little bits with reporters, but it can annoy you sometimes when your phone doesn't stop ringing. Your private life can be disrupted but that's just something you've got to accept, playing for Manchester United.'

The amiable centre-back took this open approach one step further when filming *Captain's Log*, a video diary of the momentous season when United finally lifted the long-awaited league title in

1993. With the camcorder on hand to document some memorable scenes, previously uncharted access to the club's inner sanctum was provided for viewers. Who can forget the images of the impromptu party at the skipper's house when Aston Villa's challenge faltered on the eve of Blackburn Rovers' visit to Old Trafford?

Bruce had by then long since endeared himself to the United faithful. In fact, he did so instantly when declaring he would walk across broken glass from Norwich to Manchester in order to represent the Reds when a move was mooted. Celtic and Tottenham Hotspur were also keen on the Canaries' captain, and it took much wrangling with chairman Robert Chase before a deal was finally brokered for £825,000. The centre-back made it clear his preferred option was to move to Old Trafford and the deal was processed in the tail end of 1987, despite some concerns arising from the player's medical. Worryingly, X-rays uncovered a knee problem, only for Alex Ferguson to cite Bruce's fine appearance record as evidence that he was not susceptible to injury, while also rightly reasoning that bravery was one of the stopper's chief assets.

After adjusting to life at a club of United's stature, his wholehearted commitment drew acclaim from many observers. Robson later attempted to take some of the credit for the transfer by revealing he had alerted Ferguson to the player, because he noted his consistently high ratings in the Sunday newspapers when performing for Norwich. Robson fully endorsed Bruce's acquisition and then his ascent to the job he had held with such distinction as it became clear he would not be a regular in the starting line-up.

Bruce had been captain at Gillingham and Norwich and also skippered the England B side against Malta. One of the best uncapped players of his generation, his leadership qualities were patently obvious and he was, in some respects, a throwback to the past. Here was a man willing to put his body on the line and who would always go the extra mile to ensure success for his club. Above all else, he was a real team player and immensely popular.

Writing in his autobiography, the defender expressed great satisfaction in first wearing the armband relatively early in his United career, but he also revealed Ferguson's carefully considered psychology regarding the assignment of the role. It was no mere bauble in the Scot's eyes but an important aspect of life at United.

'It was an honour first bestowed on me when Bryan was injured during the 1989-90 season,' recounted Bruce. 'It came as a major disappointment when, next season, I lost the captaincy to Neil Webb. Alex Ferguson called me in one day to announce that Webby was going through something of a bad patch so he wanted to boost his confidence. He was making him captain. Such a move might have done little for my confidence, but I suppose I should have taken it as a compliment that he considered me strong enough to withstand the blow.'

Webb never did recapture the form he initially showed when arriving from Nottingham Forest, ostensibly due to a painful snapping of his Achilles while on England duty. Bruce hid his initial disappointment and regained the leadership of the team for one of the most remarkable results of Ferguson's reign, as Arsenal were trounced 6-2 at Highbury in the Rumbelows Cup, with Lee Sharpe scoring a hat-trick. The exhilarating exhibition of attacking football in the capital offered evidence that things were beginning to click for the manager, and so it would prove.

Bruce was a key contributor in 1990-91 when European Cup-Winners' Cup success followed the previous campaign's FA Cup triumph, Ferguson's first trophy win as United boss. By emerging as a dead-eyed penalty marksman, allied to his aerial threat from set-pieces, Bruce plundered an astonishing 19 goals in all competitions – he was third top scorer overall in the season and was joint top in the league and Cup-Winners' Cup campaigns, matching Brian McClair's hauls of 13 and four goals in those respective competitions. Only Mark Hughes forcing his goalbound header over the line from close range prevented him from reaching the 20-mark in the glorious win over Barcelona in the Rotterdam final, as Robson rolled back the years with his own superb showing.

However, Robson's colossal influence on the team was beginning to recede and Bruce was assisted by some forceful personalities as the manager moulded an all-conquering side. He proved an able deputy for Robson when the midfielder was absent for long spells due to injury. Unfortunately, Bruce would also suffer fitness problems himself and a hernia operation kept him out for a chunk of the last Division One season as United went head to head with Leeds United for the title.

Typically, he attempted to postpone surgery and played through the pain barrier but was below par in matches against Oldham Athletic and QPR as United leaked seven goals. He soldiered on regardless until late January and returned ahead of schedule, living up to his promise that he was a quick healer, to make his comeback in the second leg of the Rumbelows Cup semi-final against Middlesbrough, and a trip to Wembley was secured after extra time.

Consequently, Bruce lifted his first silverware as captain when United defeated Nottingham Forest in the final in April 1992, as Brian Clough's side were also missing their regular leader Stuart Pearce, whose absence was sorely felt, even if a young Roy Keane was in their line-up. Bruce's uncompromising treatment of Nigel Clough may have upset the striker's father, who later confronted him in the toilets at a function both men attended, but the United man got his hands on the trophy and it was the first-ever success in the competition for the club. Bruce had actually already tasted success in the League Cup before and was voted Man of the Match in the 1985 final against Sunderland during the early part of his Norwich career.

Many pundits expected United to use the triumph as a stepping-stone to winning the title that season and, in some respects it was, but the wait would be prolonged for another year. During an arduous run-in, the Reds won just two of the final six league games that followed Wembley success, including three consecutive defeats – doubling the number of losses Alex Ferguson's men had suffered throughout the league programme – and Leeds were crowned champions with a four-point cushion.

In an attempt to erase the agony, the Reds pushed for success again in the inaugural Premier League campaign, despite a poor start to proceedings. Perhaps betraying a tendency to lean on Robson for support at key times, Bruce revealed in the first copy of the official *United* magazine that his New Year's resolution for 1993 was 'to make a decision on my own without Bryan Robson or my wife Janet!' Any deference to the ex-England skipper was understandable as Bruce learned the ropes and may explain why the baton was relayed so smoothly.

In fact, others were highlighting the on-field performances as an illustration that he had already emerged from Robbo's shadow. 'In the absence of Bryan Robson, he emerged as a captain of equal stature,' wrote Peter Ball in *The Times*. 'His leadership qualities proving outstanding, driving and cajoling his team-mates with his enthusiasm and, at the same time, leading by example, rallying the faint-hearted with his courage.'

As United hoped this would finally be their year, with Eric Cantona inspiring the team after his shock switch from champions Leeds, the skipper was at the heart of the drama. Understandably, neurosis began to grip the Reds again as March became a difficult and disconcerting period. A month that had started in jubilant fashion with victory at Liverpool then hosted four games without a win. Even a sensational performance in dismissing Bruce's former club Norwich's title challenge at Carrow Road failed to eradicate the jitters completely.

The home game against Sheffield Wednesday would be pivotal,

finally unlocking the door to untold success, and Bruce as captain would step to the fore in one of the most influential and memorable interventions in United's storied history. Trailing amid the dying embers of the vitally important game, United rallied and Bruce plundered a perfectly placed header. When he repeated the trick some seven minutes into injury time, it whipped Old Trafford into a frenzy the like of which may never be seen again. Robson may have been on the pitch by then after coming off the bench, but it was his stand-in who earned the plaudits with a contribution that will never be forgotten. Fellow title challengers Aston Villa, meanwhile, drew with Coventry City as the momentum switched to United. 'Every United fan I speak to shakes my hand and says: "Sheffield Wednesday, tenth of April 1993 at ten to five,"' Bruce later revealed. '"Thank you for those two goals."'

With no time for reflection, an Easter Monday trip to Highfield Road to face Coventry City provided a conundrum for the manager. Ferguson decided Robson would return and regain the armband, in addition to Cantona's No.7 shirt, trivial alterations in some people's eyes, only to be told to reverse his plans by the man himself. 'Bryan told me he felt the team shouldn't change its shape and that he was happy to be sub,' revealed the boss. 'I respect the experience and knowledge he's got and, when he told me that, he recognised he was dropping himself. I think it was more frustrating for me than for him. I was keen to play him but he was right.'

Surely it was only fair that Bruce would not be deprived of the captaincy after his heroics a couple of days earlier? Denis Irwin struck the solitary goal as United retained the 4-4-2 formation that had proved so devastating during the season and the title was wrapped up after wins, and two more clean sheets, against London duo Chelsea and Crystal Palace. 'I sensed a belief and determination which wasn't as evident twelve months ago,' confessed the skipper.

As a reward for his selflessness and distinguished service, in addition to his contribution to the triumph, Robson was granted the chance to share the honour of lifting the trophy with his colleague in front of an emotional Sir Matt Busby and an appreciative crowd. Many United fans must have felt that life could not get any better and yet, with the monkey finally off the team's back, it unequivocally did just a year later.

One of the greatest club sides in history overcame some anxious moments, none more so than when trailing Oldham Athletic deep into stoppage time in the FA Cup semi-final at Wembley, to do the Double for the first time ever. Bruce, like full-back Irwin, played in a club record 62 games during a mammoth campaign – 61 of those as a starter – and he contributed seven goals. It was irrefutable evidence of the pair's durability, consistency and reliability.

Only Aston Villa's 3-1 win in the League Cup final in March had denied United an unprecedented domestic Treble, with Bruce disappointed to be substituted late on at Wembley as Ferguson went for broke by introducing Brian McClair. Nonetheless, the team's battle-hardened defender was a pillar of a truly magnificent side and he lifted the two main pieces of silverware at the end of the term, as United capped off an epochal campaign with FA Cup glory in a 4-0 thumping of Chelsea back at Wembley, with the influential Cantona scoring two penalties.

The sense of achievement was not lost on Bruce who revealed his pride to the press at being the first English captain to lead a 20th-century team to the Double. He did, however, reveal the source of the statistic and the notification came after a long night of celebration. 'I didn't realise it until Ned Kelly, United's security chief, told me on the Sunday morning and shook my hand. It was a lot to take in. I was still in a drunken stupor over breakfast! I keep having to pinch myself to believe it. Never in my wildest dreams did I imagine something like this would happen to me.'

Allowing for some celebratory excess, the centre-back was a sobering influence whenever matters became serious. A family man –

his son Alex would go on to have a career at the top level of the game – and a mature personality, it is no surprise he engendered a tremendous amount of respect from his colleagues. Urging outrageously talented individuals to produce extra effort was perhaps not necessarily one of his primary concerns. Ensuring the smooth running of the side certainly was.

'On the pitch, I wouldn't say that the duties of captain are particularly obvious in a side like ours,' said Bruce when quizzed on the tasks he was expected to perform. 'All the lads know exactly what's to be done and they can motivate themselves really well. Off the pitch, the main duty seems to be sorting out ticket allocations for players and their families, which can be a real bind! A lot of people think we can get our hands on wads of tickets but that just isn't the case. Those reading this might be quite surprised to learn that we only get about three each for every game.'

This was a chore that clearly annoyed him as he also referenced it in his autobiography – 'if ever there was a fishes and loaves job, this is it!' – but he also addressed his responsibilities in greater detail in the book. 'Perhaps the public at large does not understand what being a captain of a football team entails,' he wrote. 'There are plenty of things that are not involved like being privy to the manager's thoughts on tactics and team selection. Our manager keeps his thoughts very much to himself on such matters there.'

He went on to explain how he saw his main function as being the link between management and the squad, with the players sometimes using him as a conduit to Ferguson, or the boss using Bruce to pass on a message. In those early days in the role, with Bryan Robson still there, the club captain also played an influential part. Having Robson around also ensured that the role of dealing with the media was shared between them, though post-match that job was usually given to the man with the armband, something he admitted he enjoyed doing.

Bruce continued: 'Players tend to look to the captain to act as their mouthpiece when they want an opinion expressed or if they want something like a day off. It is the captain who has to approach the manager, providing he himself believes there is a good case to be put forward. This role of a go-between is an important aspect of leadership, meaning there is more to being a captain than just calling "heads" and then shouting encouragement to the rest of the team. The captaincy is an honour but it is also a responsibility. I happen to relish that responsibility and regard the job as being just as much a part of my play as the actual business of performing on the field. It is one aspect of football that is either in a player or not. You cannot train a captain. The man either has leadership qualities or he has not.'

When Robson moved to Middlesbrough at the end of the Double-winning 1993-94 campaign, there was simply no doubt that Bruce was the right man to continue in the job full time. 'He's got natural leadership qualities,' said the manager. 'Some people can lead a team – even if they themselves are playing badly. When you pick a captain, you have to choose someone who is respected by the players and who can address the players as well as addressing the media. Steve Bruce has got all those qualities. He's a great representative for the team. He is one of those players whose determination has made him a top player. That's made him a hero with the fans. They appreciate what he contributes to the team.'

Without Robson to accept some of the media burden, he was in demand again. The *Captain's Log* video had covered all of the camaraderie and excitement of the final weeks of the inaugural Premier League season and provided an insight into the personality of the players, and of Bruce in particular. It was so well received that he agreed to a repeat project in 1995 with ten games to go.

'It was quite popular last time and I got the impression that a lot of people enjoyed it, so we might as well give it another crack,' he said. 'Hopefully, it will bring us the same luck as it did at the end of that season. Most players enjoyed being filmed and I tried not to be too intrusive, which was very important. I mean nobody was shown up or were filmed with their underpants off or anything like that! As time went on, the players trusted me with the camera and were totally relaxed about it all.'

However, things did not go to plan and there was no happy ending on this occasion, only crushing disappointment in the league and FA Cup, inside the space of a week, with both competitions going down to the wire. A draw at West Ham on the final day meant heartbreak as the Reds failed to capitalise on leaders Blackburn's defeat at Liverpool and the team failed to lift themselves for the Wembley final against Everton, losing to a Paul Rideout header.

Of course, there will always be pain for any successful team when competing regularly for honours, especially with such small margins separating glory and despair. Bruce was the perfect man to raise spirits as his career had seen more soul-searching lows. As a rookie midfielder, he had embarked on a plumber's job before Gillingham offered him his big break as a teenager and he knew the other side of football only too well.

How would United respond to the disappointment of that season? Ferguson's answer was to offload Mark Hughes, Andrei Kanchelskis and Paul Ince, three key members of the Double-winning side a year earlier, and he promoted promising youngsters in their place. A greater pressure was placed on the senior figures left in the dressing room and questions were inevitably asked about the manager's brave reshuffle.

An opening-day defeat at Aston Villa in August 1995 was pinned on the inexperience of the 'kids', but Bruce's absence, in hindsight, may have been more of a mitigating factor. He returned as the team embarked on a five-match winning run in the Premier League but was sidelined again around the festive period, missing the New Year's Day hammering at Tottenham. The 4-1 loss proved trialist William

Prunier was no deputy for the captain, but David May began to earn the faith of Ferguson and, as another fantastic season drew to an exciting climax, Bruce found himself out of the line-up.

The sturdy 35-year-old was being tested for pace, even though he was used to brushing off any sniping from the doubters. His partnership with Gary Pallister had been the bedrock of so much success and yet some were arguing that it had run its course. 'Pally's quick but his partner is verging on slow?' Bruce said, after the heart of the defence was identified as a potential weakness. 'They've been saying that for twenty years.'

However, the writing was on the wall and he accepted a lucrative offer to join Birmingham City as he began to consider an eventual move into coaching and management. Many top stars have departed Manchester United and the mourning for their exit is often brief as new idols quickly take over the mantle. This was clearly not the case with the veteran centre-back and his departure created a lingering sense of dejection that few players commanded during Ferguson's reign.

'He was the one I went to for advice,' revealed David Beckham. 'I was gutted when he left because he was always very good to me.' Peter Schmeichel, who had many rows with his skipper, was even more upset. 'He is a very good personal friend and a terrific leader,' said the Dane. 'I've had a few disappointments during my time in England, but Steve's transfer to Birmingham must rank as the biggest. I think it's sad and disappointing to watch him at Birmingham, a team not a tenth of the quality of the one he left behind. He deserves better than this. Fortunately, he still lives next door so we meet almost every day!'

Central defensive partner Pallister, whose own United career benefited hugely from his pal's presence, obviously agreed: 'He's been missed by everyone at the club. He seemed to get better as he got older.' Even Ferguson himself was unusually sentimental about losing such an ally. 'I didn't really want Steve to go,' he confessed. 'I could have got twenty games out of him but, at his age, I couldn't guarantee him a regular place which was what he wanted. Real sorrow overtook me at being parted with such an honourable man.'

Probably the biggest compliment that can be paid to Bruce is that he was one of the first names on the teamsheet in that all-conquering 1993-94 line-up. He was the only non-international in the side but that was largely irrelevant because, even among the great and gifted stars, he was the most reliable and always one of the most popular. 'I'm not blessed with great footballing skills but I believe the game should be played with skill and imagination and I like to be part of a team which plays that way,' he contended. 'But you need other things to provide a balance in a team and I think I can provide some of those.'

It would be wrong to refer to Bruce as an unsung hero, unless you were focusing explicitly on his lack of international recognition. The defender may have lacked the glamour of the man who took over the armband in 1996, the charismatic Cantona, but his contribution to United's success was equally relevant, even if you discount his late show against Sheffield Wednesday in that pivotal 1993 fixture, which convinced everybody of the club's destiny.

Chapter 10

Le Roi

'I can't think of anyone who I would rather wear my crown.'

Denis Law

The undisputed catalyst for Manchester United's spell of domestic dominance during the 1990s, Eric Cantona proved an inspirational and charismatic figure who won the league in five of the six years in which this sporting iconoclast illuminated English football. In the other, he was suspended for an assault on a spectator that rocked the game, but the furore would, ultimately, not define his stay at Old Trafford nor reduce his magnetic appeal to the club's faithful.

Already a champion with Leeds United, at the Reds' expense, the *enfant terrible* arrived in Manchester in 1992 during the first year of the Premier League, with Alex Ferguson's side crying out for a new striker to solve an alarming goal drought. Cantona was not first option, he may not even have been on the shortlist at all, but a well-documented enquiry by Leeds boss Howard Wilkinson regarding Denis Irwin resulted in the Frenchman crossing the Pennines for around £1 million.

On gazing upon his new home, he puffed out his chest, turned up his collar and exuded confidence, instantly enchanting everybody with his flair, arrogance and intelligence, allied to an admirable work ethic and ruthless winning streak running like an undercurrent beneath the surface of his enigmatic façade. As early as New Year's Day in 1993, less than a couple of months after his shock arrival, the effect on his manager had been intoxicating. The new boy hypnotised Ferguson and everybody else with his charisma. 'More than at any time since I was playing, the club is alive,' the boss drooled. 'It's as if the good old days are back and the major factor, as far as I'm concerned, is the Frenchman.

'Eric Cantona is so clever it's untrue and the lovely thing about special players is they're infectious. The things he tries, the others try and it's the way the team are playing that's got middle-aged fans jumping about like two-year-olds.' It is fair to say the manager realised he had found himself a bargain and other men of stature were also entranced. 'I would pay to watch Cantona play,' admitted George Best. 'There are not many players over the years I would say that about. He's a genius.'

If he was a key figure in that first title triumph, he was even more influential in the following Double-winning season, scoring two penalties in the FA Cup final against Chelsea, but there were also high-profile brushes with authority. Not only was he dismissed as United exited the European Cup at the hands of Galatasaray, but he was also sent off in consecutive Premier League games against Swindon Town and, albeit harshly, Arsenal.

Ferguson's team were potentially primed for another Double in 1995 when his temper flared again at Selhurst Park in a January fixture that would have a profound effect on Cantona's career. A petulant kick at his marker Richard Shaw resulted in another red card and, as he left the field, he was subjected to a foul-mouthed tirade by a Crystal Palace fan. An astonishing kung-fu kick on the spectator,

Matthew Simmons, would have major repercussions for the player and the club and threatened to end his spell in England under the darkest of clouds.

Initially handed a jail sentence, he was ordered to undergo community service instead, on appeal, and was banned for the remainder of the season by United. Much to the frustration of everybody at Old Trafford, the Football Association decided to extend this suspension to nine months amid much media outrage at the offence. Almost everybody expected Cantona to walk away in the face of such severe punishment and further enhance his reputation as an unruly troublemaker, something that had tainted his time in his native France.

Ferguson was at his persuasive best in talking his talisman into staying during a heart-to-heart chat in Paris and it was a rehabilitated individual who rejoined his team-mates in October with much to prove. The Old Trafford faithful revelled in the situation and roared their support on his return against Liverpool, displaying *tricolores* all around the famous stadium, and he assisted a goal for Nicky Butt early on before, inevitably, stealing the show with an equaliser from the penalty spot. 'I felt I had all the people, all the fans, behind me,' he would later admit. 'In those periods, everything you have can break down. What I did was not very nice. I didn't play for nine months and I had to pay some fines, but it was more important that the people who had followed me before the incident still supported me. It was very important to me that the fans did that.'

The adoration from the spectators proved well placed, and even Denis Law approved of a new man taking over his mantle as 'The King'. 'I can't think of anyone who I would rather wear my crown,' said the legendary marksman. Law's sense of bedevilment only enhanced his standing with the fans and the new idol enjoyed similar acclaim. The United supporters like their heroes to be unconventional and unpredictable characters, and if they rile everyone else then all the better – it adds to the excitement.

All this was the backdrop to a tale of redemption that would not look out of place in a work of fiction. Not only would Cantona lead a young side to another Double, masterfully fulfilling his new role as the team's undisputed leader, but he had an individual impact on the climax of an English season that has arguably never been matched. The early months of 1996 saw the centre-forward in his pomp and his form reeled in Newcastle United and helped induce Kevin Keegan's televised meltdown in the face of some classic Ferguson mind games. The team's main man would become the captain in the campaign's closing stages and he lifted the FA Cup aloft after another moment of brilliance, beautifully timed in the dying seconds, accounted for Liverpool at Wembley.

Cantona is a complex character who was destined to have a major impact at United, but his elevation to the captaincy came after a spell of relative mediocrity by his own lofty standards, which caused many to question whether he could retain the spark he had shown before the Simmons incident. After his return from the ban, he was in the team knocked out of the League Cup by York City, as a 3-1 win at Bootham Crescent failed to overturn a shock three-goal deficit in the home leg, and United had already been bundled out of Europe by Rotor Volgograd before he had even set foot on a pitch again.

The Reds were not firing on all cylinders with youngsters such as David Beckham, Nicky Butt, Paul Scholes and the Neville brothers being bedded into the team, but there had been a glimpse of the future in a 4-0 battering of Galatasaray in December of the previous year. The tie had been a dead rubber, with the Reds already eliminated from the Champions League, but Cantona was in his element, orchestrating the play with a vibrant, youthful side around him and providing tactical advice for those lifted by his mere presence. After the initial adrenaline surge of his high-profile return, however, his form dipped and he became peripheral at times towards the end of 1995.

'When I came back, I had two good months,' he accepted. 'Then I had a barren month or two. We knew that would happen.' His manager noticed a change in character since the incident, spotting that his striker had become a little more introverted and less prone to the explosions of temper that would regularly land him in trouble with the match officials. 'He has always been a quiet person and he's still quiet, but what's happened to him has been the kind of experience that can't help but have an effect on your life,' stated Ferguson. 'They say even a bad experience can be good for you and maybe some good has come out of it.

'Perhaps his attitude to injustice has been altered. Since he came back into the team, there have been refereeing decisions that he hasn't agreed with but he's chosen not to argue. I've seen him walk quietly away from incidents that might have drawn a different reaction before.' But had the fire been extinguished to the detriment of his ability to dictate the play?

It was actually eight games after the comeback penalty before the calmer Cantona scored again, another spot-kick in a 1-1 draw at Nottingham Forest and, although the Reds produced some excellent results, Newcastle were riding high at the top of the table. Even a double by the France international against Sheffield Wednesday failed to yield three points, and consecutive defeats to Leeds United and Arsenal resulted in a do-or-die clash with the leaders on 27 December. The festive showdown went the home side's way at Old Trafford and the gap at the top was reduced to seven points.

Arguably the fixture that generated the most belief, however, came in the following month when a Monday night visit to the capital to face West Ham United was approached with some trepidation. The Hammers always took much delight in upsetting Ferguson's men and Cantona would meet with another hot and hostile reception. He struck on eight minutes, decisively, from beyond the far post, to reward some fabulous wing-play by Ryan Giggs and even acted as a peacemaker when the sparks flew in the 77th minute. Julian Dicks launched a two-footed tackle on Andy Cole to prompt a retaliatory challenge from Butt that saw the teenager red carded.

As an incensed Cole and an aggressive Keane became embroiled in a row with Hammers hard-man Dicks, Cantona was the unlikely figure stepping in to placate the warring factions and earned praise in the press, who felt he was a reformed character. Referee Steven Lodge described a man once viewed as a disgrace to the sport as 'acting as a superb ambassador to defuse a potentially difficult situation,' while even Dicks admitted he changed his perception of the forward and now had 'great respect' for him.

Around this time, rumours resurfaced regarding a possible move to Inter Milan. The Serie A giants had attempted to exploit his enforced absence by luring him to the Continent and made a fresh approach in January. He later admitted to holding 'extensive talks' with president Massimo Moratti and was flattered by the interest. However, the choice to remain in Manchester left him without any regrets as he focused his attention on fuelling the club's title bid.

He scored a brace in an entertaining 4-2 win over Wimbledon on his first return to Selhurst Park, the scene of his crime against Palace. This was also a match where he took over the armband when Steve Bruce was forced off to receive 14 stitches in a head wound sustained in a clash with Dons striker Dean Holdsworth. If Cantona needed any extra fillip, this was it. Clearly forgiven for his misdemeanour, he was charged with the responsibility of inspiring younger colleagues to glory and applying the pressure on leaders Newcastle.

The most vital of fixtures arrived at St James' Park in early March, and United withstood a barrage of pressure as Peter Schmeichel found the form of his life in goal. Cantona struck the all-important winner, volleying in a Phil Neville cross, and he also scored in the next five league games, including a late equaliser at QPR and the only goal in home wins over North London duo Arsenal and Tottenham

Hotspur. The Gunners' boss Bruce Rioch ruefully concluded: 'They seem to take their lead from Cantona.' Ferguson was equally forth-right in his assessment. 'All the other players recognise that Eric, individually, has put us on top of the league,' he smiled.

Come the final day, with Keegan and his Newcastle team crack-ing under the strain, and a comfortable 3-0 success at Middlesbrough regained the title. Bruce lifted the Premier League trophy in his track-suit, as he had been struggling with a hamstring strain and was out of the side. The centre-back learned from Ferguson he would not fea-ture in the FA Cup final on the pitch beforehand, despite being fit. 'The manager just told me there and then, out on the pitch before kick-off,' said Bruce. 'To be fair to him, it was his way of saying: "Steve, thanks very much, this is it for you."'

So, with Bruce out for a third successive match, the Reds approached the Liverpool encounter with Cantona as skipper and the stage was set for one last dramatic intervention from the 29-year-old. A dull affair had failed to catch light until Beckham's corner was punched out by David James. Somehow, Cantona contorted his body as the ball approached and managed to manufacture a volley that seared through a crowd of players like a heat-seeking missile until the net billowed. 'I don't think that another player would have scored a goal like that,' purred Ferguson, as he enjoyed a whisky to mark the triumph. 'He controlled the ball with such accuracy.' There was no time for a response – United had clinched a second Double at their fiercest rivals' expense. It was a sixth 1-0 victory with a Cantona goal since 22 January.

There was the matter of who would actually lift the trophy to be resolved, with Bruce politely declining the stand-in's request to lead the team up the steps. Cantona tried to convince the defender that it was still his responsibility but, instead, Bruce watched from the pitch with a mixture of pride and disappointment as the match-winner did the honours. 'It was a truly beautiful moment to lift the cup,' the man with the armband commented. 'One of the moments of my life. I didn't want to pick the cup up. I wanted Steve to do it. But he said: "No, you go – I've done it before." I think, in my whole football career, this has been the best weekend of my life. It will always be something special for me. I feel very proud for everybody at the club, the players and the fans. And I think that we deserved the Double after a long season. We believed we could do it when no one else did – and that was the most important thing.'

It may have been a magical experience for the stand-in skipper, but others felt the privilege of being the man to raise the silverware, cementing a place in history forever to be shown on archived footage on televisions across the world, was not so important. 'It was a typically generous Cantona gesture which typically Steve, the club captain, passed on,' said future captain Keane. 'We'd won the cup and nobody really cared who picked it up.' As with Robson before him, full-time skipper Bruce's United career came to an end when he was left out of an FA Cup final squad.

Middlesbrough player-manager Robson was himself full of praise for the way a job he had made his own was handled by the influential striker. 'Eric has proved to be a great captain,' enthused the Old Trafford legend. 'Just look what a guiding force he has been. He has been a source of inspiration for all the young players in the side. Eric's vision is superb and United's game revolves around him. He is one of the club's greatest players.'

The Football Writers, some of whom clamoured for a lifetime ban a year earlier, voted him their Footballer of the Year, remarkably United's first winner of the award since Best in 1968. 'I had a lot of things to prove this season,' stressed Cantona. 'Everybody knows last year there was a lot of criticism so that can be very positive. I always try to put a thing that way. We learn from everything and a bad thing can be turned into a good thing. It was very difficult at the moment but, if we think about the future, we use it to put the future into the sun.' A man who famously talked of sardines and trawlers always did have a rather poetic way with words.

The youngsters were on the crest of a wave, but there were also words of warning from the main man. 'The most important season for them is next season,' he predicted in a rare televised interview with the BBC's Des Lynam. 'After one win in the championship, maybe they think that's it. Next season will be more difficult in their heads, I think.'

As a captain, his philosophy on conducting interviews contrasted starkly with that of his predecessor. A man who once said: 'I don't give a damn. I don't have to justify myself to the journalists or the TV,' was never going to entertain fulfilling this duty with any great regularity. Instead, he often maintained the language barrier was an obstacle that could not be overcome and largely shunned this obligation, preferring to lead by example on the field. 'There are two precise reasons for this silence and I want to keep them to myself,' was his typically mysterious response to a year of blanking the media following his return from suspension. 'But I can say that talking is not really necessary. The essential thing is to succeed at the sporting level.'

Nonetheless, his interviews remained fascinating and often enlightening, particularly when adding to his mystique and the fear that he could walk away from the game at any time. 'When we win, I want to stay in football but, when we lose, I want to quit,' he stated in a matter-of-fact way in 1996, warning the fans that he was capable of making snap decisions.

Perhaps in an attempt to increase a sense of responsibility and duty to his colleagues, Ferguson handed him the armband on a permanent basis ahead of the 1996-97 season. 'There are different types of captains,' explained the manager. 'Over the years, I have seen goalkeepers wearing the armband. Some see the last line of defence as people who see more of the game. Sometimes it's because of their seniority. Captains are all different. Bobby Moore wasn't a shouter – he led by example. It's the same with Eric. He captained us to the Double last season and, over the years, his experience on the training ground has been fantastic. The players adore him.'

It became a natural succession as, aside from his match-winning feats, it really did appear as though he was willing to turn over a new leaf when it came to his disciplinary record. As he entered his thirties, a calmer and altogether more serene figure could emerge. At least that was the plan, with chairman Martin Edwards endorsing the move. 'Nobody thought Eric would completely transform,' he admitted. 'We felt that, if we had to live with Eric, we would have to live with the odd indiscretion. What happened was that Eric received one booking in the whole of the season and I think that is quite remarkable. We have got to take our hats off to him.'

The captaincy was a task he embraced and the players also dismissed any issues with the language barrier. 'All the lads could understand Eric, so I don't think that comes into it,' said Butt. 'A captain is someone you look up to on the pitch for help.' Bruce said much the same when passing on the armband. 'Honestly, Eric speaks perfect English. He just uses that excuse to his advantage now and again.'

The Marseille-born forward did acknowledge he occasionally struggled to get his point across, although he too suspected it was only a minor handicap. Here was an individual whose actions always spoke louder than words. 'Maybe sometimes I want to say something and I cannot find the word,' he confessed. 'In football, you have to think really quickly.' In time, overseas captains would become far more established in the Premier League, but in 1996 the concept did still feel a little unusual to some observers.

A first game in charge of the team on a full-time basis certainly went smoothly in any language as Newcastle were hammered 4-0 in the Charity Shield at Wembley. Even the presence in the Magpies' line-up of Alan Shearer, who opted for a record move to St James' Park despite United's concerted attempts to sign him from Blackburn Rovers, in no way impinged on the Reds' superiority. Blackburn had even responded to United's interest in Shearer by making their own cheeky £4 million bid for Cantona over the summer, only for it to be understandably rejected out of hand.

Although Cantona scored a goal and conducted affairs with his customary aplomb in his first game as club captain, he became embroiled in an unsavoury incident with Philippe Albert and was perhaps fortunate not to receive a red card. It was more fuel for those who felt he could be a liability in the role, despite his heroics in clinching the Double. 'It was innocuous,' contested his manager. 'Something and nothing.' Ferguson would always defend his players, in any case, in such circumstances. 'Eric is an emotional man,' he once said. 'It's very difficult to change that in a player because you can destroy the very things that make them winners. You are asking them to be something they are not.'

The precocious Beckham, another goalscorer at Wembley in the Shield victory, stole the show in the first league outing for United's first-ever permanent foreign captain with his stupendous strike from the halfway line at Wimbledon, even if the Frenchman also netted on another return to Selhurst Park. 'What meant the most to David was Cantona shaking his hand after the game and saying: "Beautiful goal, David,"' revealed the midfielder's father Ted, highlighting the respect his son had for the skipper.

The callow youngsters were starting to blossom, inspired by their leader but gradually becoming less and less reliant on the centre-forward for his game-changing interventions. 'Eric was most important because they made him as much as he made them,' explained Sir Bobby Charlton. 'He had all these young players and they weren't afraid. I'm sure Eric told me that he really had very little to do. He couldn't believe it and it was just magical really.'

Cantona was deified in many quarters and one artist almost took this God-like status literally. Manchester-born Michael Browne's ten feet by eight feet impression of a 15th-century Italian Renaissance painting – Piero della Francesca's *Resurrection of Christ* – depicted the Frenchman as Jesus with the Nevilles, Butt and Beckham also featuring as foot-soldiers. Another youngster, John Curtis, is in the background, with Alex Ferguson portrayed as Julius Caesar.

The magnificent painting attracted criticism, but Browne countered: 'To the person on the street, it will be tongue in cheek. I don't believe people will take it seriously as an insult.' Cantona certainly did not view things that way because he purchased it and it has since been housed at the National Football Museum, which recently made Manchester its permanent home. It illustrated the awe he generated and, while perhaps labouring the point, his impact on the development of the Class of '92 was crucial to their success.

'Eric is the player we go to,' admitted Gary Neville, one of those who shared his colleague's appetite for hard work on the training pitch. 'He's the captain and a man other teams fear.' Lee Sharpe had left in 1996, but felt he could identify why these younger charges were so enthralled with the classy Frenchman. 'It's because the manager gave him this free role,' said the left-winger, who made the opposite journey over the M62 to Leeds. 'Letting him express himself, do his flicks and score his goals, I think that's why the lads looked up to him so much. They thought: "If I can be anyone, that's who I want to be. I want to be treated like that. I want to play like that. I want to be loved like that."'

Ryan Giggs, who was more established in the team, like Sharpe, used to share a car with Cantona but admits they never had deep and meaningful conversation during their journeys. 'Eric lived my side of Manchester so I would often give him lifts or pick him up for training or games,' he revealed. 'So I spent a little bit of time with him. He was great. He had this aura around him and he was obviously just different from the rest of the players. But, within the team and the squad, he was just another team-mate. He was pretty quiet and I was pretty quiet so there wasn't much conversation. I'd just stick the radio on!'

Cantona did not need to outline his philosophy on life or football to his colleagues, he merely radiated a sense of presence that commanded respect. It thrilled him to be in the company of those who followed his example, having been considered an outsider at some of his clubs in France. 'When I see them, these boys from Manchester,' he said, 'when they touch me, when they speak to me in hushed voices, I want them to go away happy and convinced that they have met a player who is more like them than they know.' Somebody who had been surprisingly overlooked for Euro 96 after once captaining his country enjoyed having kindred spirits at United.

The youngsters continued to shine. Beckham netted again, to earn a point at Derby County and Nicky Butt followed a flying header in the Charity Shield with another strike in a 4-0 win at Leeds that led to Howard Wilkinson, the man who brought Cantona to England, leaving his post. The United No.7, predictably, also got in on the act.

Help was at hand in attack with new recruit Ole Gunnar Solskjaer making an immediate impression and, when both Cantona and Beckham were on the scoresheet in a 2-0 Champions League victory at Fenerbahce, a run of five clean sheets suggested there were no problems on the horizon. However, one of the worst spells of Ferguson's reign in charge followed, beginning in a 5-0 humiliation at Newcastle, with Albert taking glee in chipping Schmeichel for the final strike. There was another clash with the Belgian, despite already having a yellow card to his name. 'He seemed to be upset with all the things going on around him,' taunted Albert. 'Especially in the second half.'

Few could blame Cantona for losing his temper and things did not get any better. An incredible 11 goals were shipped in two league games as Southampton won 6-3 at The Dell. Cantona then presided over United's first-ever European defeat at Old Trafford, at the hands of Fenerbahce, and he was cautioned for a third successive league match as a Chelsea side boasting Gianluca Vialli piled on more misery at the Theatre of Dreams. After starting the season so brightly, United were now plunged into crisis with some reporters pointing to the captain's indiscipline as a sign that he was reverting to his bad old ways.

Schmeichel revealed in a telling interview in November that mid-fielder Keane was emerging as a more important figure than the charismatic captain, something that seemed unfathomable when the Double was secured. 'Eric gets an enormous amount of respect and deservedly so,' explained the United No.1. 'The players look up to him. But I think our most influential player is Roy Keane. We've had problems once or twice when he wasn't in the team.'

Keane himself studied the actions of his skipper and appreciated he would bring a different personality the role. 'Eric did not speak to anyone away from the club and, even with the players, he only said something if it needed to be said,' the Irishman stated. 'But he had everyone's respect so it worked. I don't think I could be quite that reserved.' However detached, the striker was determined to inspire the team to greater heights in the Champions League.

After the proud European home run was ended, Juventus also left Manchester with three points less than a month later, ensuring a visit to Vienna to face Rapid became a must-win affair. The skipper, often criticised for his performances in continental competition, scored in a vital 2-0 success on a freezing night in Austria to ensure progression into the knockout stages and a place for an English side in the last eight of Europe's premier competition for the first time since 1985.

Nevertheless, confidence was not particularly high as Christmas approached until Sunderland came to Old Trafford. After 97 days without a Premier League goal, Cantona was at his imperious best, following up a penalty goal with the most arrogant of chipped finishes over Lionel Perez. As the ball kissed the far upright on its way into the net, he adopted the pose of a Roman emperor as he put his hands on his hips and slowly surveyed the crowd. It was a celebration that screamed The King was back.

'When you're confident, you find freedom,' he wrote in *La Philosophie de Cantona*. 'From freedom of expression comes genius, euphoria and fire.' There was no mistaking his genius on this occasion and the Stretford End roared their approval, sensing his form would reach the dizzy heights of the previous campaign at around the same time as he hit a purple patch in 1996.

His former club Leeds were next at United's home and succumbed to the French star's winner in the final game of the year, his penalty converted with customary elegance. The striker once revealed he would always look to see which way a goalkeeper's knees would bend before deciding where to place his finish, explaining why he often sent them the wrong way from the spot. He only ever missed twice from 12 yards for the Reds, against Blackburn and Leeds, and later atoned by scoring from open play on both occasions.

The team clicked into top gear in a fabulous 4-0 pummelling of Porto in Europe and, although he claimed one and created two others, it was an outstanding team display that effectively sealed a semi-final place with the second leg still to come. However, although he scored in three games around the tie against Borussia Dortmund, the Reds fired blanks and suffered a narrow 1-0 loss in Germany. The situation was retrievable but there was no way past the German defence in the second leg either and another 1-0 defeat ended United's European dreams.

Cantona was uncharacteristically poor and erratic in front of goal, spurning several chances to turn things in United's favour. 'Just when we needed a bit of luck, it wasn't there,' bemoaned Ferguson. The player spoke of his belief that his side were superior to the Bundesliga outfit and the fact he was surrounded by young players under the age of 23 meant it was only a matter of time before the elusive European triumph was acquired. 'With such young players, the next ten years will surely belong to us,' he predicted.

The Premier League was still secured, a memorable win at Anfield had made it a formality, but something was nagging away at the captain. There were no concerns with his fitness – he played in more games (50) than anybody else and no outfield player could match his 36 starts in the league. Yet he was no longer leading scorer as that distinction belonged to Solskjaer, who finished a remarkable debut season with 19 goals. Cantona claimed 15, with 11 coming in the league, and it was sufficient with Beckham weighing in with more than his fair share too.

The idea that the reigning Football Writers' Footballer of the Year was a spent force was misplaced. He had supplied more assists than anybody else in the Premier League (16) with only two of these coming from dead-ball situations. After all, United were champions again, and he was the man who led the team in majestic fashion. As one headline rather neatly summarised, his contribution was valuable but not invaluable.

It was insufficient for the temperamental striker and he hung up his boots at the end of the season, with a year still remaining on his contract. 'I have always planned to retire when I was at the top and, at Manchester United, I have reached the pinnacle of my career,' he stated. At 31, his time as the team's biggest name was over and his final appearance came in a testimonial for David Busst, who had broken his leg while representing Coventry at Old Trafford. Fittingly, he scored a penalty.

'After analysing the whole situation, I've concluded that he's made the right decision,' considered Ferguson in his book: *A Will to Win – The Manager's Diary*. 'I always predicted that, one day, he would simply up sticks and go and that's exactly what happened.' The boss was not merely putting on a brave face for the legions of fans who were in shock at the dramatic turn of events. He had noticed a change in his star man and added in his autobiography *Managing My Life*: 'He was subdued and did not seem to be enjoying his football. Although never extrovert around the other players, he had always been a vibrant presence, quietly conveying authority and an intense commitment. Now, somehow, the spark had gone.'

Beckham, who was emerging as a star in his own right and would inherit the famous No.7 jersey, attempted to articulate how much his game had been lifted by the presence of his enigmatic team-mate. 'It was obviously upsetting when he left because we all learned from him,' explained the midfielder. 'He was a role model for all of us, even the older lads. Just by being there, he had an influence on us. What he could do with people's confidence was unbelievable.'

Cantona appeared to have made the right decision, going out at the top, and leaving with another title winner's medal safely secured. Yet he had his doubts. 'Sometimes I think I quit too young because I love the game,' he later recounted. 'But I didn't have the passion to go to bed early, not to go out with friends, not to drink and not to do a lot of things.' This must have been something that gnawed away at him, questioning his own professionalism, and friends claimed he piled on the pounds soon after quitting.

'Perfectionism is a need,' he had insisted, earlier in his career. 'It's not something you can teach. Some people need it, some don't. It's a question of character and of personal pride.' Hurt by the failure in Europe, albeit at the semi-final stage in his last season, he would leave the fans wanting more. It ensured a cult-like status among the crowd that will persist for generations, with his name still chanted long after his sudden departure, despite new heroes emerging and more glory being attained.

During an interview with the much-respected *L'Equipe* in his homeland, Cantona emphasised why his arrival at Old Trafford created a perfect storm. He was the missing link, the supplier of the arrogance that rid an under-achieving club of its neurosis and fear of failure. In return, the Reds provided the perfect platform for his extraordinary gifts, allowing a freedom of expression that was denied during his past, which saw him cut a frustrated, misunderstood figure until being liberated by the shrewdest of managers in Ferguson.

'I was forever in search of a club like Manchester United,' he admitted. 'United is great and difficult at the same time. Great because we always have a chance of winning something. Difficult on that account, because we always have to win.' Maybe Eric Cantona could be described with the same two words – great and difficult – but he had a profound effect on the evolution of Ferguson's reign.

However, although The King had abdicated the throne, he would merely pave the way for a new man to assume the captaincy and one who would court controversy and relentlessly pursue silverware in similar fashion.

Chapter 11

The Perfectionist

'Roy is the boss of United in the dressing room. He is
the main man here.'

Ruud van Nistelrooy

If ever the term 'born winner' could be applied to a footballer, it
would be most relevant in describing Roy Keane's relentless drive to
succeed. An individual so motivated to win and willing to extract the
maximum effort from his own body while demanding the same
unflinching commitment of his colleagues, he is the epitome of the
perfect captain. In sharing similar qualities to Sir Alex Ferguson, their
partnership would bring unparalleled success to the club, even if the
relationship between two combustible characters would end in an
unavoidable supernova.

Nevertheless, there are few finer examples of the stars being
aligned so perfectly in the combination of captain and manager – and
it would deliver the club's greatest-ever achievement. Their goals were
the same and Keane was in a position to instil the desired mix of fear
and respect in the dressing room, extending the manager's presence to
an all-encompassing aura that enveloped the club. Strict discipline was

maintained at the training ground and, of course, these values were reinforced on matchday. 'On the pitch, he was Ferguson's alter ego, bringing to the team all the rage for perfection and impatience that the manager demanded,' suggested David Lacey of the *Guardian*. Steve McClaren, assistant manager of the club in 1999, agreed: 'He mirrors the manager on the pitch. They are winners.' With this pair in command of United, success was largely guaranteed.

In retrospect, Keane's appointment as Manchester United captain seems an obvious choice and a natural progression for the hugely influential midfielder as he approached his peak years. When he signed for the club in 1993, the best young player in the league was deemed Bryan Robson's heir apparent, and so it would prove.

Yet Ferguson mulled over alternative options in the wake of Eric Cantona's sudden retirement. Peter Schmeichel was an outstanding candidate; Gary Pallister, in terms of seniority, could have been handed the role; while Denis Irwin was a model of professionalism and reliability. There were nagging doubts over Keane's suitability. Could the Irishman handle the extra responsibility? Was he the right role model for others? Would he learn to curb his explosive temper?

After all, he had been sent off in matches against Crystal Palace, Blackburn Rovers, Middlesbrough and Southampton and had shown that when the red mist descended, it would sometimes lead to a card of the same colour. The stamp on Gareth Southgate in 1995's FA Cup semi-final replay was an unsavoury incident and particularly disappointing as tensions were running high beforehand, with the players urged to set a good example after a Palace fan had tragically been killed before the first game, but it is worth remembering it was Keane's first dismissal since joining the club two years previously.

But Ferguson, never afraid to make bold decisions, made the call convincingly. 'I have no qualms about Roy being captain,' insisted the manager. 'He's one of the greatest players of all time at United and he can make a great captain as well. He has got the enthusiasm and the drive that Steve Bruce and Bryan Robson had and, having played alongside these people, he has learned a lot.

'Peter Schmeichel did come into my thoughts and he would have made a good captain because of his leadership qualities, his presence and his standing in the dressing room. But I prefer an outfield player as captain. Gary Pallister was in my mind, but he's had a run of injuries and I wanted to keep continuity. In the end there was only one choice – Roy Keane.'

Nonetheless, there was still an air of controversy when Keane learned of the manager's decision during a summer tour of the Far East, absorbing the news long before it broke in England. 'When the gaffer told me I would be the new captain, I looked at it as being a great honour and a challenge,' he said. 'I'm hoping that being captain won't change my game. There will be extra responsibilities off the field, but if I can follow in the footsteps of Robbo, Brucey and Eric, then I should be fine.

'At times, I have been silly but I've always been a bit of a bawler and I'm always trying to gee up my team-mates. I've had silly bookings too, but I get very passionate about the game and, in the past, I have gone too far. When I get booked, it's usually when I'm going for the ball and that's a part of my game.

'I've got to calm down a bit and clean up my act,' he recognised in an interview with the official club magazine. 'But I was going to do that anyway. People are saying I've been given the captaincy to calm me down and it may be that extra responsibility does have that effect, but I was going to cut out the unnecessary disciplinary points in any case. I've got to an age where I've got to show a bit more restraint. It's up to me to find a way to be enthusiastic and mature at the same time.

'I thought it might be my turn,' he said of the role. 'I realised I was in the running so it wasn't exactly a surprise but it was still a great honour. I'll have to grow into the job. I'm one of the senior pros and I feel like one, too. My head keeps telling me I'm still a young lad with my best years in front of me. I just wish I could get my body to tell me the same thing.'

When writing his autobiography, Keane would contradict these initial comments and made the most prescient of observations about the armband. 'I was surprised when Alex Ferguson chose me,' he claimed. 'To be offered the captaincy of Manchester United was a huge compliment and, of course, an equally large responsibility. On the field, I was confident I could meet my obligations. However, the club captaincy also demands diplomatic skills off the field which I felt might prove a greater challenge.'

The 25-year-old had skippered the side when Cantona was suspended in the early part of 1997 and was popular with the supporters, even if he finished only third in the Sir Matt Busby Player of the Year voting behind David Beckham and Ole Gunnar Solskjaer. He joked about the backing from the supporters, betraying a sense of caution over how he would be portrayed when taking over the mantle as skipper from such distinguished names in the club's history. 'I do [have a good relationship with the fans] but we'll have to see what it's like after I've been captain for a few months,' he conceded, perhaps only half in jest.

Keane appeared to ensure a seamless transition to life after Cantona, lifting a trophy in his first game in charge after a win on penalties over Chelsea in the Charity Shield. One head-high challenge on Gustavo Poyet could have brought greater censure and widespread condemnation, but he was reprieved and went on to score in the shoot-out. Not only did he also net in wins against Coventry City and West Ham United inside the first two months of the season but the team performed magnificently, keeping clean sheets in the opening five league games.

Certainly, Schmeichel seemed perfectly happy with the manager's call as he took particular pleasure from the shut-outs. The Dane would, in 1999, stand in for his colleague on one of the club's greatest-ever nights and was overwhelmingly supportive of his new skipper. 'When Eric was suspended last season, Roy filled in so it was just a straight swap this summer,' was the goalkeeper's take on events. 'His appointment may have attracted a lot of criticism, but I think he has done very well so far and I hope that continues.'

Just when everything was looking rosy, Keane's notoriously short temper snapped, as did his cruciate knee ligament, when kicking out at Alf Inge Haaland as he chased a ball into the box during the Reds' first defeat of the season at Leeds in late September. The pair had been together at Nottingham Forest and endured a thorny relationship as the Norwegian illustrated by shouting at the stricken United man as he lay prone in agony inside the Elland Road penalty area, urging him to get to his feet. It was a moment Keane would not forget, to his detriment.

Of course, many felt this was vindication for the belief that he was too hot-headed, and could never be truly trusted to lead the side. The overriding feeling for Ferguson was one of dejection, rather than anger on his part. 'It's a great disappointment to lose such an important player for such a long time,' he conceded. There was plenty of time for reflection as Keane would not play again all season as he embarked on the long road to recovery following surgery.

'The manager does come into the treatment room but, while I wouldn't say he ignores you, he does have more important things on his mind,' accepted Keane. 'You are injured, you are not involved. I understand that and I accept it. It was not a problem. I only went to three or four games at Old Trafford and some away but with the punters, not the team.'

United faltered in his absence and the Charity Shield proved the only piece of silverware garnered all season. Arsenal did the Double under Arsene Wenger, successfully chasing down the Reds' commanding 11-point lead, while Monaco ended any hopes of long-sought Champions League success in March at the quarter-final stage. By that point the FA Cup trail had ended at the second attempt in the fifth round against Barnsley, a side beaten 7-0 earlier in the season, with an autumn defeat at Ipswich Town ensuring a League Cup run never got started.

Keane was clearly sorely missed and his return at the start of 1998-99 provided a timely boost for the unforgettable season that was about to unfold, even if it started badly with a 3-0 loss to top dogs Arsenal in the Charity Shield. Three consecutive draws in the league failed to offer any real glimpse that this would be the club's greatest-ever term, and a second 3-0 reverse to the Gunners in a matter of months, this time at Highbury, reduced expectations further.

The final game before Christmas ended in a 3-2 defeat to Middlesbrough but the side would remain unbeaten from that point onwards, with Keane to the fore during a stupendous run of form. He blotted his copybook with another red card, coming in the last-ever FA Cup semi-final replay, against respected rivals Arsenal. One of the finest spectacles the famous competition has ever produced would never have taken place had Keane's perfectly legitimate strike at Villa Park in the first game been allowed to stand, but it would have deprived the viewing public of a contest that simply had everything.

The captain's tired lunge at Marc Overmars brought a second yellow card from referee David Elleray and he trudged off with the Arsenal fans mercilessly mocking his exit. Sent off in a second FA Cup semi-final after the incident against Palace four years earlier, he could only watch the drama unfold without him as Schmeichel saved Dennis Bergkamp's last-minute penalty before Ryan Giggs claimed a sensational solo winner for the ten men in extra time. 'You could argue my indiscipline came very close to costing us the Treble,' Roy conceded.

However, the bid for glory on three fronts remained intact – in fact, momentum towards it had merely gathered pace – and a week later the one game that is frequently heralded as the finest of his career came at Juventus's Stadio delle Alpi in the semi-final of the Champions League. United looked dead and buried after conceding two early goals to Filippo Inzaghi, to trail 3-1 on aggregate, but Keane brilliantly headed in a Beckham corner to reduce the deficit and breathe life back into the bid for European glory.

This one moment encapsulated Keane's persona. There was no real celebration – why would there be with the team still losing? – only the dead-eyed determination to arc the run that allowed him to meet Beckham's cross and then head straight back to the halfway line to await a quick restart. If that was insufficient to illustrate his self-lessness, what followed in the second half reinforced the stereotype of a man utterly driven to succeed with no huge regard for personal satisfaction.

A booking, accrued for a foul on Zinedine Zidane, ruled him out of any chance of playing in the final, assuming United could get there. There was a flash of anger, directed at Jesper Blomqvist for his mis-placed pass, and then only another reason to channel the aggression into cajoling his colleagues. Keane's thoughts did not focus on the missed opportunity to lead his side out in Barcelona; instead he con-centrated on how he could help his team get there. There are numerous examples of Keane dominating matches, but this was an alluring definition of a hugely complex character trait that drove the Irishman on and defined him as player and captain; it was his ability to channel emotion, often of darker composition, into inspiring lead-ership.

The reaction resonated with supporters and recalled a similar sit-uation nine years earlier when Paul Gascoigne gave an emotional response to what would have been a similar fate with England at the World Cup. Both were undeniably great players but the contrast was stark. Only one was a leader, instilled with mental fortitude that could instantly erase such personal anguish, and the team's need was far greater at this point. The shock did not even register as, within a minute, Dwight Yorke headed the equaliser to edge the visitors in front on away goals. The Reds scored again, through Andy Cole with five minutes remaining, and Keane was hailed as a hero, even if Cole and Yorke had been the ones largely responsible for exposing the flaws in the Bianconeri's defence.

That said, it was a flawless individual display by Keane in repelling Juve's impressive threat in the midfield areas with players like Zinedine Zidane, Edgar Davids, Antonio Conte and Didier Deschamps. Keane tackled tigerishly despite being on a yellow card and passed with metronomic smoothness and unerring accuracy. Exuding calmness and confidence, he dictated United's play and controlled matters with his intelligence and experience, linking particularly effectively with Beckham. A proud Ferguson declared in his first autobiography *Managing My Life*: 'Pounding over every blade of grass, competing as if he would rather die of exhaustion than lose, he inspired all around him. I felt it was an honour to be associated with such a player." High praise indeed.

Keane disagreed, often emphasising the fact he performed far better in other matches when the game is brought up in interviews, and, in 2003, he even contested: 'It's like praising the postman for delivering letters.' It was a clear reference to the fact he felt chasing about the pitch was merely part of his job description.

Regardless, United were marching on. Victory over Tottenham Hotspur on the final day of the league season, inevitably coming from behind again, sealed the title and Keane led the team out at Wembley six days later in a bid to complete a third Double in the club's history, with the Irishman heavily involved in all of them. A rather facile win over Newcastle United followed, but the skipper was injured by a late Gary Speed tackle early in the first half and was substituted in the ninth minute for Teddy Sheringham, who scored one of the goals and assisted the other for Paul Scholes.

Keane still lifted the trophy but, ironically, would have missed the chance to perform in the Nou Camp against Bayern Munich in any case, due to ligament damage in his right ankle. In his absence, more late drama, the kind of which had never really been witnessed before in such a showpiece final, completed an unprecedented trophy haul for an English club and ensured legendary status for those involved, not least Ole Gunnar Solskjaer for his winner.

Instead, Schmeichel would get his hands on the cup on his final appearance for the club. 'There's a good chance I might be captain,' he said on the eve of the game. 'But I'd far rather just be goalkeeper and have Roy in the team.' The legendary No.1, surely the club's greatest-ever goalkeeper, decided to share the moment with the boss. 'I didn't want to be the man to lift the Champions League trophy,' he claimed. 'I wanted Sir Alex to be there because he was the one who gave me and everyone else in the team the chance. To lift it with him was paramount. This was the last thing I did for Manchester United and I could not have asked for a better ending.'

Keane was persuaded to join Paul Scholes, who was also suspended after his booking in Turin, in showing the cup off to the ecstatic, almost disbelieving, United fans in the magnificent Nou Camp stadium, but the pair looked uncomfortable in their grey suits and neither would have demanded such a gesture, preferring to remain in the background as substitute David May choreographed the celebrations in front of the packed stand of supporters.

'I could easily lay aside my personal disappointment at missing the final,' Keane insisted. 'In truth, it was an honour to captain the team that had delivered for a great club and a great manager. I guarantee, on that night when Ole scored the winner, no one in that ground was thinking about me and nor should they have been. It wasn't about me. You've got to look at the bigger picture. It's about the club.'"

European glory meant everything to him, it was the true benchmark of a team's greatness. Perhaps coming from a club like Nottingham Forest, hardly a giant of the game but a side that had won the trophy in consecutive years under Brian Clough, emphasised his conviction that United should have been crowned kings of the Continent on more than one occasion in his era. It was a situation the manager was eager to address as well and, while there was relief at bridging a 31-year gap, the signal from the top was clear – to dominate the Champions League in a similar manner to what had been achieved domestically.

'People keep reminding us of how great a team there was in 1968, so it would be nice to win the European Cup just to keep those people quiet,' Keane had admitted at the start of the Treble-winning season and this, in his view, would merely be the beginning of confirmation of the current charges' quality.

The relentless pursuit of more prizes was always at the forefront of Keane's mind, mirroring the insatiable desire of his manager, and he scored the only goal of the game in the Inter-Continental Cup final against Palmeiras in Tokyo later that year. The Club World Championship was an altogether unhappier experience, but United were peerless in the domestic division and coasted to another title. A key hurdle had been overcome as early as August when he starred in a superb 2-1 victory over Arsenal at Highbury. Locking horns with Patrick Vieira, he was at his marauding best and scored both goals to collect three precious points and deliver a message of intent to the championship pretenders.

If validation of Keane's talents was needed, it provided further weight to his argument for a steep pay increase as part of his latest contract negotiations. The protracted talks were a distraction, particularly with the media enjoying an unfortunately public unravelling of the situation. Chairman Martin Edwards hinted at a departure when stating: 'It is a question of motivation. He wants a new challenge.' Bayern Munich, most notably, and the top Italian clubs were willing to provide that platform for, in Ferguson's words, the top midfielder in the world.

The manager remained confident a contract would be brokered, stressing that 'reality paints a different picture' from the stories in sections of the press. However, Keane grew impatient and outlined his demands in one candid interview. 'The club has a wage structure but they will have to move on to continue to be successful,' he warned. 'United have to move with the times; nobody wants them to wait another thirty years to win the European Cup.

'It will come back to United and whether they can move towards what some of these other clubs are prepared to offer me. If not, we'll see. As much as I love United, I won't be afraid to move.' A matter of weeks before he could sign a pre-contract for a foreign club under the Bosman Ruling, the skipper settled on a four-year deal worth £50,000 per week.

'They've come up with a contract I felt I was deserving,' he informed MUTV. 'I pushed for it and, hopefully, I can repay the manager and the fans with some more silverware. I felt I was being maybe forced into looking abroad a little. I've always put my career first and not money, which I have done again this time.'

With the wrangle reaching a positive conclusion, United could concentrate on matters in hand and streaked clear at the Premier League summit. There were more negative headlines when the skipper led a furious protest against Andy D'Urso when the referee awarded a debatable penalty to Middlesbrough in January. Sir Alex commented how every story relating to respect for officials for years afterwards would unfairly carry the picture of Keane with the veins in his head bulging as he complained vociferously to the man in black.

In a rare move by a referee, D'Urso was persuaded to speak about his experience in a tabloid newspaper and claimed: 'If I had stood my ground, I would have been pushed over. I felt under pressure.' The manager realised his players had gone too far and addressed the situation privately. Even his firebrand captain later admitted: 'I was a bit crazy then. Hopefully, I've got a bit more control now.'

In that game, Mark Bosnich saved Juninho's spot-kick and Beckham snatched a late winner. United were unstoppable and confirmation of the latest title triumph came as early as 22 April at The Dell with a 3-1 win over Southampton, and the final margin of success in the table would be a colossal 18 points. But the celebrations were tempered with a sense of frustration for the captain.

He was still brooding over the previous fixture, a 3-2 reverse to Real Madrid that ended aspirations of retaining the Reds' European crown at the last-eight stage. What made matters worse was Keane scored an own goal, diverting an Ivan Helguera cross past stand-in keeper Raimond van der Gouw. By also squandering a simple chance to atone for his error, this was a night to forget for somebody so utterly hell bent on striving for perfection. It was a rare blip as he managed to stamp his class and authority on a campaign in which he was at the absolute peak of his impressive powers.

The first Player of the Year of the new millennium – he was the dual winner of the Football Writers' and PFA awards – was never going to rest on any laurels. 'Talk is cheap,' he complained. 'You have to do the business in Europe and we didn't do that. I remind myself of the disappointments to spur me on. It's not good looking at the good moments and forgetting what else happened and it's no use thinking that I was voted Player of the Year and being happy with that.'

United won the final five matches of the season but started the following campaign with a defeat to Chelsea in the Charity Shield, with the captain dismissed for another infringement on Poyet, the same player he had clashed with in his first game as permanent skipper. After vowing to clean up his act, he tested referee Mike Riley's patience all afternoon. A foul on the Uruguayan sparked a mass confrontation involving players from both sides and he was incensed by a challenge from Jimmy Floyd Hasselbaink, which warranted at least a yellow card.

Just past the hour mark, he committed a crude foul from behind on Poyet to earn a straight red card and become the last man sent off at the old Wembley. At least the Uruguayan did not bear a grudge, revealing after his retirement that the Irishman was his toughest opponent: 'Manchester United were a totally different team without Roy.'

However, the Reds reigned supreme again in the top flight and would wrap up a third successive title in convincing fashion. There were some eye-catching scorelines at Old Trafford along the way, including a 6-0 win over Bradford City, 5-0 against Southampton and, most notably, a 6-1 hammering of Arsenal, with the midfielder scoring one of the goals and enjoying another chance to put one over the Gunners and his midfield rival Patrick Vieira. Not that these landslide victories would have seen him change his demeanour or outlook. 'During a game, even if we're two- or three-nil up, I find it hard to relax because there is a job to be done,' he insisted.

There were still much-publicised glimpses of the captain's dissatisfaction when his high standards were not being met, on or off the field. In November 2000, he launched into a famous tirade against the Old Trafford fans following an unconvincing victory over Dynamo Kiev that clinched a nervous passage into the next round of the Champions League. 'There were one or two stray passes and they were getting on players' backs,' he protested. 'It's out of order. I don't think some of them can even spell football, let alone understand it. Away from home, our fans are fantastic but, at home, they have a few drinks and probably the prawn sandwiches and they don't realise what's going on out on the pitch.'

The acerbic comments were later interpreted as an attack on the corporate hospitality element of the crowd, rather than committed regulars in the cheaper seats, but it was a risky move to criticise the supporters, even if it was done as an attempt to protect his teammates and improve the Old Trafford atmosphere. 'If something had to be said, I would say it,' he later countered. 'People might have said that the manager gave me a free rein, but it came naturally to me anyway. People talk about the captaincy but I would have done the same things anyway, because it's about doing what is right for the team.'

Meanwhile, another domestic cakewalk in 2000-01 did not satisfy Keane, who was furious with a Champions League exit at the hands of Bayern Munich, the Germans exacting some revenge for their 1999 heartbreak with quarter-final progression. Ferguson's side were already champions before travelling to Bavaria for the second leg and the setback infuriated the skipper, who immediately pointed an accusing finger at some of his colleagues. Rather than shielding them from criticism, he opened a whole debate on whether they were likely to conquer Europe again.

'The players gave it their all tonight but we are just not good enough and maybe it's time to move on,' he conceded in his post-match interview. 'Maybe it's the end of the road for this team, although I'm not sure.'

Whether this was a heat-of-the-moment comment, the timing appeared unhelpful and the season petered out, with United winning only one of the last five league games and losing the final three matches. Keane took his frustrations out on familiar foe Haaland in the next fixture after Munich, the Manchester derby, and received another red card for a poor challenge on the Scandinavian. It would not be the sole punishment for the offence.

Keane wrote in his autobiography in the following year of a desire for revenge on his former Forest team-mate for the Elland Road altercation and the pre-meditated nature of the affair prompted the Football Association to impose an additional five-game suspension and mete out a fine of £150,000. To term the book explosive would be a huge understatement. One of numerous insightful anecdotes related to Bosnich, with the Australian arriving an hour late for training on his first day. Outraged, Keane tells the tale of how he ordered a taxi to lead the way to The Cliff, in order that he could follow behind in his car and keep track of the route. He was close to an hour early and would later introduce a policy of all the players arriving around 30 minutes in advance of their scheduled start. 'The little things matter,' he stressed.

Ghost writer Eamonn Dunphy attempted to accept responsibility for the passage regarding Haaland, claiming he exaggerated Roy's words and added a little poetic licence with a stream of four-letter expletives. Publicly, Sir Alex backed his player. When responding to talk of a legal threat by the Norwegian, the manager argued: 'He told it like it was. I don't think there is a case to answer.' However, it was an unwelcome distraction and an episode that could surely have been avoided.

Dunphy explained the manager and his captain were kindred spirits: 'They are two hungry people, driven and unique, there has never been a bond like it in football.' The Irish television pundit also compared the eponymous subject of the book to Bob Dylan, a rebel and anti-hero in many respects, who rails against the status quo. This was interesting considering Keane lists Dylan's 'Positively 4th Street' as one of his favourite songs. The confrontational opening lyrics – about fair-weather friends who just want to be on the winning side – possibly strike a chord with the man from Cork.

In Keane's eyes, the team is more important than any individual and the club even bigger still. Winning matches and trophies is merely a duty. Woe betide anybody not pulling their weight but still accepting the adulation and basking in the glory, 'bluffers' in his parlance. This appears an important facet of Keane's character and his convictions. 'Too many players forget what defeat means to the people who pay our wages,' he complained. 'We were being paid to play, paid to play for Manchester United.'

The 2001-02 season saw United lose out to Arsenal in the title race, with Sylvain Wiltord regaining the trophy with a winner on the

Reds' home turf, but it may have been Keane's last season if he had not been talked out of leaving the club by his manager. Newcastle won a thriller 4-3 at St James' Park in September and he was dismissed late on for lashing out at Alan Shearer. At a low ebb, he discussed quitting with his boss. 'I told him I wanted to pack it in,' he revealed in his autobiography. 'He said it was a knee-jerk reaction.' Thankfully, Sir Alex was right.

Only an away-goals defeat to Bayer Leverkusen prevented Sir Alex from reaching the Champions League final in his native Glasgow, and Keane had scored in the second leg in Germany but it proved insufficient and, predictably, he was far from happy when reviewing the overall term, despite going so close in Europe's premier competition.

'There are a lot of cover-ups and sometimes players need to stand up and be counted,' he explained in another interview with MUTV. 'I'm not sure that happens a lot at this club, but it's the least we should be doing. Good players don't necessarily make good teams. That's my opinion. I don't care what anyone else thinks.' Some suspected he felt Juan Sebastian Veron, a club-record signing, needed to show his true worth, but it is unlikely he would have been targeting only one individual with his latest verbal volley.

The stinging criticisms were not falling on deaf ears as he continued to have the respect of the dressing room. 'We all listen to Roy,' explained Solskjaer in 2002. 'He's a fantastic leader and a fantastic captain. When he talks, everyone listens.' Ruud van Nistelrooy, who had marked his debut season at the club with 36 goals, offered a similar view, stating: 'Roy is the boss of United in the dressing room. He is the main man here. His football brain is perfect.'

Another striker, the prolific Cole, left the previous year but would never contest the skipper's vocal manner of forcibly getting his point across. 'He didn't just lead by example, he gave everyone a lash of his tongue when he was ready,' declared Cole. 'When you played with him as your captain, all he wanted was to win and he wanted the best from you as a team-mate. So when he came and vented his frustration at you, you knew why. It wasn't personal. He just wanted the best for you as well as his football team.

'He was a very good leader and, at times, I don't think people appreciated what he did. He would sacrifice his body for his team-mates.' However, despite an understanding of this abrasive attitude at United, the darkening of his mood would have ramifications for the Republic of Ireland's World Cup campaign during the summer.

Demanding absolute perfection from those around him, he left the training camp in Saipan ahead of the tournament in a row over the facilities and missed out on leading his country on the biggest stage of all. What was most disappointing was the fact he deserved to parade his talents in such a setting because his display in knocking Louis van Gaal's Netherlands out of the competition had been truly world class.

Jason McAteer, never one to take things too seriously, joked about his team-mate's intensity when revealing: 'He started saying things like: "You all just go with the flow." I asked Roy what goes with the flow and he replied: "Dead fish." Sometimes, I think he thinks he's Alex Ferguson.'

Meanwhile, another senior member of the Ireland side, Niall Quinn, stated: 'I've never had a personal relationship with Roy. No one in this squad has.' The comments from the Irish camp echoed his own sentiments on friendships within football and his path would soon cross with both McAteer and Quinn in a league fixture at Sunderland's Stadium of Light at the end of August.

McAteer successfully got under his international colleague's skin during a niggly encounter and Keane reacted to the provocation by planting an elbow on the former Liverpool midfielder. Sir Alex could not defend the player's actions, admitting referee Uriah Rennie had no option but to brandish the red card and a fine of two weeks' wages was imposed. As the FA ban for the comments relating to the Haaland tackle coincided with this latest suspension, the sensible decision was taken for Keane to undergo a hernia operation in an attempt to cure a problem that had been troubling him for some time.

Although he returned in late December, as a substitute at Blackburn Rovers, it was an unhappy Christmas. The Reds lost at both Ewood Park and Middlesbrough's Riverside Stadium, but the midfielder showed few ill effects from the surgery and led the side to another title, his seventh and final Premier League triumph. He failed to score in his 30 starts in all competitions as his role had now been permanently changed in order to maintain his influence but limit his workload. 'We don't need the old Roy Keane anymore,' explained the manager. 'We need Roy to organise the midfield more. He is cautiously realising that he will be of more value to us now using his experience in a sitting role.'

A 2-0 win at Tottenham Hotspur virtually wrapped things up in the league in April 2003, and Keane collected the silverware on the final day after victory at Everton, running the length of the field with Beckham to celebrate the winning free-kick in what proved to be the England star's final appearance for the club. He would have only brief flirtations with elation, however, revealing that he moves on within a matter of seconds after winning something. 'Even getting the trophy, you want to get it out of the way and get back,' he claimed. 'It can be a nuisance.' Regardless of this comment, which may have been tongue in cheek, he certainly enjoyed acclaiming the club's goals and titles over the course of his career.

The Champions League run that season was ended by Real Madrid, 6-5 on aggregate, but only after a tremendously entertaining second leg at Old Trafford. This exit would not provoke the same ire from the captain, only frustration instead. At least United had bowed out with their heads held high during a marvellous exhibition of attacking football as Brazilian Ronaldo received a standing ovation from the sporting home faithful. 'It's clearing that final hurdle and we've not been able to do that,' he admitted. 'We keep getting these lessons, yet we keep giving these goals away. The penny has to finally drop.'

In 2003-04, Keane only managed 25 starts in the league as United ceded the title to Arsenal's 'Invincibles' and finished in third spot behind Chelsea. However, he led the team to another FA Cup triumph, his fourth at the club, as underdogs Millwall were swept aside 3-0 in the final at the Millennium Stadium. 'It is always nice to win,' he said in characteristically understated fashion afterwards. 'The last one is always the nicest.' Although the semi-final triumph over Arsenal really unlocked the door to another trophy, it was a relief to end the season on a high, even if a joyous occasion was tinged with sadness.

It was the skipper's idea to change into shirts carrying the No.26 with the name Davis for the presentation, as a tribute to young forward Jimmy Davis who lost his life in a car accident at the start of the season while on loan at Watford. 'It is important we remember how lucky we are,' commented Keane, with Gary Neville adding: 'Hopefully, what we did today will make Jimmy's parents smile for a moment.'

It showed respect and a sense of understanding for the wide-reaching role of a Manchester United captain. He may have cultivated an image of a fearsome loner, but there was a human side to his approach as well. Remembering how he had been treated by senior professionals earlier in his career, from Stuart Pearce at Forest to Bruce and Robson at United, he would offer friendly advice to those attempting to settle in their new surroundings, particularly if arriving from overseas.

'I have to say there are big commitments for the captain at Manchester United but, as long as you don't take your eye off the ball in terms of what you are about and that is a player, being a good leader on the training pitch and helping foreign players and their families. I was comfortable doing that,' he said.

Darren Fletcher admits there was another side to the hard-man image and one that remained unknown to the wider footballing public. 'Roy was the ultimate captain and a real leader,' the Scot explained. 'He set standards in the dressing room and, on the pitch, he demanded a lot of every player. He led by example and, if you weren't pulling your weight, he was in your face and letting you know about it.

'But people didn't see the softer side to him, when he gave you compliments and told you that you were doing well. He did it some-times one on one and sometimes in training, around the rest of the players. He did that with me a few times and it made you feel on top of the world when he singled you out for praise in front of the rest of the squad. That's the side not a lot of people saw.'

Another leading dressing-room personality, Rio Ferdinand, spoke of a lighter edge to the skipper, revealing: 'Roy was a big character but, at the same time, he was also the joker in the pack.' Gary Neville recalls informing people in his mobile contacts list of a new phone number; Keane texted back: 'So what?' It is not difficult to identify his wicked sense of humour, particularly when he assumes the role of a television pundit. Even after some of his most cutting remarks, there is often a sly grin to be found on the face of somebody who is always compelling and revels in stirring controversy.

The reality was that he did not necessarily need to socialise with his colleagues during his playing days and, particularly as captain, kept a healthy distance in order to maintain an air of authority that was presumably deemed necessary to exert control and influence. 'People think a captain has got to be mates with people, you don't,' he argued. 'You just have to have the respect of your team-mates and you earn that on the training ground. When you work with people every day of the week, that is when you get the respect. I always kept a boundary because I think that's how it should be. You need a boundary and that was just accepted.'

In the following 2004-05 campaign, Chelsea overhauled Arsenal with United lagging behind in third, 18 points off the title. However, there was a small degree of consolation in the form of a stunning 4-2 victory at Highbury, with Keane and Vieira taking centre stage beforehand. The great combatants clashed in the tunnel and the United man squared up to the France international in front of referee Graham Poll, who tried to maintain order before the first whistle had even sounded. All of it was captured by television cameras and it was a compelling insight into Keane's fearsome protection of his team-mates and his pumped-up pride as skipper of United.

It later transpired that Vieira had started the fracas by hounding Gary Neville during the warm-up, taking exception to previous rough treatment of Jose Antonio Reyes. 'Patrick Vieira is six feet four inches and he's having a go at Gary Neville,' revealed Keane. 'So I said: "Have a go at me." If he wants to intimidate our players and thinks Gary is an easy target, I'm not having it.' The aggressive stance only further endeared him to the United faithful, recognising this was a man willing to go to war on behalf of his colleagues. Perhaps a sign of Keane's maturity came early on in that game, when he charged towards the advancing Ashley Cole in United's area and the Irishman had the wherewithal not to dive in but instead to usher his opponent out of play.

But there was no redeeming FA Cup glory that year, as the Gunners gained revenge for February's defeat by shading a penalty shoot-out after a final dominated by the Reds at the Millennium Stadium in Cardiff. Keane converted his spot-kick to maintain the pressure on Vieira's fifth kick, but his counterpart beat Roy Carroll to deny his adversary a final winners' medal at the club. It also proved to be the Arsenal favourite's last act for the club as he joined Juventus in that summer.

At least the performance offered the belief that Wayne Rooney and Cristiano Ronaldo were starting to fulfil their enormous potential. Rooney, who had joined at the start of that campaign from Everton after starring in Euro 2004 for England, enjoyed working with Keane and was not intimidated by him despite still being in his teens.

'He was vocal on the pitch and helped me off it,' said Rooney. 'He was a great captain. I've had a few [dressing downs] off him. We've had a few debates. Sometimes, when you want to win, it's not always sitting down and talking quietly. You have a go at each other to try to get the best out of each other. If you saw the way he was with the senior players, it was the same as with the younger players. He wasn't afraid to tell everybody how he wanted them to play. I fully respected him and I wasn't fearful. It was desire and passion.'

United responded well to the unjust defeat in the final and began 2005-06 in tremendous form, conceding only one goal in the opening eight games. Keane's simmering frustration, however, boiled over in October and signalled the end of his illustrious Old Trafford reign. He had been unsupportive of the idea of a pre-season training camp in Portugal and publicised the fact he was thinking of leaving when his contract expired in the summer.

Sidelined by an ankle injury sustained during a goalless draw at Liverpool in September, he watched the side toil at Middlesbrough and suffer an embarrassing 4-1 beating as Ronaldo's late effort provided scant consolation for a sorry team display. MUTV asked the skipper to 'Play the Pundit' in their regular feature designed to reflect on the previous match and provide insider analysis of the highlights.

Typically, Keane spoke frankly about his colleagues' shortcomings and the programme was pulled before going to air, never to see the light of day. Fletcher was one of those in the firing line, but reiterated that he was willing to accept constructive criticism. 'Roy was probably the biggest influence on my career,' he insisted. 'He would come down hard on me if I ever did anything wrong, but he made me realise what it meant to be a Manchester United player.'

Sir Alex maintained the player had overstepped the line – the Scot's stance being that criticism in the dressing room was one thing, but to take it into public was another – and a rift developed, with Keane finally leaving by mutual consent in mid-November. The 34-year-old joined Celtic, a club he had always expressed affection for, and they provided the opposition for United in his testimonial that May.

Keane and Sir Alex had been the perfect combination and the breakdown in their relationship caused sadness among fans and an element of delight in the press. The midfield enforcer has explained that he did not enjoy the close relationship with the boss that many outsiders would have envisaged. 'People have this image of me when I was at United that I was, in some way, closer to the manager than other players but it was not the case,' he revealed. 'There has to be an element of trust from the captain to the manager, be it organising training, so the manager can let the captain get on with it. There would not be any cosy chats or meetings for cups of tea or anything like that. I think there is possibly a lot of trust involved that the manager knows the captain is taking care of things.'

One of Keane's strongest traits, imploring maximum effort from others and lambasting those who fell short of the required level, contributed to the end of his distinguished career at Old Trafford. Sir Alex once said: 'The demands he puts on others are unbelievable. He is quite simply the best player I have ever had.' Yet he felt that line had been crossed. Somebody who believed the dressing room should remain sacrosanct was clearly perturbed by the targeting of named individuals on a television show, even if Keane's overriding sentiment would have been to try to rectify the mistakes at Middlesbrough. 'At all times, I have endeavoured to do my best for the management and the team,' he said pointedly, when making his exit.

However, Keane's reputation as one of United's greatest captains is undiminished. The most successful skipper in the club's history was the driving force as United set new standards in excellence and achievement, and he was an inspirational leader. It is impossible to separate Keane the captain from Keane the player in many respects, which elevates him to the same standing as Robson, rather than those who were not necessarily defined by the role despite their brilliance, such as Denis Law or Eric Cantona.

Fellow countryman Irwin, who also hailed from Cork, is able to compare Keane to Robson having played alongside both men for many years. 'I was blessed when I came here in 1990 because I had four years under Robbo and he was a fantastic leader, a great captain and a fantastic man,' he enthused. 'Roy was exactly the same, leading by example and he probably got the players by the scruff of the neck more than Robbo did. He was probably more vocal too, but it was great to work under the pair of them. Steve Bruce and Eric Cantona were captains for a while as well, but they were the two that stick out the most.'

Numerous plaudits have been paid for Keane's role as leader of the Treble team and after the turn of the millennium. 'For me, Roy Keane is the best captain I've ever played under,' said Beckham. Life was never dull with Roy as skipper and his achievements while wearing the armband may never be matched. A true leader and an inspiration, he takes his place among Manchester United's true greats. Writing in Keane's testimonial programme, 1968 European Cup-winner Paddy Crerand, who has a similarly short fuse, concisely assessed his contribution to the United cause: 'He will be one of the great heroes here forever and ever.'

Chapter 12

Red Nev

'I've been a United fan all my life and fulfilled every
dream I've ever had.'

Gary Neville

Gary Neville talks nineteen to the dozen, to the extent that Sir Alex
Ferguson once remarked to his trusty but talkative right-back: 'I bet
your tongue says a prayer when you go to sleep at night.' It was something of a running joke among team-mates, envisaging their futures
after their football boots had been hung up, that a career in the media
inevitably awaited Neville because of his indomitable passion for the
sport. 'You can't stop him talking,' they would say with a mixture of
weariness and affection.

Many a true word is spoken in jest, because Neville has forged a
brilliant second career as a media pundit with Sky Sports, while also
finding the time and energy to coach the England national team
since retiring from a glorious playing career at Old Trafford in 2011.
But it isn't just stream-of-consciousness stuff on the hugely popular
Monday Night Football analysis show, in which Neville is the unde-
niable star; his incisive, insightful assessments have transformed

football punditry on our TV screens. Neville chases down the game's tactical topics and talking points with the same breathless relentlessness to which former opposing wingers would readily attest.

He has approached his media career with the same gusto, desire and application to improve and be the best he can be as he did as a young Bury lad at United's Littleton Road and The Cliff training grounds in Salford in the early 1990s. What shines through in his new role is his undiluted passion for a sport he has immersed his life in. He neatly positions his palpable love of United as both burden and badge of honour, particularly during the troubled 2013-14 season, but his views are never tainted by bias. His analysis and delivery also highlight his intelligence, sharp mind, self-deprecating wit and, perhaps above all, that really he is just very likeable. So much so, even Manchester City and Liverpool fans praise his analysis and observations.

This transformation to far-reaching respect right across the football community was amusingly unimaginable during a playing career in which he riled opposing supporters every bit as much as he roused those in the red of United. He veritably revelled in the fact fans on both sides of the divide recognised and responded accordingly to his unstinting loyalty and heart-on-sleeve commitment through the prism of their own allegiances.

That Neville is so convincing, so compelling to watch on screen, is no trick of the camera; it's an in-built effervescence that took comparatively rudimentary talents as a young player, which he openly admits were nothing like the natural gifts of teenage teammates Ryan Giggs or Paul Scholes, and carved out a glittering one-club playing career spanning 602 games and encompassing every trophy the English game has to offer, and more besides, with Sir Alex Ferguson describing him as 'the best right-back of his generation'.

The characteristics required for him to succeed made him a

natural fit for the armband when Roy Keane left the club in a turbulent fashion in late 2005. Keane, in many respects, embodied the torrents of change washing through the club and the team at that unsettled time. The Irishman's career was rapidly drawing to a close, while the foundations for the next great Sir Alex team were precisely that: not exactly bricks and mortar, they appeared to be more at the architectural design stage. Keane, a remaining pillar of the previous structure, represented the frustration of an older generation impatient to wait for the new one to catch up to his exacting standards.

The scene Keane left behind at Old Trafford was broadly described in the media as a 'crumbling empire' – hardly the propitious circumstances in which you might imagine realising a dream of leading out your boyhood club. The team had touched the bottom of the pool in perhaps the deepest transitional dip since Sir Alex's earliest years in the job; the dying embers of the post-Treble era had ceased to glow, while the goalscoring express train that was Ruud van Nistelrooy was waiting impatiently for the brilliance of Cristiano Ronaldo and Wayne Rooney to fully bloom.

With the benefit of hindsight, success via a series of further influential signings – notably Nemanja Vidic, Michael Carrick and Patrice Evra – was just around the corner, but perhaps only Sir Alex possessed the vision and foresight to see the light at the end of the tunnel as United ambled through four seasons without a league title, and Jose Mourinho's Chelsea bulldozed their way to claim 2004-05's Premier League crown and looked stridently intent on retaining it the following year. It was United's disappointing 4-1 defeat against Middlesbrough in October 2005 that drew Keane's ire. It was followed with a lacklustre 1-0 away loss to Lille in the Champions League and only a tubthumping, backs-to-the-wall, Darren Fletcher-inspired 1-0 win over Chelsea at a baying and defiant Old Trafford had lifted spirits around the club.

In Europe, United went on to draw 0-0 with Villarreal in

November and, the following month, lost 2-1 to Benfica to exit the competition at the group stages for the first time in a decade. That was Neville's first start as the official club captain, and it was a match which came on the back of two emotionally charged domestic outings at Old Trafford, against West Brom and Portsmouth, in which the sad passing and funeral of George Best were marked with a sea of floral tributes laid beneath the Holy Trinity statue, while you could have heard a tear drop inside the stadium during an immaculate minute's silence.

Such an emotionally raw and hazily unclear backdrop was, on first inspection, an unenviable setting for Neville's emergence as United's next skipper. But few figures in the modern game possess such an inherent understanding of the philosophy of their club, connected to United's past as a lifelong local fan from a family of Reds, and a torchbearer for the future schooled as part of the famed Class of '92, who, like their forebears the Busby Babes, were a symbol of the soul of Manchester United.

The decision to name Neville captain wasn't wholly straightforward for Sir Alex, who had a number of contenders among his squad. Van Nistelrooy had already led the team through the troubled waters of the past couple of months, while Giggs, himself a shining beacon of everything United, was also a possibility. Ferguson tactfully dealt with the dilemma: 'I've had a chat with Ruud, but I think it's the right decision, with the service Gary has given this club. Ryan was a consideration too. But Ryan is not going to play every week. You cannot expect him to run up and down the touchline all the time. He will play a lot of games, but we need to keep him fresh. That is why I have reached the decision I have.'

Van Nistelrooy wholeheartedly concurred with the choice. 'I took great pride in leading the team out in a difficult period,' said the Dutchman. 'We had to bounce back from a four-one defeat at Middlesbrough and everything that happened after that. I enjoyed it a lot and did it with great pride, but I would make the same decision as the manager. I think Gary is the perfect captain for our team. He has been at the club his whole life, he has won everything in football and has great experience and great character. You can't wish for any more in a captain.'

For Neville, this was the pinnacle, the realisation of his devotion to the United cause, but also recognition of his service and his respected voice in the dressing room. For Sir Alex, where Keane had once taken the manager's form on the field, Neville offered a different kind of leadership, albeit no less attuned to Ferguson's philosophy. 'The principles of our manager run through this club,' Neville said. 'It runs through our team: the work ethic, the loyalty, the way in which players carry themselves every day. The manager has created the strong dressing room at United with the type of characters he wants. The club, historically, has got great ideals. It's a brilliant club to play for. It's very easy to come to work every day. I play for Manchester United – a great incentive.'

Neville was a perfect fit for United, an essential cog in the bigger machine, because in Sir Alex's eyes talent alone wasn't enough. A relentless hunger to be a winner had to course through your veins, and Gary's blood vessels were bursting with the stuff. That was perhaps rooted in his childhood and the competitive sporting nature of his family. So, to arrive at the point of him becoming captain, it is essential to understand how Neville's life and education, both as youth footballer and then successful professional, had prepared him for that moment.

Gary grew up in Bury, north Manchester, the older brother of twin siblings, Phil and Tracey. It's patently clear that sport was and still is at the core of the Neville household. Dad Neville Neville was a league cricketer in nearby Bolton, while mum Jill was a keen netball player, a sport Tracey took up and went on to represent England at the World Championships and Commonwealth Games, including 2002's Manchester edition.

The eldest Neville was born on 18 February 1975 and, by the time he was just four years old, was already nagging his dad to take him to Old Trafford. As he grew a little older and attended matches more regularly, Gary insisted on arriving early at the ground, brimming with the matchday buzz that consumes young lads hooked on the game. After pie and chips at the Marina Grill at the top of Sir Matt Busby Way, Gary would be one of the first in the queue to get into the old K Stand and head straight for his spot in the stands, while his dad had a pint with his mates. Gary sat there and soaked up the sights and sounds – not that there was much to see or hear as the stadium was often mostly empty at that time, but it didn't matter. Those early trips to Old Trafford instilled in him a boyish passion for *his* club that he would fiercely defend against anyone – and that did not fade in adulthood.

'When you first walk into that ground at the age of five or ten ... you fall in love with that team running out in that red shirt, in that great stadium,' Neville wrote in his autobiography, *Red*. 'That was what drew you to the club and made you think, "Wow, that's got me." And it's an addiction you have for life. Walking into the stadium, that's what gripped me, the size of it – I was in awe of the whole place. I just love everything; the badge, the history.'

At that time, of course, United were not the dominant force in English football. Merseyside rather than Manchester regularly provided the league winners in Gary's school days. In fact, by the time he celebrated his tenth birthday, he had been alive to witness – not that he would have wanted to – seven Liverpool league triumphs. That's not a fact dredged up for the purposes of sporting masochism, it's just it shaped Neville, like many Reds at that time. Liverpool won leagues and European Cups while United were perennial under-achievers. And it hurt, not least because at Chantlers Primary School in Bury, Gary had to contend with an inordinate number of Liverpool-supporting fellow pupils, despite being just a few miles from Old Trafford. Kids naturally follow the successful teams but this inevitably led to arguments, debates and squabbles on the playground, with Neville giving every bit as good as he got, and then some. Gary attributes his intensity to a bullish stubbornness in the Neville genes, a badge of honour on his father's side of the family, but those early days spent defending his team's cause was the perfect proving ground for honing his love of United.

It wasn't just pupils that bore the brunt of Neville's argumentative streak. He constantly challenged rules and authority, as brother Phil pointed out when the pair were still at United together: 'You weren't allowed to wear trainers at school, so Gary wore trainers; you had to wear a blazer, Gary wore a jumper. He was very opinionated, too. Gary's so intense. He's relentless. If he's doing something he does it very stressfully, even just going out for a meal. He's constantly organising things and, when he has organised it, he's still worrying about it. Sometimes, he just needs to chill out a bit.'

On the pitch, few players inspired admiration in Neville quite like Bryan Robson, and he was just six when he was at Old Trafford to see Robbo unveiled on the pitch as he signed his contract before the match against Wolverhampton Wanderers in October 1981. Little did an awestruck Neville realise it then but, 12 years later, he would be playing alongside Robson in a European Cup tie against Galatasaray at Old Trafford, his second appearance for United.

There was plenty of hard work ahead before he would reach those heady heights but Robson's combative, wholehearted performances captured Neville's imagination. United's other idolised players throughout the 1980s also played a key part in his emerging characteristics as a footballer – Norman Whiteside and Mark Hughes were among those he looked up to. They were proper men, physical footballers giving their all for the cause in a team that constantly felt it had a point to prove in the shadow of its North-West neighbours.

Most of all, their blood-and-sweat commitment embodied the passion Neville had for his team even at a young age.

In his own fledgling career, the challenge was taking his obvious aptitude and the force of his personality and channelling that to wring every last drop out of his abilities. Gary freely conceded he wasn't even the best sportsman in his own family. A keen footballer and cricketer, he always felt it took the full extent of his resources of determination to impress, whereas sporting progress came more naturally to young Philip. That might have been true or it may have been part of Gary's mental make-up that drove him on to constant improvement, but he cites a struggle to make the county football team, or, aged 13, to play cricket in the Bolton League, albeit against men. Meanwhile, Phil represented England schoolboys at football and Lancashire at cricket all through the age groups. Phil starred alongside Andrew Flintoff with bat and ball and would almost certainly have made a successful career as a cricketer.

Gary's self-deprecation and downplaying of his abilities could have been a defence mechanism against what he perceived to be the possibility of failure in the starkly unforgiving environment of youth football. More likely, it was a stick used to beat himself with to ensure his standards never wavered or fell below the very maximum he was capable of producing.

Nevertheless, he was 11 when he attended trials at Littleton Road in Salford to earn a place at United's Centre of Excellence. His name was put forward, along with a few other schoolmates, by his head teacher. Back then, he was a midfielder and considered himself in the mould of his hero, Robson. He was invited to The Cliff for two sessions a week, but soon felt intimidated by the quality of talent around him, notably the street-tough, technically superior Nicky Butt and Paul Scholes, who had also joined the Centre of Excellence. At 14, however, Neville had done enough that his dad was informed in a meeting with Brian Kidd, then in charge of United's youth set-up, that not only was he being offered schoolboy forms to the age of 16, he was also given a further two-year apprenticeship beyond that.

It would have been too much to expect of a 14-year-old boy giddy with excitement about next week, never mind next year or the next decade, to have the sagacity to foresee the dynasty Alex Ferguson was creating. Yet Neville and the likes of Giggs, Scholes and Butt were all benefiting from the progressive plans to overhaul the club's entire structure – 'don't build a team, build a club' was the manager's mantra – and, in turn, these young kids were becoming steeped in Ferguson's vision and values. They were surrounded by coaches like 1968 European Cup winners Kidd and Nobby Stiles, no-nonsense Yorkshireman Eric Harrison, who would drive Neville to unrelent-ing betterment, as well as occasional sessions from then-assistant boss Archie Knox, who barked instructions in his gruff Scottish brogue and drilled into his young students the confidence to pass with pace and take the ball under pressure. It was a no-holds-barred appren-ticeship for life in the first team, mentally and physically demanding but, ultimately, deeply rewarding.

Harrison's role in Neville's development, and indeed of the feted Class of '92 as a group, cannot be overstated. 'Gary didn't have the greatest technique,' Harrison recalled, 'but we worked so hard together, just him and me, getting him to pass the ball down a white line to improve accuracy, or he would go off on his own and hit a ball against a wall, left foot, right foot, left, right, left, right – things like that. The hunger has to be there. If you don't have the hunger, you've got no chance. I know I used to slate them every now and again, but they were successful. If I'd been namby-pamby with them, who knows?'

Neville and the rest of his team-mates got the impression Harrison was applying a particularly stern brand of tough love on this increasingly lauded group. 'I was definitely tougher on them,' Harrison has since conceded. 'I had a job and it was to get players into the first team and make the team more successful than it was. I was hard. My wife came down to The Cliff one Saturday morning with me. She doesn't like football, but we were going to the Trafford Centre in the afternoon and she heard me shouting and bawling. Back in the car, she said: "You're a disgrace! You wouldn't speak to your children like that, would you?"'

Nevertheless, Harrison's approach was beginning to pay dividends. 'The idea was that you've never made it,' Neville said, looking back on those formative years. 'With a young player, sometimes you hear people saying: "He's made it." Our idea was that you'd never made it. You can perform well at United and still be out if you don't fit the plan. There are no passengers. It's a conveyor belt, and if you're not contributing to the success of the club in some way, you won't be here much longer.'

All the while, the Class of '92 were forming friendships that would last a lifetime, creating an unbreakable bond that was only ever enhanced every time they crossed the white line and had to rely on each other – against kids their own age, men in the 'A' and Reserve teams or, eventually, in the first team. The higher the stakes, the stronger the bond became. They pushed each other on and that was their great secret; these weren't just talented individuals, the collective was the key.

Neville connected with few others as he did with David Beckham, an unlikely alliance in many respects, given Beckham was seen as a flash cockney while Neville was the archetypal northerner. Yet they soon discovered a shared penchant for hard work in training and, just as importantly, a fanaticism about United – though Neville initially hadn't thought that last point was possible for a southerner. Their innate understanding together not only helped in their development as young players, it proved an invaluable asset down United's right flank for years.

Not all friendships flourished from the off. While promoting *The*

Class of '92 film that charmingly chronicled the group's astonishing story, Nicky Butt said: 'I hated Gary the first time I saw him! The first time I met him, I was playing against him, for Manchester Boys against Bury Boys. There was just this lad at the back, who was a good footballer, but who never, ever shut up talking all the way through the game. He still does that today – he never shuts up. But I couldn't stand him back then. I wanted to tackle him, I wanted to show how good I was against him. Then, one day, I met him at the training ground and it just clicked and he became one of my best mates. And he is still one of my best mates now.'

Friendships cemented, this exciting group of youngsters quickly began to raise hopes around the club that a very special crop of players was emerging. In 2011, looking back on the careers of Neville and Scholes following their retirement – though Scholes would later make a U-turn, of course – Sir Bobby Charlton relived their emergence ahead of a gala tribute evening in their honour. 'At a club like Manchester United, you often think "I wonder what's in the future? We might be playing okay today but what about the longer term?"

'The odd young player used to come through and I was always interested to see what they were like. Alex would invite me to see the youngsters train and I would always ask the coaches what our chances were in the FA Youth Cup. One day they said: "We have six certainties to be great figures in the game." What they were telling me was serious stuff, but initially I thought they were getting carried away.

'I went to the first match they played in the FA Youth Cup, against Sunderland at Roker Park [on 27 November 1991]. I drove up to watch them and after twenty minutes we were four-nil up. Butt was rampaging through midfield, Beckham came on later passing the ball like he does, and Gary seemed to be the leader at the back – it was just magical to watch. I thought to myself, "It's right what they were telling me – they weren't kidding." I was genuinely excited and you could see then these lads were going to be special. I watched every game they played because it was such a fantastic moment for the club. It was a purple patch, something magical was unfolding. Gary was a bit different. Even at a young age he was inspirational. He was the leader. Gary has been a real bonus for United because of his depth of feeling for the shirt.'

The first instance of Neville writing his name into the club's history came in that tournament, the FA Youth Cup, which has such an emotional pull on United after the Busby Babes won the inaugural trophy and successfully defended it a further four times between 1953 and 1957. Once again, it proved the start of something special for the club as Neville helped United to 3-1 and 3-2 victories over Crystal Palace in 1992's final over two legs.

That was a real high for Gary and his team-mates but, just five months later, the excitement would be cranked up a notch. Neville was just 17 and became the first of his age group to make the jump to first-team football – Giggs, just over a year older than Gary, had done it some 18 months earlier against Everton in the old First Division. Neville's opportunity came in the UEFA Cup against Torpedo Moscow at Old Trafford on 16 September 1992. It was a drab 0-0 draw and, just two weeks later, United would exit the competition on penalties, but Neville replaced Lee Martin in the 88th minute, took one throw-in that came to nothing and still admitted that if he had died the next day, he would have done so happy.

Yet if he had seemingly overcome all hurdles in his way to make that first small step, it was nothing compared to the next giant leap: breaking into United's first team and staying there. And not just any United side, but one boasting Schmeichel, Parker, Bruce, Pallister, Ince, Robson and Hughes, who were joined by Keane and Cantona. They were not just supremely talented players, they were the last bastions of true-grit footballers – fearsome competitors, ferocious winners. Be it with strength or skill, they could beat teams either which way.

Still, Neville had a way of making an impression, as Keane later recalled: 'When Gary came into the dressing room at about eighteen he seemed more like he was thirty-eight – he already had plenty to say. People say I moaned a lot, Nev was worse! But his professionalism was outstanding and there was a big group of players in that dressing room who were very driven. That approach makes the fans take to you and, in Gary's case, perhaps a little more because the badge seemed to mean a little bit more to him.'

However, it would be nearly 14 months before Neville tasted first-team action again, and almost 20 before he was handed his first club start, against Coventry City in a dead-rubber final league game of the Double-winning 1993-94 campaign. But United's young hopefuls often travelled to senior games, assisting kit man Norman Davies and, in so doing, they witnessed at first hand what it took to be a United player, and to be a winner. United's 26-year wait for the league title was over and the club was experiencing success that, without fully knowing it, these talented teens would soon be expected to emulate.

Neville's real breakthrough came in the doomed 1994-95 campaign. United had problems at right-back. After two good seasons, the regular incumbent Paul Parker was beset by injuries and, between August and January that season, Ferguson used seven players in the position: Parker, David May, Keane, Denis Irwin, Gary, Phil, and John O'Kane. May, newly signed from Blackburn Rovers, started the season at right-back before Neville appeared in the seminal 2-1 League Cup win at Port Vale. This was the game when Ferguson unleashed many of the Class of '92 on an unsuspecting public, with Davies, O'Kane and Scholes all making their debuts, alongside other alumni, also including Beckham, Butt and Keith Gillespie – a decision that caused huge controversy at the time, as the manager was accused of disrespecting the competition.

Chopping and changing ensued but, from March onwards, Gary

began to tighten his grip on the position, starting each of the last ten games. He had been pointed in that direction by Harrison, who observed that the injuries being suffered by Parker meant he was more likely to get a game there, than at his usual position in the centre where Bruce and Pallister missed just one game each in the two previous seasons. It was tempered by the fact United lost the league on the final day of the season at West Ham and then, less than a week later, fell flat in the FA Cup final against Everton. It was a harsh lesson.

Still, for Neville, harsh lessons often proved a prelude to progress. The next season, following Alan Hansen's infamous 'you can't win anything with kids' jibe after the opening-day 3-1 defeat to Aston Villa, Neville played 39 times alongside his fresh-faced cohorts and the manager's blend of youthful sparkle, vast knowhow of Schmeichel and Irwin, drive of Keane and genius of Cantona brought home the double Double. The Class of '92 had come of age, but this was just the beginning.

The league title was retained with relative ease in 1997, but it was accompanied by another pang of European disappointment after losing twice to Borussia Dortmund in the semi-finals when victory seemed within reach. Cantona called it a day and the next season brought more frustration, losing to Monaco in the quarter-finals in Europe and conceding the title to Arsene Wenger's Arsenal by a solitary point. Neville and Beckham made more appearances than anyone else that season, notching 45 and 50 outings respectively, establishing the pair as cornerstones of the team. But if Neville's run in the side over four seasons had brought with it highs and lows, it was mere preparation for the rollercoaster ride that was the epochal 1998-99 campaign. Gary was as consistent and reliable as ever, starting more games (54) than any other outfield player in United's ranks and showed his capacity to play at centre-back to assist Jaap Stam's acclimatisation to English football.

Neville was a pivotal figure in the dressing room in cultivating an atmosphere of belief, determination and the never-say-die spirit that coloured red the second half of that unforgettable campaign, culminating in 11 days of pure magic to clinch the Premier League, FA Cup and Champions League trophies. 'Those days were the best you could ever hope for as a football player,' Gary recalled. 'It was unbelievable. We won the league, went out in Mulligans in town, won the FA Cup final easily, then went to Barcelona the day after.

'We just knew it was the biggest moment of our lives but, once the game started, I felt like our legs had gone. It felt like one step too far. Then, with fifteen minutes to go, the manager made some changes and the game altered. When Teddy Sheringham scored, I thought: "We're in it," and, when Ole Gunnar Solskjaer got the second, I just couldn't believe it. People ask about my best moment as a United player and, after my debut, it was probably turning onto Deansgate on the trophy parade and thinking: "Oh my god!" There must have been five hundred thousand people hanging off buildings and lampposts, screaming, delirious, drunk, and we'd not slept – we'd just gone right through and not slept.'

As with any sportsman exposed to career-defining success, Neville and company faced the mental and physical challenge of replicating it – that's the greatest season in English football history. The departure of Schmeichel left a gaping hole United took six years to fill, while a general lack of new signings elsewhere in the team in the post-Treble bubble contributed to a sense of inertia. That wasn't helped by the lack of competition domestically as United breezed to three titles in a row in 1999-00 and 2000-01 by 18 and 10 points respectively. 'If it was possible to be bored as you win the league, we were bored in those two seasons after the Treble,' Neville said. Keane stated that some players were slacking and, aligned to a lack of sufficient strengthening, United were left ruing consecutive European quarter-final exits in 2000 against Real Madrid and 2001 against Bayern Munich.

That period had a psychological impact on Neville. The exertions of the Treble season took their toll physically, as an underlying groin injury required an injection after 1999's Champions League final. His form suffered and a nadir was reached at the World Club Championship in Brazil when Neville gifted goals to Edmundo and Romario against Vasco da Gama, prompting a text from Paul Scholes back home which simply read: 'Fiasco da Gama.' Joking aside, those errors played on Gary's mind and a first prolonged spell of uncertainty ensued as he admitted: 'In some games, I just wanted the whistle to blow.' He would recover but the team's uncertainty would continue. The 2002-03 league triumph was Neville's sixth, a decade after his debut season, but it would be a further four years before he would get his hands on the trophy again. By then, he had taken over as captain.

In the highlights reel of Neville's career, one incident guaranteed to find a place in the montage also sums up the depth of his feeling for United. It came in January 2006 in a league game against Liverpool at Old Trafford. The clock read 89 minutes and 59 seconds when Rio Ferdinand slammed home a header from Giggs's inswinging free-kick to secure a 1-0 win. Neville was back defending on the halfway line but, when the goal went in, he ran across in the direction of the travelling Liverpool fans and pumped his fists and clutched the badge on his shirt. It was pure elation, but no doubt a response to countless years of abuse from Liverpool fans as the pantomime villain of United. There was no malice, just rivalry, as Neville put it. But the incident landed him in trouble with the Football Association. Neville, by that point a representative for the Professional Footballers' Association, contested a £5,000 fine for improper conduct, insisting: 'I know people say five thousand pounds is nothing to a footballer, but I'd have contested it if it was fifty pence.'

He went on to add in typically forthright fashion: 'You are caught up in the moment and for a few seconds you can go bananas. What are you meant to do? Smile sweetly and jog back to the halfway line? I laughed when I heard someone say that it was not the behaviour of a thirty-year-old, because they are probably the same people who have accused us of lacking passion in recent games. No disrespect to Liverpool was intended.

'Last week, I had to put up with a Liverpool lad taunting our fans during the Manchester derby but at no point did I even consider that Robbie Fowler should be punished. The stick is part of the game. One week you take it on the chin, the next you give it out. That is how local rivals have always been – and always should be. I have to put up with Liverpool fans singing plenty of songs about me, none of them tasteful, and I struggle to believe that I have caused them any grave offence with an exuberant celebration. Increasingly people seem to want their footballers to be whiter than white and there are calls for sanctions over every little incident. Do they want a game of robots?'

The following month, Gary lifted his first trophy as club captain. The 4-0 League Cup triumph over Wigan Athletic may not have been scaling the heights of previous successes, but it was a kick-starter to greater glories. 'It doesn't get much better than that,' Neville beamed. 'Lifting the trophy as captain with my team-mates behind me for the club I've supported all my life. It was special for me and special for the team because we've taken criticism in the last few years. Hopefully this is the start of us winning bigger trophies. We're aware of where we have to be and that is winning championships and European Cups.'

That was exactly where United were headed. Ronaldo returned from the World Cup that year with his talent fully realised and Sir Alex's next great team was on the brink of world domination. Neville was an integral part of the title-winning side of 2006-07, right up until a March fixture against Bolton Wanderers when a late challenge by Gary Speed damaged the Reds skipper's ankle ligaments. Initially the prognosis was for an April return but, although he donned the kit to lift the Premier League trophy in May alongside Giggs, he wouldn't play for over a year as the ankle issue wouldn't resolve itself and secondary injuries hindered his comeback, which eventually arrived in the form of a late substitute appearance in 2008's Champions League quarter-final tie with Roma at Old Trafford – as a central midfielder. He took the captain's armband and received a rousing reception from the crowd – all those years dreaming of being the next Bryan Robson, fleetingly lived out. The brutal truth was that, at 33, injuries are much harder to overcome and Neville's match schedule had to be managed carefully. He would still prove an influence, but his season appearance tallies naturally fell to 25-30 games as Wes Brown and then Rafael took the other openings.

His influential voice still rang out in the dressing room at Carrington, especially passing on knowledge to the squad's younger players or even occasionally by representing them in contract negotiations. But by September 2010, he was playing once a week rather than twice, so the decision was taken that he would remain club captain while Nemanja Vidic took on the team captaincy, in much the same way Noel Cantwell and Denis Law shared duties in the 1960s.

Neville said: 'I'm captain one week, then it's Giggsy, then Rio, then Edwin. That's not ideal. You need someone who can lead the team out every single week, so it makes sense for this to happen. I'm unfortunately not going to play every week.'

That fact was brought into sharp focus by the turn of the year. On New Year's Day, Neville lined up for only his fourth appearance of the season, in what would be his final game, against West Bromwich Albion. Neville was lucky not to see red for tripping Graham Dorrans as he darted into United's penalty area. At half time, Gary sat in a toilet cubicle in the away dressing room wishing it was all over and, from there, his decision was made. Injuries and the subsequent disruption to his training schedule had taken the edge off his game. The time was right, he said, to call it a day. The announcement came a month later on 2 February 2011. At 35, fifth in United's ranks of all-time appearance makers, red through and through, this was the end.

Sir Alex paid glowing tribute to one of the club's finest servants: 'He won eight championships and was an integral part of the team that captured the Treble. But Gary's contribution goes much deeper than winning trophies, important though that is. What also counts is what he brought to the dressing room and training ground in setting standards that the others just naturally followed. We haven't had a more loyal and dedicated player in my time at Old Trafford, and typical of what he brought to the table to help us to our achievements was the manner of his departure when he thought it was time for him to go. Some people can be honest with their appraisal of others, not always with themselves.'

In Neville's case, the denouement, the last line of his own chapter in United's history, is not what endures. 'United has given me my life and being part of it is more than I could ever have asked for,' he said. But he gave everything for United, as fan, player and captain, which is why he takes fitting place among the club's great leaders.

Chapter 13

The Ultimate Warrior

'I don't ever think about getting hurt. I do what I have to do.'

Nemanja Vidic

Nemanja Vidic played his last game for Manchester United covered in blood. It was almost an artist's impression of the all-action playing style that made him hugely popular with supporters and a totemic figure in the Reds' defence for eight-and-a-half years during the club's most trophy-laden spell.

Some called him a throwback to the days of yore, and Vidic's bravery, physical aggression and willingness to put his body on the line, as well as his imperviousness to haemophobia, quickly commanded cult status. His fighting qualities, sheer consistency and dependability – barring one lengthy absence due to a serious knee injury in United's *annus horribilis* in 2012 – also earned him the armband, first as team captain in September 2010, then as club skipper when Gary Neville retired later that season.

His defensive partner, Rio Ferdinand, was arguably the more rounded defender – all refined, technical sophistication – but there were just as many supporters on the terraces gladly glorifying the guts and gore of Vida as there were swooning over Rio's cerebral centre-back play. Nemanja may have been softly spoken but there was something elemental about this Serbian hardman; a defender in its purest, most visceral form. And those qualities would prove ideal when wearing the armband.

That is not to say he was not a very astute player; Nemanja was unpretentiously assured on the ball and an excellent reader of the game. Those attributes were often simply muscled out of focus by his lean, mean façade. It would be somewhat gauche to align his physically aggressive approach on the pitch with the embattled backdrop of the war-torn former Yugoslavia in which he grew up. More tellingly, his childhood instilled characteristics of a different kind: mental fortitude, intense purpose and a resolute determination to make something of his life and his profession – and, perhaps more than anything, it nurtured a deep passion for football. 'It was hard,' he said of growing up in the region. 'Maybe it is because life was hard that I got where I wanted to be. I fought to be in this position, to play for such a big club and to be recognised. If everything had gone easily, maybe it would not have worked out like this.'

Born on 21 October 1981 in Užice, a small city of around 60,000 inhabitants some 100 miles south-west of Belgrade, Nemanja's teenage years in particular were characterised by the political and military unrest in the region throughout the 1990s. He has given stark descriptions of life in Užice and later, when he moved to Belgrade to pursue his dream of becoming a professional footballer. 'In the nineties, football was everything,' he said. 'It was the best way to show the world who we were. At the time, there were a lot of bad things happening in our country – murders, bombings, war – and it was important that Red Star Belgrade and the national team played well to counteract the negatives. It was the best way to show that Serbians also love football and sporting events. Football is still the number one sport in Serbia and everybody wants to play for Red Star or one of Europe's top clubs. Football is a big part of life for our young people.

'Back then, it was very important to us in a different way. Even with everything going on in the country, people were still playing football. Red Star had football matches and people were going to watch games, even though there was a war on. It was amazing. I remember when the bombing started and, for the first month, we were too scared to go out and play football because we didn't know what was happening. Nobody knew where the bombs would be. But after a month people relaxed a little more and they realised the targets were military and government buildings, or bridges. So then we thought it was okay to go to the stadiums and play football – we knew they wouldn't bomb there. People still wanted to lead their lives and watch football.'

Football was a cause to unite the people, although such was the passion for the beautiful game that it occasionally turned a little ugly, as Vida recalled: 'Some people say the match between Dinamo Zagreb and Red Star Belgrade in May 1990 escalated the war! There was a big fight, fans tore up seats, some got onto the pitch, even players were involved, and there were serious injuries. I remember watching the match on TV and seeing Zvonimir Boban kick a policeman, which caused a lot of trouble. At that time, there was a very, very cold relationship between Croatia and Serbia, but now I think most of the bad feelings have stopped and people realise going to war was not the right thing to do. The nineties were just a very unstable time and politics went very, very wrong. I cannot speak for everyone on this, though. These events are bigger than me and they are bigger than football.'

Young Nemanja's obsession was for his beloved Red Star. He idolised the famous team that won the European Cup in 1991, beating Marseille 5-3 on penalties at Stadio San Nicola in Bari, Italy. The team contained club greats such as Robert Prosinecki, Dejan

Savicevic, Darko Pancev, Sinisa Mihajlovic, Vladimir Jugovic and Miodrag Belodedici. Two weeks before Red Star lifted the European Cup, Mark Hughes had scored twice in Rotterdam to clinch United's 2-1 win over Barcelona in the European Cup Winners' Cup final, teeing up a meeting with Red Star in the Super Cup later that year. Brian McClair scored the game's only goal at Old Trafford in November but, aged just ten at the time, Nemanja does not recall watching the game, so when he arrived in Manchester he asked MUTV, the club's television channel, for a DVD of the match and watched it on repeat with gleeful nostalgia.

Nemanja's earliest memories of playing football are aged six, when he kicked a ball around outside the block of flats where he lived in Užice. In his teenage years, his burgeoning talent was spotted by Red Star and he joined their youth set-up and quickly rose through the ranks. Zoran Filipovic was a prolific striker for the club during the 1970s and returned to the *Marakana*, the unofficial nickname given to Red Star Stadium, as manager in 2001. He blooded several promising youngsters, among them Vidic, of whom he said: 'When I first coached Nemanja, I saw a boy with a very big talent. He never made errors during passing drills in training and, very early on, he looked suited to the type of qualities needed in English football. He had a very strong character and personality, even at nineteen. He loved to win, even when it was just games in training. He was so motivated. He was born a warrior. Because he was very young he was sometimes nervous during games, but I worked very hard with him to correct that and put him on the right road. I spoke with him a lot to help him and he matured very quickly.'

Filipovic left the club in 2003, but before he departed he told Vidic that he would go on to become captain. Sure enough, Nemanja took the armband the following season, aged just 22. 'He really needed that responsibility,' added Filipovic. 'He needed to take that next step in his career.' This rapid rise in status was no more than

Nemanja's talent deserved, but every time he stepped onto the field he spared a thought for Vladimir Dimitrijevic, who had been his closest friend in Red Star's youth team, an example of how easily everything they thought possible could be snatched away in an instant.

The two had been inseparable and 'shared the same dreams' of making a life as a professional footballer. 'Vlada' had signed a five-year contract with Red Star on his 20th birthday and made his debut for the club he loved. He was due to travel with the first team to Japan for a farewell match for Dragan Stojkovic, a club legend who had joined Nagoya Grampus Eight as his career wound down. But in a final training session before the trip, Dimitrijevic collapsed and died of heart complications. Nemanja was understandably distraught. 'We wanted to reach for the sky with our team,' he said. 'Unfortunately Vlada is gone. But the memory still remains. When I play, I think about my friend and I will do everything I can to save [my] memory about him.'

In the 2003-04 season, Vidic would realise the dreams he had shared with Vlada, as he led Red Star to the domestic Double in Serbia. His performances caught the eye of Spartak Moscow and, although his stay in the Russian capital lasted just 18 months, it was enough time for him to win the league in 2005 and take the captaincy at the Luzhniki Stadium, where, of course, he would make a triumphant and emotional return just three years later with United.

His displays were excellent for club and country, for whom he was part of Serbia & Montenegro's 'Famous Four', alongside Mladen Krstajic, Ivica Dragutinovic and Goran Gavrancic, who conceded just one goal in qualifying for the 2006 World Cup in Germany. Vidic's growing profile began to attract scouts from across the Continent. The reports coming back to Sir Alex Ferguson had the words 'courage' and 'determination' in bold, underlined and circled in red. 'He could tackle, head the ball clear. We were looking at a typical English centre-back,' the United manager noted in his book, *My*

Autobiography. So when Liverpool were suddenly also said to be keen on taking him to Anfield, United accelerated that established initial interest, resulting in an unprecedented Christmas Day announcement that a fee, reported to be £7 million, had been agreed with Spartak a full week before the January transfer window opened.

Announcing this festive gift while most fans were tucking into their Christmas turkey, Sir Alex said: 'I am delighted the two clubs have come to an agreement. Nemanja is a quick, aggressive centre-half and, at twenty-four, will be a terrific addition to the squad.' Once the move was officially pushed through on 5 January 2006, his new manager presciently enthused: 'Good defenders win you things. In my time, we have had people like Steve Bruce, Gary Pallister, Paul Parker, Denis Irwin, Ronny Johnsen and Jaap Stam at this club. Vidic is really natural and athletic. You need good defenders and that is exactly what this lad is.'

To put his new signing immediately in that bracket of quality was quite a statement. Three weeks later, Vidic's attributes were perhaps not immediately evident on his debut, a substitute appearance in United's 2-1 League Cup semi-final victory over Blackburn Rovers at Old Trafford. 'Vida hadn't played since the end of the season in Moscow, in November,' Sir Alex recalled. 'In his first game for us, against Blackburn, he was breathing out of his backside. He needed a pre-season.'

'I came to Manchester having not trained for forty days,' Vida explained. 'In Russia we had finished our season and I was resting, that was my very big problem. But I listened to every word from Sir Alex, worked very hard every day and tried to get into form because the rest of the players were already at a high level. After that I got a chance. I played twelve matches and I was not only satisfied – I was delighted!'

That summer, he could look back on a whirlwind few months settling in at his new club in which he played a cameo role in delivering League Cup success, when he came off the bench in the 4-0 final win over Wigan Athletic at the Millennium Stadium in Cardiff. United may have lost the league a couple of months later to Chelsea, whose manager Jose Mourinho had delivered consecutive Premier League crowns in his first two seasons in English football, but, for United, winning the League Cup was a crossing of the Rubicon for that team. It was the launch pad for a wealth of success that would shortly follow. For Vidic, he saw his move to United as acceptance and recognition of his talent.

'When you play for United, you have proof that you are a good player,' he said. 'Manchester United is an institution. Every one of us is very happy because we have a chance to play at Old Trafford. That is a privilege, I know that. For my club, I shall give everything – they already knew that when they selected me. In every training session, I learn something from Rio Ferdinand, Edwin van der Sar, Ryan Giggs, Paul Scholes, Ruud van Nistelrooy and all the other guys. They are phenomenal as people. You know everything about their playing ability. Being part of United is not hard, it is easy, because everybody is down to earth. People think that at big clubs people have big heads, but this is not true – we are happy because we are there and we are one family.'

It is said that contentment is the enemy of invention but, for Vidic, it was fuel for the fire burning inside him to be a success. He was hungry for more, eager to learn and desperate to develop his game. 'I shall improve,' he pledged. 'I must learn more, I must work more. Conversations with Sir Alex mean so much to me. I listen to him and accept every piece of advice. I think that I will become much better and after total adaption to English football I will show my real face. Not for my own benefit – it will be for the good of the club.'

Carlos Queiroz had returned to United in the summer of 2004, and he would play a vital part in Vidic's development as a player and as an individual in a defensive unit that was by equal measure both slick and solid. The Portuguese coach's influence at Carrington may not have always been appreciated by supporters, some of whom suggested United became too strategic, too disciplined and too defensive in a 4-5-1 or 4-4-1-1 formation, when the club's natural inclination was to throw off the shackles, cut loose and attack with abandon. But tireless work on the training ground paid dividends as United became champions of England, Europe and, eventually, the world. The Reds' back five were auto-tuned to perfection. Van der Sar, Patrice Evra, Vidic, Ferdinand and then either Gary Neville or Wes Brown were truly excellent individually, and absolutely exceptional as a collective.

'We worked a lot in training on defensive shape with Carlos Queiroz, who was a big influence on us,' says Vidic. 'He worked with us on defensive positioning and the back four or five had great balance. Patrice would go forward on that left side, almost as a winger. Then you had Rio and me in the middle, with Wes or Gary Neville on the right. They were natural defenders who could get forward as well, but with Patrice attacking a lot it gave us the right balance for them to stay more in position to stop counter-attacks coming through.

'The other reason for that was that we had Cristiano Ronaldo, so he needed defensive support behind him so he could concentrate solely on attacking. But we had a really great balance and we had Edwin behind us. He had great experience and he was talking to us all the time and could pass the ball, too. He was a great passer, like an outfield player. It was like having a midfielder and goalkeeper behind you, he could pick out passes and you always felt confident giving him the ball. That was a great time in my career. We felt really strong. We didn't think about losing a goal, that's how we felt during matches.'

Vidic's blossoming partnership with Ferdinand appeared to owe much to a classic silk-and-steel combination, Ferdinand's easy-on-the-eye continental play a velvet glove to the robust stick-your-head-where-it-hurts iron fist of Vidic. But there were many more similarities between the two players than immediately met the eye. 'First of all we worked on it,' Vidic reveals. 'I would say we were always chatty about everything in training. We talked about things. If a scenario came up we'd be asking each other, "Why did this happen?" "Where do you want me to be in that situation?" "Why do you want me there?" Then actually we started thinking like one person on the pitch because we discussed everything.

'We were so open to each other to say whatever was on our mind about the games and our performances that we just became better as individuals and as a partnership. We see the game in the same way. That really helps, that's the most important thing. As defenders, if you don't see the game in the same way then you are in big trouble. We thought the same way – where to move, when to move – when and where is the danger coming? I would say we always moved to help each other. We weren't playing selfishly to make ourselves look good, we were playing for each other and for the team. That's how I think we became a good partnership.

'We had different attributes, it's true, but if you think the same way one can have one attribute and the other has another and you work together to make the most of it. It doesn't change the way you see the game. You make the most of your skills as a player, but you can also make the most of someone else's, too. The way you watch the game and interpret it, that's all about where you move, how you move as a unit, a partnership or as a team. You're not doing things just because you want to take the ball so you're going to look better. You're doing it when it is important for the team to move. You keep your position and help your team-mate. That's not just what I did with Rio, it was the same all over the pitch. But positioning is very important for central defenders and, positionally, Rio and I understood each other. After that comes the basic qualities: tackling, jumping, heading the ball, and all the other abilities you need to be a good defender at United.'

That centre-back pairing would form an essential foundation as United wrested the title from Chelsea and Mourinho's hands in 2007 and then kept a tight grip on it for three consecutive seasons. In each of those campaigns, there were refinements to the formula, particularly in the precision clockwork defensive play. The 2006-07 title-winning season, though, perhaps produced the most attacking football, never more evident than in April 2007's 7-1 thrashing of AS Roma in the Champions League quarter-finals at Old Trafford. Sadly, United would just run out of steam and suffered a semi-final setback against AC Milan, with Vidic missing the first leg through injury and then being patched up for a 3-0 loss in the away fixture. That was followed by a heart-breaking late FA Cup final defeat to Chelsea, the first showpiece event back at the refurbished – but velcro-pitched – Wembley.

The 2007-08 campaign was the most successful of the era, clinching Premier League and Champions League success, while the 2008-09 campaign clinically took United to FIFA Club World Cup glory in December and a hat-trick of league titles in May, as well as another European final, albeit losing to Barcelona in Rome's Stadio Olimpico. Winning the Champions League the previous year in Moscow had been a neat twist of fate for Nemanja, clinching European football's most coveted prize at a ground he had briefly called home with Spartak.

During that epic season, six players made more starts than anyone else for United and their identity was significant: Ronaldo, the talisman of the team, was of course there with 46 starts, but so too was the entire back five of van der Sar (44), Evra (48), Vidic (45), Ferdinand (51) and Brown (48). United kept 31 clean sheets in 57 matches and conceded more than one goal in just seven of the other 26 games, never letting in more than two. It all culminated in rain-soaked celebration in Moscow in May.

Vidic was injured before the final and hadn't trained properly for a fortnight until two days before the all-English affair with Chelsea.

He simply had to be out there on the pitch and, while some of that final remains a bit of a blur, many moments are etched permanently in his memory. 'First, I remember that cross from Wes with his left foot and Ronaldo jumping like . . . I've never seen anyone jump like that to score a goal. He got so much height in his leap and it was a great header.' The lead lasted little more than 20 minutes as Frank Lampard equalised – somewhat fortuitously and against the general pattern of play – on the stroke of half time. Chelsea had the better of the second half and hit a post through Didier Drogba, but the Chelsea forward was dismissed after 116 minutes, during a tense period of extra time, after petulantly slapping Vidic in the face.

Match referee Lubos Michel admitted he had endured problems throughout the game with Chelsea's players and explained the incident as follows: 'The situation started when a ball was kicked out for fair play and Carlos Tevez made the gesture for United to press the throw-in. Then Michael Ballack reacted and more players got involved in a mass confrontation. No referee in the world likes to show a red card, but Drogba's slap on Vidic was violent conduct and I had no other option.'

It proved crucial as Drogba's absence from the shootout promoted John Terry to fifth spot among Chelsea's penalty takers. After Ronaldo missed, Chelsea were in control in the shootout and Terry could have won it, which is where Vidic picks up the story: 'Most of all, I remember thinking that we'd lost, but then Terry took his penalty and slipped. I saw the ball going one way and Edwin going the other and I just thought to myself, "Wow . . . that's it, we've lost." Then it hit the post. That's when it all changed.'

Anderson, Salomon Kalou and Ryan Giggs all netted to make it 6-5 to United, with Nicolas Anelka having to score to keep his side in contention. 'People ask, in that moment, what is going through your mind? It's . . . nothing. Then it's just . . . screaming and you don't know what to do with yourself. Everyone else ran and I did the same, but I couldn't believe it. Seriously, I couldn't believe it when Edwin saved Anelka's penalty and we won the European Cup. I don't think I could properly take it in.

'I think I only truly realised what we had actually achieved during the next season, when we started playing in the Champions League again. Because we won the final and, three days later, I joined up with the national team to play some games, then I went on holiday. Then it was pre-season ... OK, I enjoyed the feeling but I didn't have time to think about it and to process it in my mind. It just happened so quickly. Then you're thinking about next season and I'm saying to myself, "Come on, I want longer to think about this!" It's something I will enjoy when I finish playing, and something I will remember for the rest of my life. So, plenty of time to think about it!

'But it was very emotional for me. I played at Spartak Moscow for a year-and-a-half in that stadium and it was destiny, I believe, to play for United and win the Champions League final at the Luzhniki. That was the greatest memory I have at United, although one thing I am really sad about is that we didn't get to share that victory with the fans in Manchester with a parade around the city. That would have been great for the fans, because it was such a great achievement and the supporters were such a massive part of it, they were there with us all the way in our journey.'

It's that attitude, aligned to his palpable passion and commitment to the United cause, that made Vidic a cult figure among supporters and an obvious candidate for the captaincy. Gary Neville would make a further 61 appearances for United over the following two-and-a-half seasons, but Sir Alex sought a regular, a certainty in United's line-up, and Vidic was a pillar of stability.

At the time, United were built for success – or attempting to achieve it – on all fronts. Amid a period in which the Reds dominated the Premier League, reached three Champions League finals in four seasons, won two League Cups and the Club World Cup, squad rotation was a natural – essential – part of life in the first team. That was a big part of Sir Alex's thinking when picking who would take the armband from Neville. Ferdinand had endured injury problems between 2009-11, van der Sar's career was winding down and Giggs's output was carefully rationed. Vidic's style, consistency, character and position appealed to his manager. 'We had to choose someone we felt was going to be fit and playing every week,' he said. 'That is difficult when you rotate the squad the way we do. We felt Vidic was closest to that. And he is a defender and I always think they make better captains.'

Mike Phelan, assistant manager at the time, was also involved in the decision-making process, and described it as a 'question-and-answer session to find out who was the one we all thought should be captain'. The final decision would be the manager's, but they sought opinions from a number of sources and it was discussed among the players, too.

'The captaincy at United is a very honourable thing,' said Phelan. 'It also comes with a lot of work. You're a figurehead in certain situations, within the game or outside the game, and he handles those situations. You can sometimes be a spokesperson, although you don't have to be because there are a lot of people who can do the talking at United. But Vida's very level-headed, strong-willed and he was just the candidate that the dressing room felt happy with.

'He's a rock-solid defender and you counted on his appearances, his consistency, his strong mentality and fearless approach. He's conscientious; he not only wants to do well for himself but for the team as well – he's very team-oriented. The decision was made purely on consistency; he's a consistent performer. He was an obvious choice. His responsibilities have grown over the years of his development and it was the next step in what he would consider to be his progress. We were confident that how he handled that would be there for everyone to see.'

Even so, Vidic wasn't the sort to shout about it from the rooftops or revel in the 'Captain. Leader. Legend' hype of some of his contemporaries in the game. In fact, with van der Sar, Neville, Giggs, Scholes and Ferdinand all still at the club, Vidic seemed almost bashful about his elevation to the top role within the playing squad, even though he would treat it with the utmost seriousness.

'It is a big achievement for me,' he said. 'No one is going to say they don't want to be United captain and I am very happy with it. It is a major responsibility, but I have always liked responsibility. I am not a player who shies away from it. Nothing has really changed in that respect. We all know the captains of the team are Neville, Giggs, Scholes and Rio. They are the real leaders. The other players follow how they do things. They don't have to do anything special. They just have to be themselves to be an example for the rest of the players. When they are not on the pitch, I just try to do my best and use the experience I have gained in the years I have played for Manchester United.'

Nemanja is refreshingly humble and, in person, only an understated but undoubted steely determination gives any indication of the player he inevitably turns into when he crosses the white line on matchday. He is also exceptionally likeable, which is never a bad thing. Liked and respected – can a captain ask for more? He wasn't one to shout and scream, at least not off the pitch, and instead preferred to let his actions do the talking. 'You have to always be together as a team, that's important,' he said. 'If you have a bad result, you have to concentrate on doing the right things – in training and with your behaviour, then in the matches. You try to lead by example – first in the dressing room, then out on the pitch.

'At a club like United, there are so many players who are experienced and mature, and they help the team try to achieve great things. Those players make sure the team is always focused and prepared. Football has changed, generations change. You can't be fighting in the dressing room or anything like the things you used to hear about in football. You lead by example now and respect your team-mates. If you respect them, you get respect back. That's the way at United. Not just with team-mates but people around the club, the staff. You support your team-mates, talk to them, encourage them.'

It didn't take long for Vidic to prove his credentials – not that he needed to, of course. In 2010-11, his first season as captain, no one started more matches (47), and he missed just three of the Reds' 38 league matches en route to winning the title by nine points from second-placed Chelsea, finally overtaking Liverpool's league haul with a glorious 19th English crown. Ferdinand missed half of United's league games that season and Vidic was the experienced man keeping it all together in the heart of defence as his team remained unbeaten at Old Trafford. No team boasted a better defensive record on home soil than the Reds, conceding just 12 goals in 19 games in Manchester. Even at the other end, Vidic was influential as he weighed in with five goals and finished the campaign as United's sixth-top goalscorer. Perhaps most notably, he scored in May's 2-1 win over Chelsea which all but secured the title. As with so many of his performances that season, it was a captain's display if ever there was one.

He spoke passionately and eloquently about the privilege of getting his hands on the trophy later that month. 'It is a great honour for me to be the captain of such a big club,' he said. 'I was very proud when I was given the captaincy and I am enjoying the role. But, at the end of the day, if you are captain and you don't win a trophy, it is not a great feeling. I am very glad we won such an important trophy for us. It was one of our main targets to win the Premier League and go above Liverpool.'

Vidic's contribution would be recognised when he was named Premier League Player of the Season and there was a suggestion in some quarters that, if the voting for some of the game's other individual accolades was collated later in the season, he might have added more to his growing personal collection. He had previously won the Sir Matt Busby Player of Year award in 2008-09, as voted by fans, and collected the Players' Player accolade that year too, in addition to his first Premier League Player of the Season trophy. Vida was included in the Premier League Team of the Year four times and received nominations for the Ballon d'Or in 2008 and 2009 and was chosen in the FIFPro World XI in 2008-09 and 2010-11.

Vidic was almost peerless in the category of indefatigable defensive forces, but even the toughest sporting warriors are not immune to injury and, in December 2011, United's troubled season took a turn for the worse. Injury problems were rife during a 2-1 defeat to Basel that resulted in the Reds' exit from the Champions League, and Vidic was carried off in agony after he suffered a ruptured cruciate knee ligament as he landed awkwardly in a challenge with Marco Streller. He underwent surgery later that month and was ruled out for the rest of the season, with Sir Alex lamenting: 'It's a real loss. He's such a dominant character.'

While the Serbian's presence had been vital in overthrowing Liverpool's record league haul the season before, his absence would be acutely conspicuous in light of the new challenge from another North-West neighbour; the emerging power of Manchester City. A painful final day of the season saw City take the title on goal difference. Had Vidic been fit it is difficult not to conclude that April's decisive 1-0 defeat to Wigan Athletic and the 4-4 draw against Everton might not have happened had the skipper been there to steady the ship through choppy waters.

Nevertheless, he returned the following season and, despite another knee operation early in the campaign, fought back to help United to title number 20 and he shared the honour of lifting the trophy with Sir Alex in the great man's last home outing as boss. Nemanja's final season, the disappointing 2013-14 campaign, was a downer to end on but it certainly cannot taint his service or success as a captain and his enjoyment of playing for and leading United.

'I'm immensely proud to have been a part of this club,' he says. 'I played and trained with the best players – top-class players – during my time at United and that helped me to improve. You always had to be really focused, and that's just in training! Then when you went out onto the field in a match sometimes you would be playing against players who aren't as good as the ones you face every day. So it's easy! No, I'm joking, but it's a big thing at United, the quality. That really helped me to improve.

'I have so many nice memories at United. Winning the Champions League is one of the best on the pitch, and, in my last few months at United, after I knew that I would be leaving to play for Inter Milan, I had time to think about it all and realise how big a part of my life the club has been.' It's typical of the man that he doesn't put the personal glory of lifting the Premier League title as captain at the top of his considerable list of achievements at Old Trafford. 'It was very special, of course, but the Champions League is something you might only win once in a lifetime. This club has won it three times, so it is a part of history. I'm very proud of that.'

Vidic is an incredibly tough act to follow as a United captain, so what advice did he impart for his successor? 'I don't know if it's for me to say how someone else should captain United,' he says. 'How I saw the captaincy for me is that my job was to perform on the pitch, to be an example on the pitch to the younger generation and also in the way I trained and lived. Your actions are important as they shape how people judge you. You are judged on your actions rather than words and that should be the case for the United captain.' In that case, Vidic did a very good job of it indeed.

Chapter 14

The Born Winner

'I believe he will put his heart and soul into the captaincy role.'

Louis van Gaal

Wayne Rooney is, unequivocally, the most talked-about footballer of his generation in the British game. His every move is scrutinised by the media in both the sports pages and the gossip columns and his promotion to Manchester United captain was, in itself, a major event.

Dubbed the last of the street footballers, his was a rags-to-riches tale that enchanted the press from the very outset as his electrifying performances at Euro 2004 for England raised hopes that he could lead his country to glory and a first international trophy since 1966. Failing to dampen any enthusiasm around the 18-year-old prodigy, coach Sven-Goran Eriksson merely added to the already out-of-control hype.

'I don't remember anyone making such an impact on a tournament since Pele in the 1958 World Cup,' said the Swede. 'He deserves all the attention and all the front-page headlines. I sometimes feel I shouldn't say too much, but he has been absolutely incredible.' Unfortunately, people would forever be saying too much about a player who had the world at his feet and it was something he would have to grow accustomed to.

The die was cast that summer. Rooney would carry the nation's expectations on his broad but young shoulders and this unfair level of pressure would naturally intensify only further when, a couple of months later, he traded his boyhood club Everton for Manchester United on transfer-deadline day for a record fee for a teenager in excess of £25 million. Sir Alex Ferguson boldly stated: 'We have got the best young player this country has seen in the past thirty years.' The teenager secured the platform he craved on a regular basis and, ever since a sensational debut hat-trick against Fenerbahce in the Champions League, has been a leading figure for the biggest club in the country.

At the time of writing, he has won five Barclays Premier League titles, the first of which arrived in 2006-07, when he played in more matches (55) than any of his colleagues and was joint-top scorer in all competitions with 23 goals, the same figure managed by Cristiano Ronaldo. A year later, the title was retained and he added a Champions League winner's medal to his trophy cabinet as Chelsea were overcome on penalties in Moscow in the final. The Club World Cup followed in December, when he scored the winner in the final against Liga de Quito after netting a brace in the 5-3 semi-final triumph over Gamba Osaka.

A third successive championship was secured, as he hit 20 goals overall, but Barcelona ended hopes of another Champions League success in Rome. The 2009-10 campaign was one of his very best as he was deployed as an out-and-out centre-forward and displayed a new-found ability for headed goals. A final tally of 26 goals in 32 Premier League appearances was outstanding, as was a record of 34 in all competitions. The trophies kept coming. In 2011, his ice-cool penalty clinched the title at Blackburn Rovers and he also found the net in the Champions League final at Wembley, albeit in vain as Barcelona again took the trophy.

Undeterred, he top-scored with 27 league goals in the next campaign, 34 in all competitions, and it is easy to forget it was his final-day effort at Sunderland which would have won yet another title had it not been for Manchester City's dramatic late turnaround against Queens Park Rangers in May 2012. Injuries ensured he played second fiddle to Robin van Persie in the goal stakes in Sir Alex Ferguson's final season in charge, but he still scooped a fifth Premier League medal and registered better than a goal every other league start. He was leading marksman for the Reds again in 2013-14 and has moved into third place behind luminaries Sir Bobby Charlton and Denis Law in the list of United's all-time goalscorers. Only Alan Shearer and Andy Cole have hit the net more often in Premier League history.

That is not to mention his numerous feats for England, nor the PFA Players' Player of the Year and Football Writers' awards he obtained in 2010. Although, much to his frustration, he has yet to win the FA Cup, he netted twice in the 2006 League Cup victory over Wigan Athletic, and headed the winner against Aston Villa in the final of the same competition four years later. Those who continue to insist he has not fulfilled his potential must have set the bar unattainably high.

Rooney lives and breathes football and has always been characterised as possessing a boyish addiction to the game. The story that he would be representing Everton's first team and then head home to kick a ball around in the street with his mates in the working-class Liverpool area of Croxteth added to the mythology surrounding him. He played with an infectious enthusiasm, refreshing innocence and a burning desire to win at all costs, never tiring of enjoying the thrill of competing in the sport he loves.

This innate passion has never left him, despite his inexorable rise to becoming the country's leading light. Sir Alex often complained that his eager striker would nag him incessantly to play, even when he planned to rest him, particularly in League Cup fixtures and any European dead rubbers. Rooney always wants to pull on the shirt and, equally, has a desire to lead from the front. He quickly made no secret of his ambition to captain the side and his first opportunity to do so came against FC Copenhagen in the Champions League, way back in 2006.

When senior figures Ryan Giggs and Rio Ferdinand withdrew from the team due to injury close to kick-off time, Sir Alex turned to a player not yet 21 to assume the role. 'Wayne is, quite possibly, the youngest player to captain United,' said the manager. 'You look for someone who could respond to it. Paul Scholes, for example, doesn't want to be captain. So it was an easy choice, giving it to some-one that it would give a lift to. He did a fantastic job, as we expected.' The night went well for the Reds. A 3-0 victory over the Danish outfit was recorded and, despite failing to get on the scoresheet, the youngster understandably relished the experience.

Indeed, his post-match interview deflected the attention to the bigger picture, extoling the virtues of three goals, three points and a step closer to qualification. It was the sort of mantra espoused regu-larly by the then incumbent Gary Neville and a million miles away from his cheeky and cocky persona around the training ground. 'I remember he joked about it last season,' revealed Ferguson, when pushed on the decision to award the youngster the armband. 'He said within earshot of Roy Keane that he should be captain and that Roy was finished!' This was a boy barely out of his teens and yet display-ing enough bravado to make such an inflammatory comment, even in jest, to a notoriously explosive character and fearsome leader.

Of course, there would be a long wait before he gained the honour on a permanent basis, eight years in fact, although he occasionally took charge on the field in the meantime. Nemanja Vidic was a natural replacement for Neville, and Patrice Evra's lofty status within the dressing room marked him out as an ideal deputy. Furthermore, the manager was honest about his reluctance to award the armband to strikers. 'I've never been a real advocate of centre-forwards being captain,' he reiterated. 'Even though Eric Cantona did a fantastic job for us. You tend to look at central defenders, midfielders or even goalkeepers.'

England offered him another route to such elevated status and he received a glowing tribute from Sir Alex after being chosen to lead his country in a friendly defeat to Brazil in Doha in November 2009. 'You can see the qualities Wayne would bring to the captaincy,' outlined the United boss. 'His determination, his hunger and his desire to do well. He always tries, no matter how the team is playing. He always gives one hundred per cent, and these are wonderful qualities for a captain.

'He exemplifies the spirit of the whole team and other players can take that on board. So there are good reasons for making him captain. I think Fabio Capello made him England captain against Brazil because Wayne was the one regular player left. That was the key to it. But top players can take that responsibility. They've got their ego, reputation and pride to defend in that respect. As captain, you don't want to let anyone down. And Wayne would be very much like that.'

Patience may not be one of Rooney's strongest virtues, and it was clear by the time of David Moyes's brief reign that he had his eyes fixed on finally realising his personal ambition to become Manchester United skipper. However, the rather pressing issue to be resolved at the start of that 2013-14 season was whether his long-term future was even going to be at Old Trafford.

As is the case with a number of players, including Keane in the past, contract negotiations do not always run smoothly and Ferguson stunned the footballing world when declaring in October of 2010 that his striker wanted to leave the club. In an amazing about-turn, Rooney instead signed a new deal four days later and displayed renewed brilliance in the red shirt, particularly when executing an unbelievable bicycle kick in the Manchester derby to earn three vital points after the turn of the year.

Neighbours City, armed with an enviable transfer budget, had been his chief suitors on that occasion, according to various stories in the press, but it was Chelsea who openly pushed for his signature in 2013 following Sir Alex's departure. With his future shrouded in doubt, he injured a hamstring on United's pre-season tour without playing a game and returned home from Thailand. A shoulder problem, sustained in a behind-closed-doors friendly with Real Betis, then kept him out of a trip to Sweden to face AIK Stockholm in another pre-season friendly. Conspiracy theories went into overdrive. Again, there were fears he could be sold rather than see his contract out, despite United's insistence this would never happen.

The fans showed their support, cheering him onto the field as a substitute in Moyes's first league game in charge at Swansea City. When he started the opening home fixture, a goalless draw with Chelsea, the rival manager still harboured hopes of luring him to Stamford Bridge. Instead, Jose Mourinho was astounded that his masterplan was destined to fail, as the Old Trafford faithful continued to back their striker. He responded with a man-of-the-match display. 'I think this club must be a very special club,' conceded Mourinho afterwards. 'In every other club in the world, when a player wants to leave, they don't support him and give him a hard time. But they have supported him all the way so I think this must be a very special club, with special fans. It was good. It was nice. It was very English. I think probably now, he decides that he wants to stay. If he makes that decision, we will be the first to respect that.'

Of course, Rooney never openly confirmed he did want to leave United. However, the affection he received from the supporters was reciprocated. 'The fans were brilliant and, to be fair, they have been brilliant to me ever since I joined the club,' he later admitted. 'There have been a couple of issues where I can understand why the fans are upset, but they have been fantastic with me and I genuinely have nothing but respect for them for that support.'

Steadfastly refusing to actually discuss the situation as the season unfolded, there could certainly be no criticism levelled at his performances. His contribution and commitment were both faultless, despite a difficult start to life without the ultra-successful Ferguson. He captained the team to a sweet victory over Liverpool in the Capital One Cup third round, which exacted some form of revenge for a league defeat 24 days earlier, but also oversaw a dismal home reverse to West Bromwich Albion, the first of eight domestic defeats at Old Trafford in 2013-14. There was no doubt that Moyes, who had great respect for his No.10, considered him worthy of taking on the role on a full-time basis at a later date.

'I think Wayne has always had the ability to be a captain,' said Moyes, who had known him since he was a schoolboy at Everton. 'He's got that love of football as the biggest thing because he loves the game and loves the ball and kicking it around. He's a natural and, in his own way, leads by example in what he tries to do. In future years, he could be the skipper here.'

For a second time, all of the thousands of column inches devoted to his future proved ultimately pointless as he did commit himself to United in February 2014, signing a five-and-a-half year contract. 'As you know, football deals don't get done quickly now,' explained Moyes. 'Very few deals get done. It's been ongoing for a while. I've probably known for three or four months that this would probably happen. In fact I've probably known, or felt it, since August. There was never going to be a chance he was going to leave Manchester United, certainly not on my watch.'

Chelsea boss Mourinho may have been disappointed at the

outcome, but Moyes, who had reconciled with the centre-forward after some acrimony following his transfer to the Reds all those years earlier, rightly saw it as a personal victory. He also understandably laughed off the ludicrous suggestion that Rooney had not only demanded the captaincy but also a say in transfer targets during the protracted negotiations. His contract resolved, the England international could now focus on the future without any distractions on that front.

Speaking on the plane flying a disheartened squad back from Athens after a shocking Champions League loss to Olympiacos, Rooney confirmed he would be delighted to succeed Vidic as skipper, with the Serbian already declaring he had signed a pre-contract agreement with Inter Milan to join the Serie A club at the end of the season. 'I've captained United a few times and, if the manager wants me to be captain, I'd have no problem with that,' he told *Inside United*, the official club magazine. 'I'd grab it with both hands.

'I think, whether you've got the armband or not, I always feel I'm quite vocal on the pitch. I try to help the players when I feel I can and say what I think. I believe that's the most important thing, to be honest and say what you feel. If you say what you believe are the right things, you need to keep doing that.' Speaking from the heart in the heat of battle came naturally to him and was something he must have observed at first hand from Keane in the past.

If a reminder was required of his ability to conjure up moments of off-the-cuff brilliance, it was provided at West Ham United when his stupendous long-range lob embarrassed Adrian in the home goal. The fact he was captain while doing so suggested the responsibility would surely not inhibit him. Moyes had no fears on that front either, even if he refused to strip Vidic of the captaincy, despite the defender's impending departure. 'Maybe Wayne wore the armband and took a wee bit of pride in that,' said the Reds manager. 'He wanted to show exactly what it means and he wanted to take responsibility. It's for him to show it and you'd have to say he showed it.'

The champions' form on the road had actually been impressive, and the two-goal deficit against Olympiacos was remarkably overturned in the second leg at Old Trafford with a van Persie hat-trick, but there was no disguising that the season had been a huge disappointment. The European run ended at the hands of holders Bayern Munich, despite an Evra wonder goal very briefly raising hopes of an upset at the Allianz Arena, and Moyes's tenure came to an abrupt end after the next fixture.

The Scot's final match in charge proved to be a defeat at his, and Rooney's, old club as Everton's comfortable 2-0 success made it an unhappy return to Merseyside, particularly as the striker was captain again in the absence of Vidic and Evra. The loss ensured Rooney would spend a year out of the Champions League for the first time in his United career, as the Reds were unable to finish in the top four of the Premier League. After weeks of speculation regarding the new manager, with Ryan Giggs taking over in an interim capacity, confirmation of Louis van Gaal's appointment appeared to dash Rooney's captaincy hopes – or at least that was the conventional wisdom in the press.

Van Gaal's skipper with the Netherlands national team was United star van Persie, and he appeared a natural choice to replace Vidic at Old Trafford, considering the Dutch pair worked to such good effect in steering their country to third place at the 2014 World Cup finals. Their special relationship was deemed decisive. After all, the pair had been spotted in the stands watching one game together in the build-up to the main event in Brazil. Some even speculated the new man's arrival would spark a fresh challenge for Rooney to keep his place in the team and his future, once again, could be thrown into doubt if he missed out on the role he craved.

Rooney's response to rumours of van Persie's likely promotion was measured, but again illustrated a passion for the armband. 'I feel I am ready for the captaincy, but it's the manager's decision,' he admitted. 'Whoever he chooses to be captain, I'll respect that and have no problems with it. If he chooses someone else, then I've honestly got no problems with that. Robin is captain of his country, he has captained Arsenal and, if he gets the nod, I'm sure he'll do a great job.' So much for any friction between the strike partnership over the armband.

The debate raged on. Paul Scholes, now far more vocal in the media than he ever was publicly in his playing days, admitted he wanted Rooney to be appointed skipper but felt van Persie was the strong favourite. 'I think van Gaal will give it to Robin,' said the former midfielder. 'He's had a lot of experience with him from Holland. He knows him well, knows him as a player, but personally I would probably go for Rooney. He's always struck me as the type who could be a captain and now is the perfect time to give him the responsibility I know he is capable of taking.'

The fact van Persie had only been at the club for a couple of seasons was perhaps an obvious issue, particularly compared with his strike partner's longevity, and van Gaal sensibly deliberated before making his appointment. 'I am always looking for opportunities to give players the captain's armband,' revealed the new manager. 'I think you have to choose, when it is possible, the English style. That is when it is possible.' Following that hint, Darren Fletcher and Tom Cleverley assumed the role on the tour of the United States before Rooney skippered the team to victory against Liverpool in Miami in the final of the International Champions Cup.

He kept the job for the final pre-season friendly, against Valencia at Old Trafford, and the official announcement of the permanence of the position came later that evening. 'I'll try to lead the players on the pitch with hard work and dedication,' he stressed. 'That's what we really want to do. We want to show the fans that we care and want to win. It's a massive role to take on. I'm aware of that, the responsibility of it, and feel I'm ready, at this stage in my career, to do it.'

Never one to make any decision rashly, van Gaal was adamant about his selection. 'Wayne has shown a great attitude towards everything he does,' said a manager who had clearly been encouraged by his first impressions of the experienced attacker. 'I have been very impressed by his professionalism and his attitude to training and to my philosophy. He is a great inspiration to the younger members of the team and I believe he will put his heart and soul into his captaincy role.'

The new 'trainer-coach', the term he personally favours, did not feel it was a case of van Persie being overlooked, merely explaining that he had wanted a British player for the role all along. 'It was not difficult,' he said. 'I didn't say it to him [Robin]. He was not there at that moment. I told it personally to Wayne, then I had to choose the vice-captain, then I had to say it to my players. This is a different situation to the Dutch national team. I think you always have to choose a native captain. I don't think there is any problem.'

As is always the case with Rooney, everybody offered an opinion on the news and most, particularly those associated with Manchester United and who had worked with him, were in agreement it was a natural step for him to take. 'There has been a sharp decline in leadership in football, but Rooney has all the attributes,' wrote Gary Neville in the *Daily Telegraph*. 'By "leaders", I mean people who are prepared not only to hold themselves accountable but hold their team-mates accountable too.

'Rooney is one of a dying breed of footballers who is willing to call his team-mates out. He can take criticism but also hand it out. His approach is the traditional one of not taking criticism personally – and expecting team-mates not to take it personally either. Van Gaal will have looked at Rooney and thought: this is a player who is not too proud to listen to criticism and not too shy to dish it out.'

Current colleagues were also quick to offer their support. 'He is a born winner who wants to win everything,' said Darren Fletcher, after being named vice-captain. 'His desire and determination on the pitch sets the example and he has a never-say-die attitude. In the last few years, he has developed a real leader's role in the dressing room in terms of the voice he has in there. He's great at helping people and giving advice to younger players – he's really developed that. He is going to be a fantastic captain for Manchester United.'

One of those younger players, Tyler Blackett, broke into the side at the beginning of the season to start the opening five Premier League games of van Gaal's reign, and also endorsed the appointment. 'I think he is stepping up well,' said the promising defender. 'He is saying the right things and helping the team by getting us up and ready for the games. I think he is still learning [the role] but he's doing well at the moment.'

Inevitably, van Gaal places great emphasis on the relevance of his on-field leader and sees the role as vital to the implementation of his fabled footballing philosophy. 'The choice of captain is always very important for me,' he revealed. 'There are always players we put in the line-up – my captain shall always play. I don't think any player is fixed. Only the captain has more privileges. No other player has privileges, I think.' For those still seeking to drive an agenda relating to Rooney's place in the side, it was a devastatingly honest revelation from the manager.

There were also many who wondered whether Rooney would become too consumed by the added responsibility, tipping the balance between displaying his rapacious appetite for victory and keeping his emotions in check. This failed to take into account a more refined playing style and increased maturity, which made him a very different footballer from the one who first exploded onto the scene as an untamed teenager.

'I'm a better footballer now than I was then,' he opined. 'When I was younger, I was raw. There were moments when I did spectacular stuff but now, overall, my play is better. When I was younger, I wasted far too much energy charging around and, in the last fifteen minutes, I'd be tired. I read the game a lot better now and there are certain situations where you can use your experience.' With more control, he was still exerting great influence and remained capable of dominating matches, particularly when dropping a little deeper.

It was no surprise that the spotlight on the United No.10 would burn brighter than ever, particularly as he also took on the dual role of England skipper in the wake of Steven Gerrard's international retirement. The 28-year-old was the first man to be named permanent skipper of both the Reds and the Three Lions since Bryan Robson. 'It's primarily a job off the field,' explained another of the country's former captains, Gary Lineker. 'You're the middle man between players and the management, the media and the public. That's where you could question whether Rooney is the right man, but his media side has improved and he handles that reasonably well now.' Coach Roy Hodgson felt it was an obvious choice. 'I've had a long conversation with him and he's prepared to accept the pressures that the England captaincy brings,' he revealed.

It would be difficult to conceive how there could possibly be even more media glare on Rooney, but the questions kept coming after an opening-day defeat to Swansea City in his first competitive match of the new era at club level. Rooney produced a good personal performance, scoring an expertly taken close-range overhead kick in the 2-1 defeat, but had seen a penalty saved against Valencia in a friendly a few days earlier and it was already being contested that the responsibility was weighing too heavily on his shoulders. His own assessment of the situation was a simpler one that would not appease any headline writers. 'I just had a bad game [against Valencia],' he conceded. 'I was the first to say that when I got into the dressing room. I didn't play well and you have those days.'

Van Gaal immediately addressed any concerns that his new skipper would be overawed, which seemed a pretty bizarre suggestion in any case. 'I think he wanted to show more than his utmost best to the public that he is Wayne Rooney, the new captain,' said the Dutchman. 'I said to him: "Let it fly, let it fly." It is more important how you perform and not the captaincy.'

Appropriately, he celebrated a tenth anniversary of his unforgettable debut for the club by making all the headlines again in a win against West Ham United in late September 2014. Scoring a superb opening goal and performing well, he blotted his copybook by receiving a red card for a foul on Stewart Downing which provided more fuel for an obsessed media who paid little attention to a morale-boosting victory acquired with ten men.

There was only one story coming out of this match. Was Rooney fit to captain United and England? Did a rash challenge undo all of his previously splendid work? It was his first sending off in five years for the Reds and yet all the talk of an uncontrollable temper resurfaced. 'I expect people to say that,' he said after the game, showing no signs of anger or anguish. 'But, at the end of the day, I was trying to break up the play. I have just misjudged it, simple as that, but I have no complaints.' Van Gaal was also posed questions after the final whistle, even being asked if he still felt he had made the right decision in selecting his skipper.

Of course, it seems unlikely there will be any doubts from the boss regarding Rooney's suitability to continue leading his side. The manager analyses everything in meticulous detail and felt a man who had been at United for a decade was capable of assisting his transition of the club during his stint in charge. It is why he enlisted Giggs as assistant manager, too, because he wants to surround himself with those who know how things work at such a footballing institution. 'There are the guardians of the culture of the club,' said van Gaal. 'Rooney is such a player. He is now captain and guardian of this culture and can transfer this culture to his fellow players. That is very important.'

The role of the United captain in this new chapter for the club appears clear. It is a case of uniting a dressing room that contains six stellar signings and ensuring the sizeable Spanish-speaking contingent learn to understand the ethos of the club and gel with the existing staff. It is not anticipated that Rooney will be expected to become fluent in a foreign language, with van Gaal instead determined the native tongue must dominate – not only on the field but around the training ground as well.

Rooney is the man entrusted to knit everything together when his manager is not there to impose his iron will. Not least on the field. It is a task he appears to be approaching with a sense of seniority and maturity. A midweek meal was organised for the first-team squad at a restaurant in Manchester to assist with the integration of Angel Di Maria, Marcos Rojo, Daley Blind and Radamel Falcao, all signed after the tour of the United States and thus missing out on the team bonding such excursions promote.

'I think it was Wayne's idea because he spoke to everyone about it,' revealed Rafael, suddenly one of the longest-serving members of the team. 'Now he is the captain here, he's doing everything like that.' Organising social events and ensuring the new faces are happy away from the pitch, even putting new team-mates in touch with suitable babysitters, Rooney has come a long way since the teenage tearaway who looked, at times, like he wanted to take on the world. Other areas look certain to come naturally to him. He will handle the increased media duties with aplomb, having learned how to effectively get his message across.

There could be new avenues for him to explore as he assesses the potential for bringing new ideas to the captain's role. Whether it is communicating with fans via his vast social media reach, or even implementing an ambassadorial element to his current position, which was alluded to in his contract announcement, these are areas he may look to exploit, but only with the primary aim in mind of achieving success and winning trophies – his overriding concern.

At a time when there is constant conjecture as to whether too much stock is placed on the captaincy in football, admittedly generated by those largely responsible for the role's elevated status in the first place, it is refreshing to have a skipper who openly acknowledges its importance and who was desperate for the job since an early age.

Wayne Rooney certainly feels he is ready to lead Manchester United into a new era and could stand on the brink of cementing his place as one of the club's greatest-ever stars. 'Only time will tell whether I can be a successful captain,' he stated. 'But I will certainly be giving everything I can to help this club win trophies.' With a bullish and honest character like Rooney, you would never expect anything less and the way his career has gone to date, you shouldn't bet against him achieving it.

APPENDIX –
Captains timeline*

1878-82 – Unknown

1882-83 – E. Thomas

1883-87 – Sam Black

1887-91 – Jack Powell

1891-92 – Bob McFarlane

1892-93 – Joe Cassidy

1893-94 – Unknown

1894-96 – James McNaught

1896-97 – Caesar Jenkyns

1897-1903 – Harry Stafford

1903-04 – John Sutcliffe

1904-05 – Jack Peddie

1905-13 – Charlie Roberts

1913-14 – George Stacey

1914-15 – George Hunter

1915-17 – Pat O'Connell

1917-18 – George Anderson

1918-19 – Jack Mew

1919-22 – Clarence Hilditch (or Arthur Whalley in 1919-20)

1923-28 – Frank Barson

1928-29 – Jack Wilson

1929-30 – Charlie Spencer

1930-31 – Jack Silcock

1931-32 – George McLachlan

1932-33 – Louis Page (also Jack Silcock)

1933-34 – Ernest Hine

1934-35 – William McKay

1935-37 – James Brown

1937-39 – George Roughton

1939-40 – William McKay

1940-44 – Football suspended due to Second World War

APPENDIX – Captains timeline

1944-45 – George Roughton

1945-53 – Johnny Carey

1953-54 – Stan Pearson (Allenby
Chilton Oct 1953 – Feb 1955)

1955-58 – Roger Byrne

1958-59 – Bill Foulkes

1959-60 – Dennis Viollet

1960-63 – Maurice Setters

1963-67 – Noel Cantwell (Denis
Law team captain 1964-67)

1967-68 – Denis Law

1968-73 – Bobby Charlton

1973-74 – George Graham

1974-75 – Willie Morgan

1975-82 – Martin Buchan

1982 – Ray Wilkins

(Feb – Oct 1982)

1982-94 – Bryan Robson (Steve
Bruce team captain Dec 1992 –
May 1994)

1994-96 – Steve Bruce

1996-97 – Eric Cantona

1997-2005 – Roy Keane (Peter
Schmeichel team captain in
Keane's absence)

2005-11 – Gary Neville (Nemanja
Vidic team captain Sept 2010 –
Feb 2011)

2011-14 – Nemanja Vidic (Patrice
Evra team captain in Vidic's
absence)

2014-present – Wayne Rooney

Many more players have captained Manchester United, some frequently, but the list above conveys official club captains or recognised team captains (players, sometimes unofficially appointed, who captained the side in the absence of the club skipper).

Acknowledgements

This was a hugely rewarding piece of work, combining years of admiring Manchester United's leaders from the stands and the press box; interviewing – at various points in the last decade or so – nine of the captains featured in this book; and months of research and writing to hopefully capture the inspiring leadership of some of the club's most colourful characters.

A big thank you in particular goes to Bryan Robson, the captain's captain, who offered his time to so insightfully describe the pride and honour he felt wearing the armband, which really informed the tone of the book.

The staff at the fabulous Manchester United Museum were, as always, a tremendous help, including the venerable curator Mark Wylie, who was a font of knowledge on the subject, particularly the years prior to the Second World War and the sketchier history of the role in its beginnings. His insight was invaluable.

At Simon & Schuster, Ian Marshall has once again proved a crucial ally throughout the process from conception to publication, providing unyielding support, vital guidance and a keen eye for detail.

Of course, all the various autobiographies, books, magazines, programmes and newspapers that are credited throughout supplied essential background on the various skippers.

Finally, a word of gratitude to the 14 captains who appear prominently in this book, and the long list of supporting cast members, for making this a thoroughly enjoyable subject to explore. We hope you enjoyed reliving their stories as much as we did.